T0275482

C++: The Programming Language

C++: The Programming Language

Language

Edited by
Waylon Warren

Larsen & Keller
www.larsen-keller.com

C++: The Programming Language
Edited by Waylon Warren
ISBN: 978-1-63549-158-6 (Hardback)

© 2017 Larsen & Keller

 Larsen & Keller

Published by Larsen and Keller Education,
5 Penn Plaza,
19th Floor,
New York, NY 10001, USA

Cataloging-in-Publication Data

C++ : the programming language / edited by Waylon Warren.
  p. cm.
Includes bibliographical references and index.
ISBN 978-1-63549-158-6
1. C++ (Computer program language).
I. Warren, Waylon.
QA76.73.C153 C15 2017
005.133--dc23

The publisher's policy is to use permanent paper from mills that operate a sustainable forestry policy. Furthermore, the publisher ensures that the text paper and cover boards used have met acceptable environmental accreditation standards.

Printed and bound in the United States of America.

For more information regarding Larsen and Keller Education and its products, please visit the publisher's website www.larsen-keller.com

Table of Contents

Preface

C++ is a computer language or program language. It provides low-level memory manipulation and is also used for object-oriented, imperative and generic programming features. C++ has helped develop many other languages like Java, C#, and D. This book presents the complex subject of C++ in the most comprehensible and easy to understand language. The topics included in it are of utmost significance and are bound to provide incredible insights to students. Some of the diverse topics covered in this text address the varied branches that fall under this category. Those in search of information to further their knowledge will be greatly assisted by this textbook.

A detailed account of the significant topics covered in this book is provided below:

Chapter 1- Programming language is a computer language aimed at communicating instructions to a device, particularly a computer. C++ is one of these programming languages, which has imperative and object oriented programing features. This text guides the reader in having an in depth understanding of C++.

Chapter 2- There are a number of programming languages which are related to C++. Some of these are C, Ada, CLU and ALGOL 68. All these languages are well structured, imperative and object oriented. This section strategically encompasses and incorporates the major components and key concepts of all the programming languages that are related to C++.

Chapter 3- C++ has a number of programming languages; some of these languages are C++03, C++11, C++14 and C++17. C++03 is the standard version of C++ globally whereas C++11 is the standard version of C++. The following chapter helps the reader in understanding all the types of C++.

Chapter 4- CLI is a programing language, which was created by Microsoft. It was created with the intention of replacing the managed extensions for C++. Some other extensions of C++, like Cilk was created with the purpose of programming languages for multithreaded parallel computing. This section also focuses on some aspects of C++, aspect C++, CLI.

Chapter 5- Computer programming has a feature called copy elision. Copy elision is a method which is essential to eliminate the unnecessary coping of objects. Templates (C++) and decltypes are other prominent techniques used in C++. The text elucidates all the tools and methods of C++.

Chapter 6- Subroutine is a sequence of programming which is assigned to perform precise tasks, packaged as a unit. Exception safety on the other hand is a set of guidelines that can be used by clients when handling safety in any programming language, specifically C++. This chapter strategically encompasses and incorporates the methods and tools of C++, providing a complete understanding.

Chapter 7- Generic programming has software such as Ada, Delphi, Eiffel, Java and C# whereas metaprogramming writes programs with the skill to treat programs as their data. Which means if a data is being analyzed it can simultaneously be modified also. C++ programming is best understood in confluence with the major topics listed in following chapter.

Chapter 8- Generic programming is a style of computer programming where the algorithms written in generic programming are written in terms of types to-be-specified-later. The other diverse aspects of C++ are metaprogramming, compatibility of C and C++, criticism of C++ and Sieve C++ Parallel programming system. This topic will provide an integrated understanding of C++ programming language.

Chapter 9- C++ Standard Library is a collection of classes and functions. This collection is written in the core language. The topics discussed in this text are C++ string handling, functional (C++), sequence container (C++) and standard template library. The diverse aspects of C++ Standard Library have been carefully analyzed in this chapter.

It gives me an immense pleasure to thank our entire team for their efforts. Finally in the end, I would like to thank my family and colleagues who have been a great source of inspiration and support.

Editor

Introduction to C++

Programming language is a computer language aimed at communicating instructions to a device, particularly a computer. C++ is one of these programming languages, which has imperative and object oriented programing features. This text guides the reader in having an in depth understanding of C++.

C++

C++ is a general-purpose programming language. It has imperative, object-oriented and generic programming features, while also providing facilities for low-level memory manipulation.

It was designed with a bias toward system programming and embedded, resource-constrained and large systems, with performance, efficiency and flexibility of use as its design highlights. C++ has also been found useful in many other contexts, with key strengths being software infrastructure and resource-constrained applications, including desktop applications, servers (e.g. e-commerce, web search or SQL servers), and performance-critical applications (e.g. telephone switches or space probes). C++ is a compiled language, with implementations of it available on many platforms and provided by various organizations, including the Free Software Foundation (FSF's GCC), LLVM, Microsoft, Intel and IBM.

C++ is standardized by the International Organization for Standardization (ISO), with the latest standard version ratified and published by ISO in December 2014 as *ISO/IEC 14882:2014* (informally known as C++14). The C++ programming language was initially standardized in 1998 as *ISO/IEC 14882:1998*, which was then amended by the C++03, *ISO/IEC 14882:2003*, standard. The current C++14 standard supersedes these and C++11, with new features and an enlarged standard library. Before the initial standardization in 1998, C++ was developed by Bjarne Stroustrup at Bell Labs since 1979, as an extension of the C language as he wanted an efficient and flexible language similar to C, which also provided high-level features for program organization.

Many other programming languages have been influenced by C++, including C#, D, Java, and newer versions of C (after 1998).

History

In 1979, Bjarne Stroustrup, a Danish computer scientist, began work on the predecessor to C++, "C with Classes". The motivation for creating a new language originated from Stroustrup's experience in programming for his Ph.D. thesis. Stroustrup found that Simula had features that were very helpful for large software development, but the language was too slow for practical use, while BCPL was fast but too low-level to be suitable for large software development. When Stroustrup started working in AT&T Bell Labs, he had the problem of analyzing the UNIX kernel with respect to distributed computing. Remembering his Ph.D. experience, Stroustrup set out to enhance the C language with Simula-like features. C was chosen because it was general-purpose, fast, portable and widely used. As well as C and Simula's influences, other languages also influenced C++, including ALGOL 68, Ada, CLU and ML.

Bjarne Stroustrup, the creator of C++

Initially, Stroustrup's "C with Classes" added features to the C compiler, Cpre, including classes, derived classes, strong typing, inlining and default arguments.

In 1983, *C with Classes* was renamed to *C++* ("++" being the increment operator in C), adding new features that included virtual functions, function name and operator overloading, references, constants, type-safe free-store memory allocation (new/delete), improved type checking, and BCPL style single-line comments with two forward slashes (//). Furthermore, it included the development of a standalone compiler for C++, Cfront.

In 1985, the first edition of *The C++ Programming Language* was released, which became the definitive reference for the language, as there was not yet an official standard. The first commercial implementation of C++ was released in October of the same year.

In 1989, C++ 2.0 was released, followed by the updated second edition of *The C++ Programming Language* in 1991. New features in 2.0 included multiple inheritance, abstract classes, static member functions, const member functions, and protected members. In 1990, *The Annotated C++ Reference Manual* was published. This work became the basis for the future standard. Later feature additions included templates, exceptions, namespaces, new casts, and a boolean type.

After the 2.0 update, C++ evolved relatively slowly until, in 2011, the C++11 standard was released, adding numerous new features, enlarging the standard library further, and providing more facilities to C++ programmers. After a minor C++14 update released in December 2014, various new additions are planned for 2017 and 2020.

Etymology

According to Stroustrup: "the name signifies the evolutionary nature of the changes from C". This name is credited to Rick Mascitti (mid-1983) and was first used in December 1983. When Mascitti was questioned informally in 1992 about the naming, he indicated that it was given in a tongue-in-cheek spirit. The name comes from C's "++" operator (which increments the value of a variable) and a common naming convention of using "+" to indicate an enhanced computer program.

During C++'s development period, the language had been referred to as "new C" and "C with Classes" before acquiring its final name.

Philosophy

Throughout C++'s life, its development and evolution has been informally governed by a set of rules that its evolution should follow:

- It must be driven by actual problems and its features should be useful immediately in real world programs.

- Every feature should be implementable (with a reasonably obvious way to do so).

- Programmers should be free to pick their own programming style, and that style should be fully supported by C++.

- Allowing a useful feature is more important than preventing every possible misuse of C++.

- It should provide facilities for organising programs into well-defined separate parts, and provide facilities for combining separately developed parts.

- No implicit violations of the type system (but allow explicit violations; that is, those explicitly requested by the programmer).

- User-created types need to have the same support and performance as built-in types.

- Unused features should not negatively impact created executables (e.g. in lower performance).

- There should be no language beneath C++ (except assembly language).

- C++ should work alongside other existing programming languages, rather than fostering its own separate and incompatible programming environment.

- If the programmer's intent is unknown, allow the programmer to specify it by providing manual control.

Standardization

C++ is standardized by an ISO working group known as JTC1/SC22/WG21. So far, it has published four revisions of the C++ standard and is currently working on the next revision, C++17.

Year	C++ Standard	Informal name
1998	ISO/IEC 14882:1998	C++98
2003	ISO/IEC 14882:2003	C++03
2011	ISO/IEC 14882:2011	C++11
2014	ISO/IEC 14882:2014	C++14
2017	to be determined	C++17
2020	to be determined	C++20

In 1998, the ISO working group standardized C++ for the first time as *ISO/IEC 14882:1998*, which is informally known as *C++98*. In 2003, it published a new version of the C++ standard called *ISO/IEC 14882:2003*, which fixed problems identified in C++98.

The next major revision of the standard was informally referred to as "C++0x", but it was not released until 2011. C++11 (14882:2011) included many additions to both the core language and the standard library.

In 2014, C++14 (also known as C++1y) was released as a small extension to C++11, featuring mainly bug fixes and small improvements. The Draft International Standard ballot procedures completed in mid-August 2014.

After C++14, a major revision, informally known as C++17 or C++1z, is planned for 2017, which is almost feature-complete.

As part of the standardization process, ISO also publishes technical reports and specifications:

- ISO/IEC TR 18015:2006 on the use of C++ in embedded systems and on performance implications of C++ language and library features,

- ISO/IEC TR 19768:2007 (also known as the C++ Technical Report 1) on library extensions mostly integrated into C++11,

- ISO/IEC TR 29124:2010 on special mathematical functions,

- ISO/IEC TR 24733:2011 on decimal floating point arithmetic,

- ISO/IEC TS 18822:2015 on the standard filesystem library,

- ISO/IEC TS 19570:2015 on parallel versions of the standard library algorithms,

- ISO/IEC TS 19841:2015 on software transactional memory,

- ISO/IEC TS 19568:2015 on a new set of library extensions, some of which are already integrated into C++17,

- ISO/IEC TS 19217:2015 on the C++ Concepts

More technical specifications are in development and pending approval, including concurrency library extensions, a networking standard library, ranges, and modules.

Language

The C++ language has two main components: a direct mapping of hardware features provided primarily by the C subset, and zero-overhead abstractions based on those mappings. Stroustrup describes C++ as "a light-weight abstraction programming language [designed] for building and using efficient and elegant abstractions"; and "offering both hardware access and abstraction is the basis of C++. Doing it efficiently is what distinguishes it from other languages".

C++ inherits most of C's syntax. The following is Bjarne Stroustrup's version of the Hello world program that uses the C++ Standard Library stream facility to write a message to standard output:

```
#include <iostream>

int main()

{

        std::cout << "Hello, world!\n";

}
```

Within functions that define a non-void return type, failure to return a value before control reaches the end of the function results in undefined behaviour (compilers typically provide the means to issue a diagnostic in such a case). The sole exception to this rule is the main function, which implicitly returns a value of zero.

Object Storage

As in C, C++ supports four types of memory management: static storage duration objects, thread storage duration objects, automatic storage duration objects, and dynamic storage duration objects.

Static Storage Duration Objects

Static storage duration objects are created before main() is entered and destroyed in reverse order of creation after main() exits. The exact order of creation is not specified by the standard (though there are some rules defined below) to allow implementations some freedom in how to organize their implementation. More formally, objects of this type have a lifespan that "shall last for the duration of the program".

Static storage duration objects are initialized in two phases. First, "static initialization" is performed, and only *after* all static initialization is performed, "dynamic initialization" is performed. In static initialization, all objects are first initialized with zeros; after that, all objects that have a constant initialization phase are initialized with the constant expression (i.e. variables initialized with a literal or constexpr). Though it is not specified in the standard, the static initialization phase can be completed at compile time and saved in the data partition of the executable. Dynamic initialization involves all object initialization done via a constructor or function call (unless the function is marked with constexpr, in C++11). The dynamic initialization order is defined as the order of declaration within the compilation unit (i.e. the same file). No guarantees are provided about the order of initialization between compilation units.

Thread Storage Duration Objects

Variables of this type are very similar to static storage duration objects. The main difference is the creation time is just prior to thread creation and destruction is done after the thread has been joined.

Automatic Storage Duration Objects

The most common variable types in C++ are local variables inside a function or block, and temporary variables. The common feature about automatic variables is that they have a lifetime that is limited to the scope of the variable. They are created and potentially initialized at the point of declaration and destroyed in the *reverse* order of creation when the scope is left.

Local variables are created as the point of execution passes the declaration point. If the variable has a constructor or initializer this is used to define the initial state of the object. Local variables are destroyed when the local block or function that they are declared in is closed. C++ destructors for local variables are called at the end of the object lifetime, allowing a discipline for automatic resource management termed RAII, which is widely used in C++.

Member variables are created when the parent object is created. Array members are initialized from 0 to the last member of the array in order. Member variables are destroyed when the parent object is destroyed in the reverse order of creation. i.e. If the parent is an "automatic object" then it will be destroyed when it goes out of scope which triggers the destruction of all its members.

Temporary variables are created as the result of expression evaluation and are destroyed when the statement containing the expression has been fully evaluated (usually at the ; at the end of a statement).

Dynamic Storage Duration Objects

These objects have a dynamic lifespan and are created with a call to new and destroyed explicitly with a call to delete.

Templates

C++ templates enable generic programming. C++ supports function, class, alias and variable templates. Templates may be parameterized by types, compile-time constants, and other templates. Templates are implemented by *instantiation* at compile-time. To instantiate a template, compilers substitute specific arguments for a template's parameters to generate a concrete function or class instance. Some substitutions are not possible; these are eliminated by an overload resolution policy described by the phrase "Substitution failure is not an error" (SFINAE). Templates are a powerful tool that can be used for generic programming, template metaprogramming, and code optimization, but this power implies a cost. Template use may increase code size, because each template instantiation produces a copy of the template code: one for each set of template arguments, however, this is the same or smaller amount of code that would be generated if the code was written by hand. This is in contrast to run-time generics seen in other languages (e.g., Java) where at compile-time the type is erased and a single template body is preserved.

Templates are different from macros: while both of these compile-time language features enable conditional compilation, templates are not restricted to lexical substitution. Templates are aware of the semantics and type system of their companion language, as well as all compile-time type definitions, and can perform high-level operations including programmatic flow control based on evaluation of strictly type-checked parameters. Macros are capable of conditional control over compilation based on predetermined criteria, but cannot instantiate new types, recurse, or perform type evaluation and in effect are limited to pre-compilation text-substitution and text-inclusion/exclusion. In other words, macros can control compilation flow based on pre-defined symbols but cannot, unlike templates, independently instantiate new symbols. Templates are a tool for static polymorphism and generic programming.

In addition, templates are a compile time mechanism in C++ that is Turing-complete, meaning that any computation expressible by a computer program can be computed, in some form, by a template metaprogram prior to runtime.

In summary, a template is a compile-time parameterized function or class written without knowledge of the specific arguments used to instantiate it. After instantiation, the resulting code is equivalent to code written specifically for the passed arguments. In this manner, templates provide a way to decouple generic, broadly applicable aspects of functions and classes (encoded in templates) from specific aspects (encoded in template parameters) without sacrificing performance due to abstraction.

Objects

C++ introduces object-oriented programming (OOP) features to C. It offers classes, which provide the four features commonly present in OOP (and some non-OOP) languages: abstraction, encapsulation, inheritance, and polymorphism. One distinguishing feature of C++ classes compared to classes in other programming languages is support for deterministic destructors, which in turn provide support for the Resource Acquisition is Initialization (RAII) concept.

Encapsulation

Encapsulation is the hiding of information to ensure that data structures and operators are used as intended and to make the usage model more obvious to the developer. C++ provides the ability to define classes and functions as its primary encapsulation mechanisms. Within a class, members can be declared as either public, protected, or private to explicitly enforce encapsulation. A public member of the class is accessible to any function. A private member is accessible only to functions that are members of that class and to functions and classes explicitly granted access permission by the class ("friends"). A protected member is accessible to members of classes that inherit from the class in addition to the class itself and any friends.

The OO principle is that all of the functions (and only the functions) that access the internal representation of a type should be encapsulated within the type definition. C++ supports this (via member functions and friend functions), but does not enforce it: the programmer can declare parts or all of the representation of a type to be public, and is allowed to make public entities that are not part of the representation of the type. Therefore, C++ supports not just OO programming, but other weaker decomposition paradigms, like modular programming.

It is generally considered good practice to make all data private or protected, and to make public only those functions that are part of a minimal interface for users of the class. This can hide the details of data implementation, allowing the designer to later fundamentally change the implementation without changing the interface in any way.

Inheritance

Inheritance allows one data type to acquire properties of other data types. Inheritance from a base class may be declared as public, protected, or private. This access specifier determines whether unrelated and derived classes can access the inherited public and protected members of the base class. Only public inheritance corresponds to what is usually meant by "inheritance". The other two forms are much less frequently used. If the access specifier is omitted, a "class" inherits privately, while a "struct" inherits publicly. Base classes may be declared as virtual; this is called virtual inheritance. Virtual inheritance ensures that only one instance of a base class exists in the inheritance graph, avoiding some of the ambiguity problems of multiple inheritance.

Multiple inheritance is a C++ feature not found in most other languages, allowing a class to be derived from more than one base class; this allows for more elaborate inheritance relationships. For example, a "Flying Cat" class can inherit from both "Cat" and "Flying Mammal". Some other languages, such as C# or Java, accomplish something similar (although more limited) by allowing inheritance of multiple interfaces while restricting the number of base classes to one (interfaces, unlike classes, provide only declarations of member functions, no implementation or member data). An interface as in C# and Java can be defined in C++ as a class containing only pure virtual functions, often known as an abstract base class or "ABC". The member functions of such an abstract base class are normally explicitly defined in the derived class, not inherited implicitly. C++ virtual inheritance exhibits an ambiguity resolution feature called dominance.

Operators and Operator Overloading

C++ provides more than 35 operators, covering basic arithmetic, bit manipulation, indirection, comparisons, logical operations and others. Almost all operators can be overloaded for user-defined types, with a few notable exceptions such as member access (. and .*) as well as the conditional operator. The rich set of overloadable operators is central to making user-defined types in C++ seem like built-in types.

Operators that cannot be overloaded	
Operator	**Symbol**
Scope resolution operator	::
Conditional operator	?:
dot operator	.
Member selection operator	.*
"sizeof" operator	sizeof
"typeid" operator	typeid

Overloadable operators are also an essential part of many advanced C++ programming techniques, such as smart pointers. Overloading an operator does not change the precedence of calculations involving the operator, nor does it change the number of operands that the operator uses (any operand may however be ignored by the operator, though it will be evaluated prior to execution). Overloaded "&&" and "||" operators lose their short-circuit evaluation property.

Polymorphism

Polymorphism enables one common interface for many implementations, and for objects to act differently under different circumstances.

C++ supports several kinds of *static* (resolved at compile-time) and *dynamic* (resolved at run-time) polymorphisms, supported by the language features described above. Compile-time polymorphism does not allow for certain run-time decisions, while run-time polymorphism typically incurs a performance penalty.

Static Polymorphism

Function overloading allows programs to declare multiple functions having the same name but with different arguments (i.e. *ad hoc* polymorphism). The functions are distinguished by the number or types of their formal parameters. Thus, the same function name can refer to different functions depending on the context in which it is used. The type returned by the function is not used to distinguish overloaded functions and would result in a compile-time error message.

When declaring a function, a programmer can specify for one or more parameters a default value. Doing so allows the parameters with defaults to optionally be omitted when the function is called, in which case the default arguments will be used. When a function is called with fewer arguments than there are declared parameters, explicit arguments are matched to parameters in left-to-right order, with any unmatched parameters at the end of the parameter list being assigned their default arguments. In many cases, specifying default arguments in a single function declaration is preferable to providing overloaded function definitions with different numbers of parameters.

Templates in C++ provide a sophisticated mechanism for writing generic, polymorphic code (i.e. parametric polymorphism). In particular, through the Curiously Recurring Template Pattern, it's possible to implement a form of static polymorphism that closely mimics the syntax for overriding virtual functions. Because C++ templates are type-aware and Turing-complete, they can also be used to let the compiler resolve recursive conditionals and generate substantial programs through template metaprogramming. Contrary to some opinion, template code will not generate a bulk code after compilation with the proper compiler settings.

Dynamic Polymorphism

Inheritance

Variable pointers and references to a base class type in C++ can also refer to objects of any derived classes of that type. This allows arrays and other kinds of containers to hold pointers to objects of differing types (references cannot be directly held in containers).

This enables dynamic (run-time) polymorphism, where the referred objects can behave differently depending on their (actual, derived) types.

C++ also provides the dynamic_cast operator, which allows code to safely attempt conversion of an object, via a base reference/pointer, to a more derived type: *downcasting*. The *attempt* is necessary as often one does not know which derived type is referenced. (*Upcasting*, conversion to a more general type, can always be checked/performed at compile-time via static_cast, as ancestral classes are specified in the derived class's interface, visible to all callers.) dynamic_cast relies on run-time type information (RTTI), metadata in the program that enables differentiating types and their relationships. If a dynamic_cast to a pointer fails, the result is the nullptr constant, whereas if the destination is a reference (which cannot be null), the cast throws an exception. Objects *known* to be of a certain derived type can be cast to that with static_cast, bypassing RTTI and the safe runtime type-checking of dynamic_cast, so this should be used only if the programmer is very confident the cast is, and will always be, valid.

Virtual Member Functions

Ordinarily, when a function in a derived class overrides a function in a base class, the function to call is determined by the type of the object. A given function is overridden when there exists no difference in the number or type of parameters between two or more definitions of that function. Hence, at compile time, it may not be possible to determine the type of the object and therefore the correct function to call, given only a base class pointer; the decision is therefore put off until runtime. This is called dynamic dispatch. Virtual member functions or *methods* allow the most specific implementation of the function to be called, according to the actual run-time type of the object. In C++ implementations, this is commonly done using virtual function tables. If the object type is known, this may be bypassed by prepending a fully qualified class name before the function call, but in general calls to virtual functions are resolved at run time.

In addition to standard member functions, operator overloads and destructors can be virtual. As a rule of thumb, if any function in the class is virtual, the destructor should be as well. As the type of an object at its creation is known at compile time, constructors, and by extension copy constructors, cannot be virtual. Nonetheless a situation may arise where a copy of an object needs to be created when a pointer to a derived object is passed as a pointer to a base object. In such a case, a common solution is to create a clone() (or similar) virtual function that creates and returns a copy of the derived class when called.

A member function can also be made "pure virtual" by appending it with = 0 after the closing parenthesis and before the semicolon. A class containing a pure virtual function is called an *abstract data type*. Objects cannot be created from abstract data types; they can only be derived from. Any derived class inherits the virtual function as pure and must provide a non-pure definition of it (and all other pure virtual functions) before objects of the derived class can be created. A program that attempts to create an object of a class with a pure virtual member function or inherited pure virtual member function is ill-formed.

Lambda Expressions

C++ provides support for anonymous functions, which are also known as lambda expressions and have the following form:

[capture](parameters) -> return_type { function_body }

The [capture] list supports the definition of closures. Such lambda expressions are defined in the standard as syntactic sugar for an unnamed function object. An example lambda function may be defined as follows:

```
[] (int x, int y) -> int { return x + y; }
```

Exception Handling

Exception handling is used to communicate the existence of a runtime problem or error from where it was detected to where the issue can be handled. It permits this to be done in a uniform manner and separately from the main code, while detecting all errors. Should an error occur, an exception is thrown (raised), which is then caught by the nearest suitable exception handler. The exception causes the current scope to be exited, and also each outer scope (propagation) until a suitable handler is found, calling in turn the destructors of any objects in these exited scopes. At the same time, an exception is presented as an object carrying the data about the detected problem.

The exception-causing code is placed inside a try block. The exceptions are handled in separate catch blocks (the handlers); each try block can have multiple exception handlers, as it is visible in the example below.

```
#include <iostream>

#include <vector>

#include <stdexcept>

int main() {

    try {

        std::vector<int> vec{3,4,3,1};

        int i{vec.at(4)}; // Throws an exception, std::out_of_
range (indexing for vec is from 0-3 not 1-4)

    }
```

```
    // An exception handler, catches std::out_of_range, which is
thrown by vec.at(4)
    catch (std::out_of_range& e) {
        std::cerr << "Accessing a non-existent element: " <<
e.what() << '\n';
    }


    // To catch any other standard library exceptions (they de-
rive from std::exception)
    catch (std::exception& e) {
        std::cerr << "Exception thrown: " << e.what() << '\n';
    }


    // Catch any unrecognised exceptions (i.e. those which don't
derive from std::exception)
    catch (...) {
        std::cerr << "Some fatal error\n";
    }
}
```

It is also possible to raise exceptions purposefully, using the throw keyword; these exceptions are handled in the usual way. In some cases, exceptions cannot be used due to technical reasons. One such example is a critical component of an embedded system, where every operation must be guaranteed to complete within a specified amount of time. This cannot be determined with exceptions as no tools exist to determine the minimum time required for an exception to be handled.

Standard Library

The C++ standard consists of two parts: the core language and the standard library. C++ programmers expect the latter on every major implementation of C++; it includes vectors, lists, maps, algorithms (find, for_each, binary_search, random_shuffle, etc.), sets, queues, stacks, arrays, tuples, input/output facilities (iostream, for reading from and writing to the console and files), smart pointers for automatic memory management, regular expression support, multi-threading library, atomics support (allowing a variable to be read or written to by at most one thread at a time without any external synchronisation), time utilities (measurement, getting current time, etc.), a system for converting error reporting that doesn't use C++ exceptions into C++ exceptions, a random number generator and a slightly modified version of the C standard library (to make it comply with the C++ type system).

A large part of the C++ library is based on the Standard Template Library (STL). Useful tools provided by the STL include containers as the collections of objects (such as vectors and lists), iterators that provide array-like access to containers, and algorithms that perform operations such as searching and sorting.

Furthermore, (multi)maps (associative arrays) and (multi)sets are provided, all of which export compatible interfaces. Therefore, using templates it is possible to write generic algorithms that work with any container or on any sequence defined by iterators. As in C, the features of the library are accessed by using the #include directive to include a standard header. C++ provides 105 standard headers, of which 27 are deprecated.

The standard incorporates the STL that was originally designed by Alexander Stepanov, who experimented with generic algorithms and containers for many years. When he started with C++, he finally found a language where it was possible to create generic algorithms (e.g., STL sort) that perform even better than, for example, the C standard library qsort, thanks to C++ features like using inlining and compile-time binding instead of function pointers. The standard does not refer to it as "STL", as it is merely a part of the standard library, but the term is still widely used to distinguish it from the rest of the standard library (input/output streams, internationalization, diagnostics, the C library subset, etc.).

Most C++ compilers, and all major ones, provide a standards conforming implementation of the C++ standard library.

Compatibility

To give compiler vendors greater freedom, the C++ standards committee decided not to dictate the implementation of name mangling, exception handling, and other implementation-specific features. The downside of this decision is that object code produced by different compilers is expected to be incompatible. There were, however, attempts to standardize compilers for particular machines or operating systems (for example C++ ABI), though they seem to be largely abandoned now.

With C

C++ is often considered to be a superset of C, but this is not strictly true. Most C code can easily be made to compile correctly in C++, but there are a few differences that cause some valid C code to be invalid or behave differently in C++. For example, C allows implicit conversion from void* to other pointer types, but C++ does not (for type safety reasons). Also, C++ defines many new keywords, such as new and class, which may be used as identifiers (for example, variable names) in a C program.

Some incompatibilities have been removed by the 1999 revision of the C standard (C99), which now supports C++ features such as line comments (//), and declarations mixed with code. On the other hand, C99 introduced a number of new features that C++ did not support, were incompatible or redundant in C++, such as variable-length arrays, native complex-number types (however, the std::complex class in the C++ standard library provides similar functionality, although not code-compatible), designated initializers, compound literals, and the restrict keyword. Some of the C99-introduced features were included in the subsequent version of the C++ standard, C++11 (out of those which were not redundant). However, the C++11 standard introduces new incompatibilities, such as disallowing assignment of a string literal to a character pointer, which remains valid C.

To intermix C and C++ code, any function declaration or definition that is to be called from/used both in C and C++ must be declared with C linkage by placing it within an extern "C" {/*...*/} block. Such a function may not rely on features depending on name mangling (i.e., function overloading).

Criticism

Despite its widespread adoption, many programmers have criticized the C++ language, including Linus Torvalds, Richard Stallman, and Ken Thompson. Issues include a lack of reflection or garbage collection, slow compilation times, perceived feature creep, and verbose error messages, particularly from template metaprogramming.

To avoid the problems that exist in C++, and to increase productivity, some people suggest alternative languages newer than C++, such as D, Go, Rust and Vala.

Programming Language

A programming language is a formal computer language or constructed language designed to communicate instructions to a machine, particularly a computer. Programming languages can be used to create programs to control the behavior of a machine or to express algorithms.

The earliest known programmable machine preceded the invention of the digital computer and is the automatic flute player described in the 9th century by the brothers Musa in Baghdad, "during the Islamic Golden Age". From the early 1800s, "programs" were used to direct the behavior of machines such as Jacquard looms and player pianos. Thousands of different programming languages have been created, mainly in the computer field, and many more still are being created every year. Many programming languages require computation to be specified in an imperative form (i.e., as a sequence of operations to perform), while other languages use other forms of program specification such as the declarative form (i.e. the desired result is specified, not how to achieve it).

```
1  /* This line basically imports the "stdio" header file, part of
2   * the standard library. It provides input and output functionality
3   * to the program.
4   */
5  #include <stdio.h>
6
7  /*
8   * Function (method) declaration. This outputs "Hello, world" to
9   * standard output when invoked.
10  */
11 void sayHello() {
12     // printf() in C outputs the specified text (with optional
13     // formatting options) when invoked.
14     printf("Hello, world!");
15 }
16
17 /*
18  * This is a "main function". The compiled program will run the code
19  * defined here.
20  */
21 void main() {
22     // Invoke the sayHello() function.
23     sayHello();
24 }
```

Source code of a simple computer program written in the C programming language, which will output the "Hello, world!" message when compiled and run

The description of a programming language is usually split into the two components of syntax (form) and semantics (meaning). Some languages are defined by a specification document (for example, the C programming language is specified by an ISO Standard), while other languages (such as Perl) have a dominant implementation that is treated as a reference. Some languages have both, with the basic language defined by a standard and extensions taken from the dominant implementation being common.

Definitions

A programming language is a notation for writing programs, which are specifications of a computation or algorithm. Some, but not all, authors restrict the term "programming language" to those languages that can express *all* possible algorithms. Traits often considered important for what constitutes a programming language include:

Function and Target

> A *computer programming language* is a language used to write computer programs, which involve a computer performing some kind of computation or algorithm and possibly control external devices such as printers, disk drives, robots, and so on. For example, PostScript programs are frequently created by another program to control a computer printer or display. More generally, a programming language may describe computation on some, possibly abstract, machine. It is generally accepted that a complete specification for a program-

ming language includes a description, possibly idealized, of a machine or processor for that language. In most practical contexts, a programming language involves a computer; consequently, programming languages are usually defined and studied this way. Programming languages differ from natural languages in that natural languages are only used for interaction between people, while programming languages also allow humans to communicate instructions to machines.

Abstractions

Programming languages usually contain abstractions for defining and manipulating data structures or controlling the flow of execution. The practical necessity that a programming language support adequate abstractions is expressed by the abstraction principle; this principle is sometimes formulated as a recommendation to the programmer to make proper use of such abstractions.

Expressive Power

The theory of computation classifies languages by the computations they are capable of expressing. All Turing complete languages can implement the same set of algorithms. ANSI/ISO SQL-92 and Charity are examples of languages that are not Turing complete, yet often called programming languages.

Markup languages like XML, HTML or troff, which define structured data, are not usually considered programming languages. Programming languages may, however, share the syntax with markup languages if a computational semantics is defined. XSLT, for example, is a Turing complete XML dialect. Moreover, LaTeX, which is mostly used for structuring documents, also contains a Turing complete subset.

The term *computer language* is sometimes used interchangeably with programming language. However, the usage of both terms varies among authors, including the exact scope of each. One usage describes programming languages as a subset of computer languages. In this vein, languages used in computing that have a different goal than expressing computer programs are generically designated computer languages. For instance, markup languages are sometimes referred to as computer languages to emphasize that they are not meant to be used for programming.

Another usage regards programming languages as theoretical constructs for programming abstract machines, and computer languages as the subset thereof that runs on physical computers, which have finite hardware resources. John C. Reynolds emphasizes that formal specification languages are just as much programming languages as are the languages intended for execution. He also argues that textual and even graphical input formats that affect the behavior of a computer are programming languages, despite the fact they are commonly not Turing-complete, and remarks that ignorance of programming language concepts is the reason for many flaws in input formats.

History

Early Developments

The earliest computers were often programmed without the help of a programming language, by writing programs in absolute machine language. The programs, in decimal or binary form, were read in from punched cards or magnetic tape, or toggled in on switches on the front panel of the computer. Absolute machine languages were later termed *first-generation programming languages* (1GL).

The next step was development of so-called *second-generation programming languages* (2GL) or assembly languages, which were still closely tied to the instruction set architecture of the specific computer. These served to make the program much more human-readable, and relieved the programmer of tedious and error-prone address calculations.

The first *high-level programming languages*, or *third-generation programming languages* (3GL), were written in the 1950s. An early high-level programming language to be designed for a computer was Plankalkül, developed for the German Z3 by Konrad Zuse between 1943 and 1945. However, it was not implemented until 1998 and 2000.

John Mauchly's Short Code, proposed in 1949, was one of the first high-level languages ever developed for an electronic computer. Unlike machine code, Short Code statements represented mathematical expressions in understandable form. However, the program had to be translated into machine code every time it ran, making the process much slower than running the equivalent machine code.

The Manchester Mark 1 ran programs written in Autocode from 1952.

At the University of Manchester, Alick Glennie developed Autocode in the early 1950s. A programming language, it used a compiler to automatically convert the language into machine code. The first code and compiler was developed in 1952 for the Mark 1 computer at the University of Manchester and is considered to be the first compiled high-level programming language.

The second autocode was developed for the Mark 1 by R. A. Brooker in 1954 and was called the "Mark 1 Autocode". Brooker also developed an autocode for the Ferranti Mercury in the 1950s in conjunction with the University of Manchester. The version for the EDSAC 2 was devised by D. F. Hartley of University of Cambridge Mathematical Laboratory in 1961. Known as EDSAC 2 Autocode, it was a straight development from Mercury Autocode adapted for local circumstances, and was noted for its object code optimisation and source-language diagnostics which were advanced for the time. A contemporary but separate thread of development, Atlas Autocode was developed for the University of Manchester Atlas 1 machine.

In 1954, language FORTRAN was invented at IBM by John Backus; it was the first widely used high level general purpose programming language to have a functional implementation, as opposed to just a design on paper. It is still popular language for high-performance computing and is used for programs that benchmark and rank the world's fastest supercomputers.

Another early programming language was devised by Grace Hopper in the US, called FLOW-MATIC. It was developed for the UNIVAC I at Remington Rand during the period from 1955 until 1959. Hopper found that business data processing customers were uncomfortable with mathematical notation, and in early 1955, she and her team wrote a specification for an English programming language and implemented a prototype. The FLOW-MATIC compiler became publicly available in early 1958 and was substantially complete in 1959. Flow-Matic was a major influence in the design of COBOL, since only it and its direct descendant AIMACO were in actual use at the time.

Refinement

The increased use of high-level languages introduced a requirement for *low-level programming languages* or *system programming languages*. These languages, to varying degrees, provide facilities between assembly languages and high-level languages, and can be used to perform tasks which require direct access to hardware facilities but still provide higher-level control structures and error-checking.

The period from the 1960s to the late 1970s brought the development of the major language paradigms now in use:

- APL introduced *array programming* and influenced functional programming.

- ALGOL refined both *structured procedural programming* and the discipline of language specification; the "Revised Report on the Algorithmic Language ALGOL 60" became a model for how later language specifications were written.

- Lisp, implemented in 1958, was the first dynamically typed *functional programming* language

- In the 1960s, Simula was the first language designed to support *object-oriented programming*; in the mid-1970s, Smalltalk followed with the first "purely" object-oriented language.

- C was developed between 1969 and 1973 as a system programming language for the Unix operating system, and remains popular.

- Prolog, designed in 1972, was the first *logic programming* language.

- In 1978, ML built a polymorphic type system on top of Lisp, pioneering *statically typed functional programming* languages.

Each of these languages spawned descendants, and most modern programming languages count at least one of them in their ancestry.

The 1960s and 1970s also saw considerable debate over the merits of *structured programming*, and whether programming languages should be designed to support it. Edsger Dijkstra, in a famous 1968 letter published in the Communications of the ACM, argued that GOTO statements should be eliminated from all "higher level" programming languages.

Consolidation and Growth

The 1980s were years of relative consolidation. C++ combined object-oriented and systems programming. The United States government standardized Ada, a systems programming language derived from Pascal and intended for use by defense contractors. In Japan and elsewhere, vast sums were spent investigating so-called "fifth generation" languages that incorporated logic programming constructs. The functional languages community moved to standardize ML and Lisp. Rather than inventing new paradigms, all of these movements elaborated upon the ideas invented in the previous decades.

A selection of textbooks that teach programming, in languages both popular and obscure. These are only a few of the thousands of programming languages and dialects that have been designed in history.

One important trend in language design for programming large-scale systems during the 1980s was an increased focus on the use of *modules*, or large-scale organizational units of code. Modula-2, Ada, and ML all developed notable module systems in the 1980s, which were often wedded to generic programming constructs.

The rapid growth of the Internet in the mid-1990s created opportunities for new languages. Perl, originally a Unix scripting tool first released in 1987, became common in dynamic websites. Java came to be used for server-side programming, and bytecode virtual machines became popular again in commercial settings with their promise of "Write once, run anywhere" (UCSD Pascal had been popular for a time in the early 1980s). These developments were not fundamentally novel, rather they were refinements of many existing languages and paradigms (although their syntax was often based on the C family of programming languages).

Programming language evolution continues, in both industry and research. Current directions include security and reliability verification, new kinds of modularity (mixins, delegates, aspects), and database integration such as Microsoft's LINQ.

Fourth-generation programming languages (4GL) are a computer programming languages which aim to provide a higher level of abstraction of the internal computer hardware details than 3GLs. *Fifth generation programming languages* (5GL) are programming languages based on solving problems using constraints given to the program, rather than using an algorithm written by a programmer.

Elements

All programming languages have some primitive building blocks for the description of data and the processes or transformations applied to them (like the addition of two numbers or the selection of an item from a collection). These primitives are defined by syntactic and semantic rules which describe their structure and meaning respectively.

Syntax

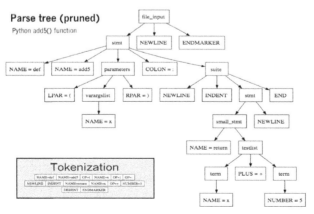

Parse tree of Python code with inset tokenization

A programming language's surface form is known as its syntax. Most programming languages are purely textual; they use sequences of text including words, numbers, and punctuation, much like written natural languages. On the other hand, there are some programming languages which are more graphical in nature, using visual relationships between symbols to specify a program.

```python
def add5(x):
    return x+5

def dotwrite(ast):
    nodename = getNodename()
    label=symbol.sym_name.get(int(ast[0]),ast[0])
    print '    %s [label="%s' % (nodename, label),
    if isinstance(ast[1], str):
        if ast[1].strip():
            print '= %s"];' % ast[1]
        else:
            print '"]'
    else:
        print '"];'
        children = []
        for n, child in enumerate(ast[1:]):
            children.append(dotwrite(child))
        print '    %s -> {' % nodename,
        for name in children:
            print '%s' % name,
```

Syntax highlighting is often used to aid programmers in recognizing elements of source code. The language above is Python.

The syntax of a language describes the possible combinations of symbols that form a syntactically correct program. The meaning given to a combination of symbols is handled by semantics (either formal or hard-coded in a reference implementation). Since most languages are textual, this article discusses textual syntax.

Programming language syntax is usually defined using a combination of regular expressions (for lexical structure) and Backus–Naur form (for grammatical structure). Below is a simple grammar, based on Lisp:

```
expression ::= atom | list

atom       ::= number | symbol

number     ::= [+-]?['0'-'9']+

symbol     ::= ['A'-'Z''a'-'z'].*

list       ::= '(' expression* ')'
```

This grammar specifies the following:

- an *expression* is either an *atom* or a *list*;

- an *atom* is either a *number* or a *symbol*;

- a *number* is an unbroken sequence of one or more decimal digits, optionally preceded by a plus or minus sign;

- a *symbol* is a letter followed by zero or more of any characters (excluding whitespace); and

- a *list* is a matched pair of parentheses, with zero or more *expressions* inside it.

The following are examples of well-formed token sequences in this grammar: 12345, () and (a b c232 (1)).

Not all syntactically correct programs are semantically correct. Many syntactically correct programs are nonetheless ill-formed, per the language's rules; and may (depending on the language specification and the soundness of the implementation) result in an error on translation or execution. In some cases, such programs may exhibit undefined behavior. Even when a program is well-defined within a language, it may still have a meaning that is not intended by the person who wrote it.

Using natural language as an example, it may not be possible to assign a meaning to a grammatically correct sentence or the sentence may be false:

- "Colorless green ideas sleep furiously." is grammatically well-formed but has no generally accepted meaning.

- "John is a married bachelor." is grammatically well-formed but expresses a meaning that cannot be true.

The following C language fragment is syntactically correct, but performs operations that are not semantically defined (the operation *p >> 4 has no meaning for a value having a complex type and p->im is not defined because the value of p is the null pointer):

```
complex *p = NULL;
complex abs_p = sqrt(*p >> 4 + p->im);
```

If the type declaration on the first line were omitted, the program would trigger an error on compilation, as the variable "p" would not be defined. But the program would still be syntactically correct, since type declarations provide only semantic information.

The grammar needed to specify a programming language can be classified by its position in the Chomsky hierarchy. The syntax of most programming languages can be specified using a Type-2 grammar, i.e., they are context-free grammars. Some languages, including Perl and Lisp, contain constructs that allow execution during the parsing phase. Languages that have constructs that allow the programmer to alter the behavior of the parser make syntax analysis an undecidable problem, and generally blur the distinction between parsing and execution. In contrast to Lisp's macro system and Perl's BEGIN blocks, which may contain general computations, C macros are merely string replacements, and do not require code execution.

Semantics

The term *semantics* refers to the meaning of languages, as opposed to their form (syntax).

Static Semantics

The static semantics defines restrictions on the structure of valid texts that are hard or impossible to express in standard syntactic formalisms. For compiled languages, static semantics essentially include those semantic rules that can be checked at compile time. Examples include checking that every identifier is declared before it is used (in languages that require such declarations) or that the labels on the arms of a case statement are distinct. Many important restrictions of this type, like checking that identifiers are used in the appropriate context (e.g. not adding an integer to a function name), or that subroutine calls have the appropriate number and type of arguments, can be enforced by defining them as rules in a logic called a type system. Other forms of static analyses like data flow analysis may also be part of static semantics. Newer programming languages like Java and C# have definite assignment analysis, a form of data flow analysis, as part of their static semantics.

Dynamic Semantics

Once data has been specified, the machine must be instructed to perform operations on the data. For example, the semantics may define the strategy by which expressions are evaluated to values, or the manner in which control structures conditionally execute statements. The *dynamic semantics* (also known as *execution semantics*) of a language defines how and when the various constructs of a language should produce a program behavior. There are many ways of defining execution semantics. Natural language is often used to specify the execution semantics of languages commonly used in practice. A significant amount of academic research went into formal semantics of programming languages, which allow execution semantics to be specified in a formal manner. Results from this field of research have seen limited application to programming language design and implementation outside academia.

Type System

A type system defines how a programming language classifies values and expressions into *types*, how it can manipulate those types and how they interact. The goal of a type system is to verify and usually enforce a certain level of correctness in programs written in that language by detecting certain incorrect operations. Any decidable type system involves a trade-off: while it rejects many incorrect programs, it can also prohibit some correct, albeit unusual programs. In order to bypass this downside, a number of languages have *type loopholes*, usually unchecked casts that may be used by the programmer to explicitly allow a normally disallowed operation between different types.

In most typed languages, the type system is used only to type check programs, but a number of languages, usually functional ones, infer types, relieving the programmer from the need to write type annotations. The formal design and study of type systems is known as *type theory*.

Typed Versus Untyped Languages

A language is *typed* if the specification of every operation defines types of data to which the operation is applicable, with the implication that it is not applicable to other types. For example, the data represented by "this text between the quotes" is a string, and in many programming languages dividing a number by a string has no meaning and will be rejected by the compilers. The invalid operation may be detected when the program is compiled ("static" type checking) and will be rejected by the compiler with a compilation error message, or it may be detected when the program is run ("dynamic" type checking), resulting in a run-time exception. Many languages allow a function called an exception handler to be written to handle this exception and, for example, always return "-1" as the result.

A special case of typed languages are the *single-type* languages. These are often scripting or markup languages, such as REXX or SGML, and have only one data type—most commonly character strings which are used for both symbolic and numeric data.

In contrast, an *untyped language*, such as most assembly languages, allows any operation to be performed on any data, which are generally considered to be sequences of bits of various lengths. High-level languages which are untyped include BCPL, Tcl, and some varieties of Forth.

In practice, while few languages are considered typed from the point of view of type theory (verifying or rejecting *all* operations), most modern languages offer a degree of typing. Many production languages provide means to bypass or subvert the type system, trading type-safety for finer control over the program's execution.

Static Versus Dynamic Typing

In *static typing*, all expressions have their types determined prior to when the program is executed, typically at compile-time. For example, 1 and (2+2) are integer expressions; they cannot be passed to a function that expects a string, or stored in a variable that is defined to hold dates.

Statically typed languages can be either *manifestly typed* or *type-inferred*. In the first case, the programmer must explicitly write types at certain textual positions (for example, at variable declarations). In the second case, the compiler *infers* the types of expressions and declarations based on context. Most mainstream statically typed languages, such as C++, C# and Java, are manifestly typed. Complete type inference has traditionally been associated with less mainstream languages, such as Haskell and ML. However, many manifestly typed languages support partial type inference; for example, Java and C# both infer types in certain limited cases. Additionally, some programming languages allow for some types to be automatically converted to other types; for example, an int can be used where the program expects a float.

Dynamic typing, also called *latent typing*, determines the type-safety of operations at run time; in other words, types are associated with *run-time values* rather than *textual expressions*. As with type-inferred languages, dynamically typed languages do not require the programmer to write explicit type annotations on expressions. Among other things, this may permit a single variable to refer to values of different types at different points in the program execution. However, type errors cannot be automatically detected until a piece of code is actually executed, potentially making debugging more difficult. Lisp, Smalltalk, Perl, Python, JavaScript, and Ruby are dynamically typed.

Weak and Strong Typing

Weak typing allows a value of one type to be treated as another, for example treating a string as a number. This can occasionally be useful, but it can also allow some kinds of program faults to go undetected at compile time and even at run time.

Strong typing prevents the above. An attempt to perform an operation on the wrong type of value raises an error. Strongly typed languages are often termed *type-safe* or *safe*.

An alternative definition for "weakly typed" refers to languages, such as Perl and JavaScript, which permit a large number of implicit type conversions. In JavaScript, for example, the expression 2 * x implicitly converts x to a number, and this conversion succeeds even if x is null, undefined, an Array, or a string of letters. Such implicit conversions are often useful, but they can mask programming errors. *Strong* and *static* are now generally considered orthogonal concepts, but usage in the literature differs. Some use the term *strongly typed* to mean *strongly, statically typed*, or, even more confusingly, to mean simply *statically typed*. Thus C has been called both strongly typed and weakly, statically typed.

It may seem odd to some professional programmers that C could be "weakly, statically typed". However, notice that the use of the generic pointer, the **void*** pointer, does allow for casting of pointers to other pointers without needing to do an explicit cast. This is extremely similar to somehow casting an array of bytes to any kind of datatype in C without using an explicit cast, such as (int) or (char).

Standard Library and Run-time System

Most programming languages have an associated core library (sometimes known as the 'standard library', especially if it is included as part of the published language standard), which is conventionally made available by all implementations of the language. Core libraries typically include definitions for commonly used algorithms, data structures, and mechanisms for input and output.

The line between a language and its core library differs from language to language. In some cases, the language designers may treat the library as a separate entity from the language. However, a language's core library is often treated as part of the language by its users, and some language specifications even require that this library be made available in all implementations. Indeed, some languages are designed so that the meanings of certain syntactic constructs cannot even be described without referring to the core library. For example, in Java, a string literal is defined as an instance of the java.lang. String class; similarly, in Smalltalk, an anonymous function expression (a "block") constructs an instance of the library's BlockContext class. Conversely, Scheme contains multiple coherent subsets that suffice to construct the rest of the language as library macros, and so the language designers do not even bother to say which portions of the language must be implemented as language constructs, and which must be implemented as parts of a library.

Design and Implementation

Programming languages share properties with natural languages related to their purpose as vehicles for communication, having a syntactic form separate from its semantics, and showing *language families* of related languages branching one from another. But as artificial constructs, they also differ in fundamental ways from languages that have evolved through usage. A significant difference is that a programming language can be fully described and studied in its entirety, since it has a precise and finite definition. By contrast, natural languages have changing meanings given by their users in different communities. While constructed languages are also artificial languages designed from the ground up with a specific purpose, they lack the precise and complete semantic definition that a programming language has.

Many programming languages have been designed from scratch, altered to meet new needs, and combined with other languages. Many have eventually fallen into disuse. Although there have been attempts to design one "universal" programming language that serves all purposes, all of them have failed to be generally accepted as filling this role. The need for diverse programming languages arises from the diversity of contexts in which languages are used:

- Programs range from tiny scripts written by individual hobbyists to huge systems written by hundreds of programmers.

- Programmers range in expertise from novices who need simplicity above all else, to experts who may be comfortable with considerable complexity.

- Programs must balance speed, size, and simplicity on systems ranging from microcontrollers to supercomputers.

- Programs may be written once and not change for generations, or they may undergo continual modification.

- Programmers may simply differ in their tastes: they may be accustomed to discussing problems and expressing them in a particular language.

One common trend in the development of programming languages has been to add more ability to solve problems using a higher level of abstraction. The earliest programming languages were tied very closely to the underlying hardware of the computer. As new programming languages have developed, features have been added that let programmers express ideas that are more remote from simple translation into underlying hardware instructions. Because programmers are less tied to the complexity of the computer, their programs can do more computing with less effort from the programmer. This lets them write more functionality per time unit.

Natural language programming has been proposed as a way to eliminate the need for a specialized language for programming. However, this goal remains distant and its benefits are open to debate. Edsger W. Dijkstra took the position that the use of a formal language is essential to prevent the introduction of meaningless constructs, and dismissed natural language programming as "foolish". Alan Perlis was similarly dismissive of the idea. Hybrid approaches have been taken in Structured English and SQL.

A language's designers and users must construct a number of artifacts that govern and enable the practice of programming. The most important of these artifacts are the language *specification* and *implementation*.

Specification

The specification of a programming language is an artifact that the language users and the implementors can use to agree upon whether a piece of source code is a valid program in that language, and if so what its behavior shall be.

A programming language specification can take several forms, including the following:

- An explicit definition of the syntax, static semantics, and execution semantics of the language. While syntax is commonly specified using a formal grammar, semantic definitions may be written in natural language (e.g., as in the C language), or a formal semantics (e.g., as in Standard ML and Scheme specifications).

- A description of the behavior of a translator for the language (e.g., the C++ and Fortran specifications). The syntax and semantics of the language have to be inferred from this description, which may be written in natural or a formal language.

- A *reference* or *model* implementation, sometimes written in the language being specified (e.g., Prolog or ANSI REXX). The syntax and semantics of the language are explicit in the behavior of the reference implementation.

Implementation

An *implementation* of a programming language provides a way to write programs in that language and execute them on one or more configurations of hardware and software. There are, broadly, two approaches to programming language implementation: *compilation* and *interpretation*. It is generally possible to implement a language using either technique.

The output of a compiler may be executed by hardware or a program called an interpreter. In some implementations that make use of the interpreter approach there is no distinct boundary between compiling and interpreting. For instance, some implementations of BASIC compile and then execute the source a line at a time.

Programs that are executed directly on the hardware usually run several orders of magnitude faster than those that are interpreted in software.

One technique for improving the performance of interpreted programs is just-in-time compilation. Here the virtual machine, just before execution, translates the blocks of bytecode which are going to be used to machine code, for direct execution on the hardware.

Proprietary Languages

Although most of the most commonly used programming languages have fully open specifications and implementations, many programming languages exist only as proprietary programming languages with the implementation available only from a single vendor, which may claim that such a proprietary language is their intellectual property. Proprietary programming languages are commonly domain specific languages or internal scripting languages for a single product; some proprietary languages are used only internally within a vendor, while others are available to external users.

Some programming languages exist on the border between proprietary and open; for example, Oracle Corporation asserts proprietary rights to some aspects of the Java programming language, and Microsoft's C# programming language, which has open implementations of most parts of the system, also has Common Language Runtime (CLR) as a closed environment.

Many proprietary languages are widely used, in spite of their proprietary nature; examples include MATLAB and VBScript. Some languages may make the transition from closed to open; for example, Erlang was originally an Ericsson's internal programming language.

Usage

Thousands of different programming languages have been created, mainly in the computing field. Software is commonly built with 5 programming languages or more.

Programming languages differ from most other forms of human expression in that they require a greater degree of precision and completeness. When using a natural language to communicate with other people, human authors and speakers can be ambiguous and make small errors, and still expect their intent to be understood. However, figuratively speaking, computers "do exactly what they are told to do", and cannot "understand" what code the programmer intended to write. The combination of the language definition, a program, and the program's inputs must fully specify the external behavior that occurs when the program is executed, within the domain of control of that program. On the other hand, ideas about an algorithm can be communicated to humans without the precision required for execution by using pseudocode, which interleaves natural language with code written in a programming language.

A programming language provides a structured mechanism for defining pieces of data, and the operations or transformations that may be carried out automatically on that data. A programmer uses the abstractions present in the language to represent the concepts involved in a computation. These concepts are represented as a collection of the simplest elements available (called primitives). *Programming* is the process by which programmers combine these primitives to compose new programs, or adapt existing ones to new uses or a changing environment.

Programs for a computer might be executed in a batch process without human interaction, or a user might type commands in an interactive session of an interpreter. In this case the "commands" are simply programs, whose execution is chained together. When a language can run its commands through an interpreter (such as a Unix shell or other command-line interface), without compiling, it is called a scripting language.

Measuring Language Usage

It is difficult to determine which programming languages are most widely used, and what usage means varies by context. One language may occupy the greater number of programmer hours, a different one have more lines of code, and a third may consume the most CPU time. Some languages are very popular for particular kinds of applications. For example, COBOL is still strong in the corporate data center, often on large mainframes; Fortran in scientific and engineering applications; Ada in aerospace, transportation, military, real-time and embedded applications; and C in embedded applications and operating systems. Other languages are regularly used to write many different kinds of applications.

Various methods of measuring language popularity, each subject to a different bias over what is measured, have been proposed:

- counting the number of job advertisements that mention the language

- the number of books sold that teach or describe the language

- estimates of the number of existing lines of code written in the language – which may underestimate languages not often found in public searches

- counts of language references (i.e., to the name of the language) found using a web search engine.

Combining and averaging information from various internet sites, langpop.com claims that in 2013 the ten most popular programming languages are (in descending order by overall popularity): C, Java, PHP, JavaScript, C++, Python, Shell, Ruby, Objective-C and C#.

Taxonomies

There is no overarching classification scheme for programming languages. A given programming language does not usually have a single ancestor language. Languages commonly arise by combining the elements of several predecessor languages with new ideas in circulation at the time. Ideas that originate in one language will diffuse throughout a family of related languages, and then leap suddenly across familial gaps to appear in an entirely different family.

The task is further complicated by the fact that languages can be classified along multiple axes. For example, Java is both an object-oriented language (because it encourages object-oriented organization) and a concurrent language (because it contains built-in constructs for running multiple threads in parallel). Python is an object-oriented scripting language.

In broad strokes, programming languages divide into *programming paradigms* and a classification by *intended domain of use,* with general-purpose programming languages distinguished from domain-specific programming languages. Traditionally, programming languages have been regarded as describing computation in terms of imperative sentences, i.e. issuing commands. These are generally called imperative programming languages. A great deal of research in programming languages has been aimed at blurring the distinction between a program as a set of instructions and a program as an assertion about the desired answer, which is the main feature of declarative programming. More refined paradigms include procedural programming, object-oriented programming, functional programming, and logic programming; some languages are hybrids of paradigms or multi-paradigmatic. An assembly language is not so much a paradigm as a direct model of an underlying machine architecture. By purpose, programming languages might be considered general purpose, system programming languages, scripting languages, domain-specific languages, or concurrent/distributed languages (or a combination of these). Some general purpose languages were designed largely with educational goals.

A programming language may also be classified by factors unrelated to programming paradigm. For instance, most programming languages use English language keywords, while a minority do not. Other languages may be classified as being deliberately esoteric or not.

References

- Stroustrup, Bjarne (2000). The C++ Programming Language (Special ed.). Addison-Wesley. p. 310. ISBN 0-201-70073-5.

- Scott, Michael (2006). Programming Language Pragmatics. Morgan Kaufmann. p. 802. ISBN 0-12-633951-1.

- Milner, R.; M. Tofte, R. Harper and D. MacQueen. (1997). The Definition of Standard ML (Revised). MIT Press. ISBN 0-262-63181-4.

- Harry. H. Chaudhary (28 July 2014). "Cracking The Java Programming Interview :: 2000+ Java Interview Que/Ans". Retrieved 29 May 2016.

- Mycroft, Alan (2013). "C and C++ Exceptions | Templates" (PDF). Cambridge Computer Laboratory - Course Materials 2013-14. Retrieved 30 August 2016.

- Stroustrup, B. (6 May 2014). "Lecture:The essence of C++. University of Edinburgh.". Retrieved 12 June 2015.

- Nicholas Enticknap. "SSL/Computer Weekly IT salary survey: finance boom drives IT job growth". Computerweekly.com. Retrieved 2013-06-14.

Programming Languages Related to C++

There are a number of programming languages which are related to C++. Some of these are C, Ada, CLU and ALGOL 68. All these languages are well structured, imperative and object oriented. This section strategically encompasses and incorporates the major components and key concepts of all the programming languages that are related to C++.

C (Programming Language)

C is a general-purpose, imperative computer programming language, supporting structured programming, lexical variable scope and recursion, while a static type system prevents many unintended operations. By design, C provides constructs that map efficiently to typical machine instructions, and therefore it has found lasting use in applications that had formerly been coded in assembly language, including operating systems, as well as various application software for computers ranging from supercomputers to embedded systems.

C was originally developed by Dennis Ritchie between 1969 and 1973 at Bell Labs, and used to re-implement the Unix operating system. It has since become one of the most widely used programming languages of all time, with C compilers from various vendors available for the majority of existing computer architectures and operating systems. C has been standardized by the American National Standards Institute (ANSI) since 1989 and subsequently by the International Organization for Standardization (ISO).

Design

C is an imperative procedural language. It was designed to be compiled using a relatively straightforward compiler, to provide low-level access to memory, to provide language constructs that map efficiently to machine instructions, and to require minimal run-time support. Therefore, C was useful for many applications that had formerly been coded in assembly language, for example in system programming.

Despite its low-level capabilities, the language was designed to encourage cross-platform programming. A standards-compliant and portably written C program can be compiled for a very wide variety of computer platforms and operating systems with few changes to its source code. The language has become available on a very wide range of platforms, from embedded microcontrollers to supercomputers.

Overview

Like most imperative languages in the ALGOL tradition, C has facilities for structured programming and allows lexical variable scope and recursion, while a static type system prevents many unintended operations. In C, all executable code is contained within sub-routines, which are called "functions" (although not in the strict sense of functional programming). Function parameters are always passed by value. Pass-by-reference is simulated in C by explicitly passing pointer values. C program source text is free-format, using the semicolon as a statement terminator and curly braces for grouping blocks of statements.

The C language also exhibits the following characteristics:

- There is a small, fixed number of keywords, including a full set of flow of control primitives: for, if/else, while, switch, and do/while. User-defined names are not distinguished from keywords by any kind of sigil.

- There are a large number of arithmetical and logical operators, such as +, +=, ++, &, ~, etc.

- More than one assignment may be performed in a single statement.

- Function return values can be ignored when not needed.

- Typing is static, but weakly enforced: all data has a type, but implicit conversions may be performed.

- Declaration syntax mimics usage context. C has no "define" keyword; instead, a statement beginning with the name of a type is taken as a declaration. There is no "function" keyword; instead, a function is indicated by the parentheses of an argument list.

- User-defined (typedef) and compound types are possible.

  o Heterogeneous aggregate data types (struct) allow related data elements to be accessed and assigned as a unit.

  o Array indexing is a secondary notation, defined in terms of pointer arithmetic. Unlike structs, arrays are not first-class objects; they cannot be assigned or compared using single built-in operators. There is no "array" keyword, in use or definition; instead, square brackets indicate arrays syntactically, for example month.

  o Enumerated types are possible with the enum keyword. They are not tagged, and are freely interconvertible with integers.

  o Strings are not a separate data type, but are conventionally implemented as null-terminated arrays of characters.

- Low-level access to computer memory is possible by converting machine addresses to typed pointers.

- Procedures (subroutines not returning values) are a special case of function, with an untyped return type void.

- Functions may not be defined within the lexical scope of other functions.

- Function and data pointers permit *ad hoc* run-time polymorphism.

- A preprocessor performs macro definition, source code file inclusion, and conditional compilation.

- There is a basic form of modularity: files can be compiled separately and linked together, with control over which functions and data objects are visible to other files via static and extern attributes.

- Complex functionality such as I/O, string manipulation, and mathematical functions are consistently delegated to library routines.

While C does not include some features found in some other languages, such as object orientation or garbage collection, such features can be implemented or emulated in C, often by way of external libraries (e.g., the Boehm garbage collector or the GLib Object System).

Relations to Other Languages

Many later languages have borrowed directly or indirectly from C, including C++, D, Go, Rust, Java, JavaScript, Limbo, LPC, C#, Objective-C, Perl, PHP, Python, Verilog (hardware description language), and Unix's C shell. These languages have drawn many of their control structures and other basic features from C. Most of them (with Python being the most dramatic exception) are also very syntactically similar to C in general, and they tend to combine the recognizable expression and statement syntax of C with underlying type systems, data models, and semantics that can be radically different.

History

Early Developments

The origin of C is closely tied to the development of the Unix operating system, originally implemented in assembly language on a PDP-7 by Ritchie and Thompson, incorporating several ideas from colleagues. Eventually, they decided to port the operating system to a PDP-11. The original PDP-11 version of Unix was developed in assembly language. The developers were considering rewriting the system using the B language, Thompson's simplified version of BCPL. However B's inability to take advantage of some of the PDP-11's features, notably byte addressability, led to C. The name of C was chosen simply as the next after B.

The development of C started in 1972 on the PDP-11 Unix system and first appeared in Version 2 Unix. The language was not initially designed with portability in mind, but soon ran on different platforms as well: a compiler for the Honeywell 6000 was written within the first year of C's history, while an IBM System/370 port followed soon.

Ken Thompson (left) with Dennis Ritchie (right, the inventor of the C programming language)

Also in 1972, a large part of Unix was rewritten in C. By 1973, with the addition of struct types, the C language had become powerful enough that most of the Unix's kernel was now in C.

Unix was one of the first operating system kernels implemented in a language other than assembly. Earlier instances include the Multics system which was written in PL/I), and Master Control Program (MCP) for the Burroughs B5000 written in ALGOL in 1961. In around 1977, Ritchie and Stephen C. Johnson made further changes to the language to facilitate portability of the Unix operating system. Johnson's Portable C Compiler served as the basis for several implementations of C on new platforms.

K&R C

The cover of the book, *The C Programming Language*, first edition by Brian Kernighan and Dennis Ritchie

In 1978, Brian Kernighan and Dennis Ritchie published the first edition of *The C Pro-*

gramming Language. This book, known to C programmers as "K&R", served for many years as an informal specification of the language. The version of C that it describes is commonly referred to as *K&R C*. The second edition of the book covers the later ANSI C standard, described below.

K&R introduced several language features:

- Standard I/O library

- long int data type

- unsigned int data type

- Compound assignment operators of the form *=op* (such as =-) were changed to the form *op=* (that is, -=) to remove the semantic ambiguity created by constructs such as i=-10, which had been interpreted as i =- 10 (decrement i by 10) instead of the possibly intended i = -10 (let i be -10).

Even after the publication of the 1989 ANSI standard, for many years K&R C was still considered the "lowest common denominator" to which C programmers restricted themselves when maximum portability was desired, since many older compilers were still in use, and because carefully written K&R C code can be legal Standard C as well.

In early versions of C, only functions that return types other than int must be declared if used before the function definition; functions used without prior declaration were presumed to return type int.

For example:

```
long some_function();
/* int */ other_function();


/* int */ calling_function()
{
    long test1;
    register /* int */ test2;


    test1 = some_function();
    if (test1 > 0)
            test2 = 0;
    else
```

```
    test2 = other_function();

  return test2;

}
```

The int type specifiers which are commented out could be omitted in K&R C, but are required in later standards.

Since K&R function declarations did not include any information about function arguments, function parameter type checks were not performed, although some compilers would issue a warning message if a local function was called with the wrong number of arguments, or if multiple calls to an external function used different numbers or types of arguments. Separate tools such as Unix's lint utility were developed that (among other things) could check for consistency of function use across multiple source files.

In the years following the publication of K&R C, several features were added to the language, supported by compilers from AT&T (in particular PCC) and some other vendors. These included:

- void functions (i.e., functions with no return value)

- functions returning struct or union types (rather than pointers)

- assignment for struct data types

- enumerated types

The large number of extensions and lack of agreement on a standard library, together with the language popularity and the fact that not even the Unix compilers precisely implemented the K&R specification, led to the necessity of standardization.

ANSI C and ISO C

The cover of the book, *The C Programming Language,* second edition by Brian Kernighan and Dennis Ritchie covering ANSI C

During the late 1970s and 1980s, versions of C were implemented for a wide variety of mainframe computers, minicomputers, and microcomputers, including the IBM PC, as its popularity began to increase significantly.

In 1983, the American National Standards Institute (ANSI) formed a committee, X3J11, to establish a standard specification of C. X3J11 based the C standard on the Unix implementation; however, the non-portable portion of the Unix C library was handed off to the IEEE working group 1003 to become the basis for the 1988 POSIX standard. In 1989, the C standard was ratified as ANSI X3.159-1989 "Programming Language C". This version of the language is often referred to as ANSI C, Standard C, or sometimes C89.

In 1990, the ANSI C standard (with formatting changes) was adopted by the International Organization for Standardization (ISO) as ISO/IEC 9899:1990, which is sometimes called C90. Therefore, the terms "C89" and "C90" refer to the same programming language.

ANSI, like other national standards bodies, no longer develops the C standard independently, but defers to the international C standard, maintained by the working group ISO/IEC JTC1/SC22/WG14. National adoption of an update to the international standard typically occurs within a year of ISO publication.

One of the aims of the C standardization process was to produce a superset of K&R C, incorporating many of the subsequently introduced unofficial features. The standards committee also included several additional features such as function prototypes (borrowed from C++), void pointers, support for international character sets and locales, and preprocessor enhancements. Although the syntax for parameter declarations was augmented to include the style used in C++, the K&R interface continued to be permitted, for compatibility with existing source code.

C89 is supported by current C compilers, and most C code being written today is based on it. Any program written only in Standard C and without any hardware-dependent assumptions will run correctly on any platform with a conforming C implementation, within its resource limits. Without such precautions, programs may compile only on a certain platform or with a particular compiler, due, for example, to the use of non-standard libraries, such as GUI libraries, or to a reliance on compiler- or platform-specific attributes such as the exact size of data types and byte endianness.

In cases where code must be compilable by either standard-conforming or K&R C-based compilers, the __STDC__ macro can be used to split the code into Standard and K&R sections to prevent the use on a K&R C-based compiler of features available only in Standard C.

After the ANSI/ISO standardization process, the C language specification remained relatively static for several years. In 1995, Normative Amendment 1 to the 1990 C standard (ISO/IEC 9899/AMD1:1995, known informally as C95) was published, to correct some details and to add more extensive support for international character sets.

C99

The C standard was further revised in the late 1990s, leading to the publication of ISO/ IEC 9899:1999 in 1999, which is commonly referred to as "C99". It has since been amended three times by Technical Corrigenda.

C99 introduced several new features, including inline functions, several new data types (including long long int and a complex type to represent complex numbers), variable-length arrays and flexible array members, improved support for IEEE 754 floating point, support for variadic macros (macros of variable arity), and support for one-line comments beginning with //, as in BCPL or C++. Many of these had already been implemented as extensions in several C compilers.

C99 is for the most part backward compatible with C90, but is stricter in some ways; in particular, a declaration that lacks a type specifier no longer has int implicitly assumed. A standard macro __STDC_VERSION__ is defined with value 199901L to indicate that C99 support is available. GCC, Solaris Studio, and other C compilers now support many or all of the new features of C99. The C compiler in Microsoft Visual C++, however, implements the C89 standard and those parts of C99 that are required for compatibility with C++11.

C11

In 2007, work began on another revision of the C standard, informally called "C1X" until its official publication on 2011-12-08. The C standards committee adopted guidelines to limit the adoption of new features that had not been tested by existing implementations.

The C11 standard adds numerous new features to C and the library, including type generic macros, anonymous structures, improved Unicode support, atomic operations, multi-threading, and bounds-checked functions. It also makes some portions of the existing C99 library optional, and improves compatibility with C++. The standard macro __STDC_VERSION__ is defined as 201112L to indicate that C11 support is available.

Embedded C

Historically, embedded C programming requires nonstandard extensions to the C language in order to support exotic features such as fixed-point arithmetic, multiple distinct memory banks, and basic I/O operations.

In 2008, the C Standards Committee published a technical report extending the C language to address these issues by providing a common standard for all implementations to adhere to. It includes a number of features not available in normal C, such as fixed-point arithmetic, named address spaces, and basic I/O hardware addressing.

Syntax

C has a formal grammar specified by the C standard. Unlike languages such as FOR-TRAN 77, C source code is free-form which allows arbitrary use of whitespace to format code, rather than column-based or text-line-based restrictions; however, line boundaries do have significance during the preprocessing phase. Comments may appear either between the delimiters /* and */, or (since C99) following // until the end of the line. Comments delimited by /* and */ do not nest, and these sequences of characters are not interpreted as comment delimiters if they appear inside string or character literals.

C source files contain declarations and function definitions. Function definitions, in turn, contain declarations and statements. Declarations either define new types using keywords such as struct, union, and enum, or assign types to and perhaps reserve storage for new variables, usually by writing the type followed by the variable name. Keywords such as char and int specify built-in types. Sections of code are enclosed in braces ({ and }, sometimes called "curly brackets") to limit the scope of declarations and to act as a single statement for control structures.

As an imperative language, C uses *statements* to specify actions. The most common statement is an *expression statement*, consisting of an expression to be evaluated, followed by a semicolon; as a side effect of the evaluation, functions may be called and variables may be assigned new values. To modify the normal sequential execution of statements, C provides several control-flow statements identified by reserved keywords. Structured programming is supported by if(-else) conditional execution and by do-while, while, and for iterative execution (looping). The for statement has separate initialization, testing, and reinitialization expressions, any or all of which can be omitted. break and continue can be used to leave the innermost enclosing loop statement or skip to its reinitialization. There is also a non-structured goto statement which branches directly to the designated label within the function. switch selects a case to be executed based on the value of an integer expression.

Expressions can use a variety of built-in operators and may contain function calls. The order in which arguments to functions and operands to most operators are evaluated is unspecified. The evaluations may even be interleaved. However, all side effects (including storage to variables) will occur before the next "sequence point"; sequence points include the end of each expression statement, and the entry to and return from each function call. Sequence points also occur during evaluation of expressions containing certain operators (&&, ||, ?: and the comma operator). This permits a high degree of object code optimization by the compiler, but requires C programmers to take more care to obtain reliable results than is needed for other programming languages.

Kernighan and Ritchie say in the Introduction of *The C Programming Language*: "C, like any other language, has its blemishes. Some of the operators have the wrong precedence; some parts of the syntax could be better." The C standard did not attempt to correct many of these blemishes, because of the impact of such changes on already existing software.

Character Set

The basic C source character set includes the following characters:

- Lowercase and uppercase letters of ISO Basic Latin Alphabet: a–z A–Z

- Decimal digits: 0–9

- Graphic characters: ! " # % & ' ( ) * + , - . / : ; < = > ? [\ ] ^ _ { | } ~

- Whitespace characters: *space, horizontal tab, vertical tab, form feed, newline*

Newline indicates the end of a text line; it need not correspond to an actual single character, although for convenience C treats it as one.

Additional multi-byte encoded characters may be used in string literals, but they are not entirely portable. The latest C standard (C11) allows multi-national Unicode characters to be embedded portably within C source text by using \uXXXX or \UXXXXXXXX encoding (where the X denotes a hexadecimal character), although this feature is not yet widely implemented.

The basic C execution character set contains the same characters, along with representations for alert, backspace, and carriage return. Run-time support for extended character sets has increased with each revision of the C standard.

Reserved Words

C89 has 32 reserved words, also known as keywords, which are the words that cannot be used for any purposes other than those for which they are predefined:

auto	double	int	struct
break	else	long	switch
case	enum	register	typedef
char	extern	return	union
const	float	short	unsigned
continue	for	signed	void
default	goto	sizeof	volatile
do	if	static	while

C99 reserved five more words:

_Bool	_Imaginary	restrict
_Complex	inline	

C11 reserved seven more words:

_Alignas	_Atomic	_Noreturn	_Thread_local
_Alignof	_Generic	_Static_assert	

Most of the recently reserved words begin with an underscore followed by a capital letter, because identifiers of that form were previously reserved by the C standard for use only by implementations. Since existing program source code should not have been using these identifiers, it would not be affected when C implementations started supporting these extensions to the programming language. Some standard headers do define more convenient synonyms for underscored identifiers. The language previously included a reserved word called entry, but this was seldom implemented, and has now been removed as a reserved word.

Operators

C supports a rich set of operators, which are symbols used within an expression to specify the manipulations to be performed while evaluating that expression. C has operators for:

- arithmetic: +, -, *, /, %
- assignment: =
- augmented assignment: +=, -=, *=, /=, %=, &=, |=, ^=, <<=, >>=
- bitwise logic: ~, &, |, ^
- bitwise shifts: <<, >>
- boolean logic: !, &&, ||
- conditional evaluation: ? :
- equality testing: ==, !=
- calling functions: ( )
- increment and decrement: ++, --
- member selection: ., ->
- object size: sizeof
- order relations: <, <=, >, >=

- reference and dereference: &, *, [ ]

- sequencing: ,

- subexpression grouping: ( )

- type conversion: (*typename*)

C uses the operator = (used in mathematics to express equality) to indicate assignment, following the precedent of Fortran and PL/I, but unlike ALGOL and its derivatives. C uses the operator == to test for equality. The similarity between these two operators (assignment and equality) may result in the accidental use of one in place of the other, and in many cases, the mistake does not produce an error message (although some compilers produce warnings). For example, the conditional expression if(a==b+1) might mistakenly be written as if(a=b+1), which will be evaluated as true if a is not zero after the assignment.

The C operator precedence is not always intuitive. For example, the operator == binds more tightly than (is executed prior to) the operators & (bitwise AND) and | (bitwise OR) in expressions such as x & 1 == 0, which must be written as (x & 1) == 0 if that is the coder's intent.

"Hello, World" Example

The "hello, world" example, which appeared in the first edition of K&R, has become the model for an introductory program in most programming textbooks, regardless of programming language. The program prints "hello, world" to the standard output, which is usually a terminal or screen display.

The original version was:

```
main()
{
    printf("hello, world\n");
}
```

A standard-conforming "hello, world" program is:

```
#include <stdio.h>


int main(void)
{
    printf("hello, world\n");
}
```

The first line of the program contains a preprocessing directive, indicated by #include. This causes the compiler to replace that line with the entire text of the stdio.h standard header, which contains declarations for standard input and output functions such as printf. The angle brackets surrounding stdio.h indicate that stdio.h is located using a search strategy that prefers headers provided with the compiler to other headers having the same name, as opposed to double quotes which typically include local or project-specific header files.

The next line indicates that a function named main is being defined. The main function serves a special purpose in C programs; the run-time environment calls the main function to begin program execution. The type specifier int indicates that the value that is returned to the invoker (in this case the run-time environment) as a result of evaluating the main function, is an integer. The keyword void as a parameter list indicates that this function takes no arguments

The opening curly brace indicates the beginning of the definition of the main function.

The next line *calls* (diverts execution to) a function named printf, which in this case is supplied from a system library. In this call, the printf function is *passed* (provided with) a single argument, the address of the first character in the string literal "hello, world\n". The string literal is an unnamed array with elements of type char, set up automatically by the compiler with a final 0-valued character to mark the end of the array (printf needs to know this). The \n is an *escape sequence* that C translates to a *newline* character, which on output signifies the end of the current line. The return value of the printf function is of type int, but it is silently discarded since it is not used. (A more careful program might test the return value to determine whether or not the printf function succeeded.) The semicolon ; terminates the statement.

The closing curly brace indicates the end of the code for the main function. According to the C99 specification and newer, the main function, unlike any other function, will implicitly return a status of 0 upon reaching the } that terminates the function. This is interpreted by the run-time system as an exit code indicating successful execution.

Data Types

The type system in C is static and weakly typed, which makes it similar to the type system of ALGOL descendants such as Pascal. There are built-in types for integers of various sizes, both signed and unsigned, floating-point numbers, and enumerated types (enum). Integer type char is often used for single-byte characters. C99 added a boolean datatype. There are also derived types including arrays, pointers, records (struct), and untagged unions (union).

C is often used in low-level systems programming where escapes from the type system may be necessary. The compiler attempts to ensure type correctness of most expressions, but the programmer can override the checks in various ways, either by using a *type cast* to explicitly convert a value from one type to another, or by using pointers or unions to reinterpret the underlying bits of a data object in some other way.

Some find C's declaration syntax unintuitive, particularly for function pointers. (Ritchie's idea was to declare identifiers in contexts resembling their use: "declaration reflects use".)

C's *usual arithmetic conversions* allow for efficient code to be generated, but can sometimes produce unexpected results. For example, a comparison of signed and unsigned integers of equal width requires a conversion of the signed value to unsigned. This can generate unexpected results if the signed value is negative.

Pointers

C supports the use of pointers, a type of reference that records the address or location of an object or function in memory. Pointers can be *dereferenced* to access data stored at the address pointed to, or to invoke a pointed-to function. Pointers can be manipulated using assignment or pointer arithmetic. The run-time representation of a pointer value is typically a raw memory address (perhaps augmented by an offset-within-word field), but since a pointer's type includes the type of the thing pointed to, expressions including pointers can be type-checked at compile time. Pointer arithmetic is automatically scaled by the size of the pointed-to data type. Pointers are used for many purposes in C. Text strings are commonly manipulated using pointers into arrays of characters. Dynamic memory allocation is performed using pointers. Many data types, such as trees, are commonly implemented as dynamically allocated struct objects linked together using pointers. Pointers to functions are useful for passing functions as arguments to higher-order functions (such as qsort or bsearch) or as callbacks to be invoked by event handlers.

A *null pointer value* explicitly points to no valid location. Dereferencing a null pointer value is undefined, often resulting in a segmentation fault. Null pointer values are useful for indicating special cases such as no "next" pointer in the final node of a linked list, or as an error indication from functions returning pointers. In appropriate contexts in source code, such as for assigning to a pointer variable, a *null pointer constant* can be written as 0, with or without explicit casting to a pointer type, or as the NULL macro defined by several standard headers. In conditional contexts, null pointer values evaluate to false, while all other pointer values evaluate to true.

Void pointers (void *) point to objects of unspecified type, and can therefore be used as "generic" data pointers. Since the size and type of the pointed-to object is not known, void pointers cannot be dereferenced, nor is pointer arithmetic on them allowed, although they can easily be (and in many contexts implicitly are) converted to and from any other object pointer type.

Careless use of pointers is potentially dangerous. Because they are typically unchecked, a pointer variable can be made to point to any arbitrary location, which can cause undesirable effects. Although properly used pointers point to safe places, they can be made to point to unsafe places by using invalid pointer arithmetic; the objects they point to may continue to be used after deallocation (dangling pointers); they may be used without having been initialized (wild pointers); or they may be directly assigned an unsafe value using a cast, union, or through another corrupt pointer. In general, C is permissive in allowing manipulation of and conversion between pointer types, although compilers typically provide options for various levels of checking. Some other programming languages address these problems by using more restrictive reference types.

Arrays

Array types in C are traditionally of a fixed, static size specified at compile time. (The more recent C99 standard also allows a form of variable-length arrays.) However, it is also possible to allocate a block of memory (of arbitrary size) at run-time, using the standard library's malloc function, and treat it as an array. C's unification of arrays and pointers means that declared arrays and these dynamically allocated simulated arrays are virtually interchangeable.

Since arrays are always accessed (in effect) via pointers, array accesses are typically *not* checked against the underlying array size, although some compilers may provide bounds checking as an option. Array bounds violations are therefore possible and rather common in carelessly written code, and can lead to various repercussions, including illegal memory accesses, corruption of data, buffer overruns, and run-time exceptions. If bounds checking is desired, it must be done manually.

C does not have a special provision for declaring multi-dimensional arrays, but rather relies on recursion within the type system to declare arrays of arrays, which effectively accomplishes the same thing. The index values of the resulting "multi-dimensional array" can be thought of as increasing in row-major order.

Multi-dimensional arrays are commonly used in numerical algorithms (mainly from applied linear algebra) to store matrices. The structure of the C array is well suited to this particular task. However, since arrays are passed merely as pointers, the bounds of the array must be known fixed values or else explicitly passed to any subroutine that requires them, and dynamically sized arrays of arrays cannot be accessed using double indexing. (A workaround for this is to allocate the array with an additional "row vector" of pointers to the columns.)

C99 introduced "variable-length arrays" which address some, but not all, of the issues with ordinary C arrays.

Array–pointer Interchangeability

The subscript notation x[i] (where x designates a pointer) is syntactic sugar for *(x+i). Taking advantage of the compiler's knowledge of the pointer type, the address that x +

i points to is not the base address (pointed to by x) incremented by i bytes, but rather is defined to be the base address incremented by i multiplied by the size of an element that x points to. Thus, x[i] designates the i+1th element of the array.

Furthermore, in most expression contexts (a notable exception is as operand of sizeof), the name of an array is automatically converted to a pointer to the array's first element. This implies that an array is never copied as a whole when named as an argument to a function, but rather only the address of its first element is passed. Therefore, although function calls in C use pass-by-value semantics, arrays are in effect passed by reference.

The size of an element can be determined by applying the operator sizeof to any deref-erenced element of x, as in n = sizeof *x or n = sizeof x, and the number of elements in a declared array A can be determined as sizeof A / sizeof A. The latter only applies to array names: variables declared with subscripts (int A). Due to the semantics of C, it is not possi-ble to determine the entire size of arrays through pointers to arrays or those created by dy-namic allocation (malloc); code such as sizeof arr / sizeof arr (where arr designates a point-er) will not work since the compiler assumes the size of the pointer itself is being requested. Since array name arguments to sizeof are not converted to pointers, they do not exhibit such ambiguity. However, arrays created by dynamic allocation are accessed by pointers rather than true array variables, so they suffer from the same sizeof issues as array pointers.

Thus, despite this apparent equivalence between array and pointer variables, there is still a distinction to be made between them. Even though the name of an array is, in most expression contexts, converted into a pointer (to its first element), this pointer does not itself occupy any storage; the array name is not an l-value, and its address is a constant, unlike a pointer variable. Consequently, what an array "points to" cannot be changed, and it is impossible to assign a new address to an array name. Array contents may be copied, however, by using the memcpy function, or by accessing the individual elements.

Memory Management

One of the most important functions of a programming language is to provide facilities for managing memory and the objects that are stored in memory. C provides three dis-tinct ways to allocate memory for objects:

- Static memory allocation: space for the object is provided in the binary at com-pile-time; these objects have an extent (or lifetime) as long as the binary which contains them is loaded into memory.

- Automatic memory allocation: temporary objects can be stored on the stack, and this space is automatically freed and reusable after the block in which they are declared is exited.

- Dynamic memory allocation: blocks of memory of arbitrary size can be requested at run-time using library functions such as malloc from a region of memory called the heap; these blocks persist until subsequently freed for reuse by calling the library function realloc or free

These three approaches are appropriate in different situations and have various trade-offs. For example, static memory allocation has little allocation overhead, automatic allocation may involve slightly more overhead, and dynamic memory allocation can potentially have a great deal of overhead for both allocation and deallocation. The persistent nature of static objects is useful for maintaining state information across function calls, automatic allocation is easy to use but stack space is typically much more limited and transient than either static memory or heap space, and dynamic memory allocation allows convenient allocation of objects whose size is known only at run-time. Most C programs make extensive use of all three.

Where possible, automatic or static allocation is usually simplest because the storage is managed by the compiler, freeing the programmer of the potentially error-prone chore of manually allocating and releasing storage. However, many data structures can change in size at runtime, and since static allocations (and automatic allocations before C99) must have a fixed size at compile-time, there are many situations in which dynamic allocation is necessary. Prior to the C99 standard, variable-sized arrays were a common example of this. Unlike automatic allocation, which can fail at run time with uncontrolled consequences, the dynamic allocation functions return an indication (in the form of a null pointer value) when the required storage cannot be allocated. (Static allocation that is too large is usually detected by the linker or loader, before the program can even begin execution.)

Unless otherwise specified, static objects contain zero or null pointer values upon program startup. Automatically and dynamically allocated objects are initialized only if an initial value is explicitly specified; otherwise they initially have indeterminate values (typically, whatever bit pattern happens to be present in the storage, which might not even represent a valid value for that type). If the program attempts to access an uninitialized value, the results are undefined. Many modern compilers try to detect and warn about this problem, but both false positives and false negatives can occur.

Another issue is that heap memory allocation has to be synchronized with its actual usage in any program in order for it to be reused as much as possible. For example, if the only pointer to a heap memory allocation goes out of scope or has its value overwritten before free() is called, then that memory cannot be recovered for later reuse and is essentially lost to the program, a phenomenon known as a *memory leak*. Conversely, it is possible for memory to be freed but continue to be referenced, leading to unpredictable results. Typically, the symptoms will appear in a portion of the program far removed from the actual error, making it difficult to track down the problem. (Such issues are ameliorated in languages with automatic garbage collection.)

Libraries

The C programming language uses libraries as its primary method of extension. In C, a library is a set of functions contained within a single "archive" file. Each library typically has a header file, which contains the prototypes of the functions contained within the library that may be used by a program, and declarations of special data types and macro symbols used with these functions. In order for a program to use a library, it must include the library's header file, and the library must be linked with the program, which in many cases requires compiler flags (e.g., -lm, shorthand for "link the math library").

The most common C library is the C standard library, which is specified by the ISO and ANSI C standards and comes with every C implementation (implementations which target limited environments such as embedded systems may provide only a subset of the standard library). This library supports stream input and output, memory allocation, mathematics, character strings, and time values. Several separate standard headers (for example, stdio.h) specify the interfaces for these and other standard library facilities.

Another common set of C library functions are those used by applications specifically targeted for Unix and Unix-like systems, especially functions which provide an interface to the kernel. These functions are detailed in various standards such as POSIX and the Single UNIX Specification.

Since many programs have been written in C, there are a wide variety of other libraries available. Libraries are often written in C because C compilers generate efficient object code; programmers then create interfaces to the library so that the routines can be used from higher-level languages like Java, Perl, and Python.

Language Tools

A number of tools have been developed to help C programmers find and fix statements with undefined behavior or possibly erroneous expressions, with greater rigor than that provided by the compiler. The tool lint was the first such, leading to many others.

Automated source code checking and auditing are beneficial in any language, and for C many such tools exist, such as Lint. A common practice is to use Lint to detect questionable code when a program is first written. Once a program passes Lint, it is then compiled using the C compiler. Also, many compilers can optionally warn about syntactically valid constructs that are likely to actually be errors. MISRA C is a proprietary set of guidelines to avoid such questionable code, developed for embedded systems.

There are also compilers, libraries, and operating system level mechanisms for performing actions that are not a standard part of C, such as bounds checking for arrays, detection of buffer overflow, serialization, dynamic memory tracking, and automatic garbage collection.

Tools such as Purify or Valgrind and linking with libraries containing special versions of the memory allocation functions can help uncover runtime errors in memory usage.

Uses

C is widely used for "system programming", including implementing operating systems and embedded system applications, because C code, when written for portability, can be used for most purposes, yet when needed, system-specific code can be used to access specific hardware addresses and to perform type punning to match externally imposed interface requirements, with a low run-time demand on system resources. C can also be used for website programming using CGI as a "gateway" for information between the Web application, the server, and the browser. C is often chosen over interpreted languages because of its speed, stability, and near-universal availability.

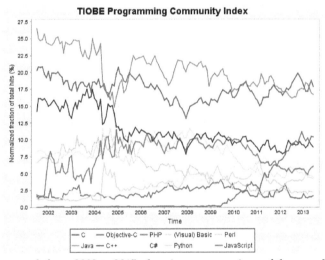

The TIOBE index graph from 2002 to 2015, showing a comparison of the popularity of various programming languages

One consequence of C's wide availability and efficiency is that compilers, libraries and interpreters of other programming languages are often implemented in C. The primary implementations of Python, Perl 5 and PHP, for example, are all written in C.

Because the layer of abstraction is thin and the overhead is low, C enables programmers to create efficient implementations of algorithms and data structures, useful for computationally intense programs. For example, the GNU Multiple Precision Arithmetic Library, the GNU Scientific Library, Mathematica, and MATLAB are completely or partially written in C.

C is sometimes used as an intermediate language by implementations of other languages. This approach may be used for portability or convenience; by using C as an intermediate language, additional machine-specific code generators are not necessary. C has some features, such as line-number preprocessor directives and optional superfluous commas at the end of initializer lists, that support compilation of generated code. However, some of C's shortcomings have prompted the development of other C-based languages specifically designed for use as intermediate languages, such as C--.

C has also been widely used to implement end-user applications. However, such applications can also be written in newer, higher-level languages.

Related Languages

C has directly or indirectly influenced many later languages such as C#, D, Go, Java, JavaScript, Limbo, LPC, Perl, PHP, Python, and Unix's C shell. The most pervasive influence has been syntactical: all of the languages mentioned combine the statement and (more or less recognizably) expression syntax of C with type systems, data models and/or large-scale program structures that differ from those of C, sometimes radically.

Several C or near-C interpreters exist, including Ch and CINT, which can also be used for scripting.

When object-oriented languages became popular, C++ and Objective-C were two different extensions of C that provided object-oriented capabilities. Both languages were originally implemented as source-to-source compilers; source code was translated into C, and then compiled with a C compiler.

The C++ programming language was devised by Bjarne Stroustrup as an approach to providing object-oriented functionality with a C-like syntax. C++ adds greater typing strength, scoping, and other tools useful in object-oriented programming, and permits generic programming via templates. Nearly a superset of C, C++ now supports most of C, with a few exceptions.

Objective-C was originally a very "thin" layer on top of C, and remains a strict superset of C that permits object-oriented programming using a hybrid dynamic/static typing paradigm. Objective-C derives its syntax from both C and Smalltalk: syntax that involves preprocessing, expressions, function declarations, and function calls is inherited from C, while the syntax for object-oriented features was originally taken from Smalltalk.

In addition to C++ and Objective-C, Ch, Cilk and Unified Parallel C are nearly supersets of C.

Ada (Programming Language)

Ada is a structured, statically typed, imperative, wide-spectrum, and object-oriented high-level computer programming language, extended from Pascal and other languages. It has built-in language support for design-by-contract, extremely strong typing, explicit concurrency, offering tasks, synchronous message passing, protected objects, and non-determinism. Ada improves code safety and maintainability by using the compiler to find errors in favor of runtime errors. Ada is an international standard; the current version (known as Ada 2012) is defined by ISO/IEC 8652:2012.

Ada was originally designed by a team led by Jean Ichbiah of CII Honeywell Bull under contract to the United States Department of Defense (DoD) from 1977 to 1983 to supersede over 450 programming languages used by the DoD at that time. Ada was named after Ada Lovelace (1815–1852), who is credited with being the first computer programmer.

Features

Ada was originally targeted at embedded and real-time systems. The Ada 95 revision, designed by S. Tucker Taft of Intermetrics between 1992 and 1995, improved support for systems, numerical, financial, and object-oriented programming (OOP).

Features of Ada include: strong typing, modularity mechanisms (packages), run-time checking, parallel processing (tasks, synchronous message passing, protected objects, and nondeterministic select statements), exception handling, and generics. Ada 95 added support for object-oriented programming, including dynamic dispatch.

The syntax of Ada minimizes choices of ways to perform basic operations, and prefers English keywords (such as "or else" and "and then") to symbols (such as "||" and "&&"). Ada uses the basic arithmetical operators "+", "-", "*", and "/", but avoids using other symbols. Code blocks are delimited by words such as "declare", "begin", and "end", where the "end" (in most cases) is followed by the identifier of the block it closes (e.g., *if ... end if, loop ... end loop*). In the case of conditional blocks this avoids a *dangling else* that could pair with the wrong nested if-expression in other languages like C or Java.

Ada is designed for development of very large software systems. Ada packages can be compiled separately. Ada package specifications (the package interface) can also be compiled separately without the implementation to check for consistency. This makes it possible to detect problems early during the design phase, before implementation starts.

A large number of compile-time checks are supported to help avoid bugs that would not be detectable until run-time in some other languages or would require explicit checks to be added to the source code. For example, the syntax requires explicitly named closing of blocks to prevent errors due to mismatched end tokens. The adherence to strong typing allows detection of many common software errors (wrong parameters, range violations, invalid references, mismatched types, etc.) either during compile-time, or otherwise during run-time. As concurrency is part of the language specification, the compiler can in some cases detect potential deadlocks. Compilers also commonly check for misspelled identifiers, visibility of packages, redundant declarations, etc. and can provide warnings and useful suggestions on how to fix the error.

Ada also supports run-time checks to protect against access to unallocated memory, buffer overflow errors, range violations, off-by-one errors, array access errors, and other detectable bugs. These checks can be disabled in the interest of runtime efficiency, but can often be compiled efficiently. It also includes facilities to help program verification. For these reasons, Ada is widely used in critical systems, where any anomaly might lead to very serious consequences, e.g., accidental death, injury or severe financial loss. Examples of systems where Ada is used include avionics, ATC, railways, banking, military and space technology.

Ada's dynamic memory management is high-level and type-safe. Ada does not have generic or untyped pointers; nor does it implicitly declare any pointer type. Instead, all dynamic memory allocation and deallocation must take place through explicitly declared *access types*. Each access type has an associated *storage pool* that handles the low-level details of memory management; the programmer can either use the default storage pool or define new ones (this is particularly relevant for Non-Uniform Memory Access). It is even possible to declare several different access types that all designate the same type but use different storage pools. Also, the language provides for *accessibility checks*, both at compile time and at run time, that ensures that an *access value* cannot outlive the type of the object it points to.

Though the semantics of the language allow automatic garbage collection of inaccessible objects, most implementations do not support it by default, as it would cause unpredictable behaviour in real-time systems. Ada does support a limited form of region-based memory management; also, creative use of storage pools can provide for a limited form of automatic garbage collection, since destroying a storage pool also destroys all the objects in the pool.

Ada was designed to resemble the English language in its syntax for comments: a double-dash ("--"), resembling an em dash, denotes comment text. Comments stop at end of line, so there is no danger of unclosed comments accidentally voiding whole sections of source code. Prefixing each line (or column) with "--" will skip all that code, while being clearly denoted as a column of repeated "--" down the page. There is no limit to the nesting of comments, thereby allowing prior code, with commented-out sections, to be commented-out as even larger sections. All Unicode characters are allowed in comments, such as for symbolic formulas ($E=m\times c^2$). To the compiler, the double-dash is treated as end-of-line, allowing continued parsing of the language as a context-free grammar.

The semicolon (";") is a statement terminator, and the null or no-operation statement is null;. A single ; without a statement to terminate is not allowed.

Unlike most ISO standards, the Ada language definition (known as the *Ada Reference Manual* or *ARM*, or sometimes the *Language Reference Manual* or *LRM*) is free content. Thus, it is a common reference for Ada programmers and not just programmers implementing Ada compilers. Apart from the reference manual, there is also an extensive rationale document which explains the language design and the use of various language constructs. This document is also widely used by programmers. When the language was revised, a new rationale document was written.

One notable free software tool that is used by many Ada programmers to aid them in writing Ada source code is the GNAT Programming Studio.

History

In the 1970s, the US Department of Defense (DoD) was concerned by the number of different programming languages being used for its embedded computer system projects, many of which were obsolete or hardware-dependent, and none of which supported safe modular programming. In 1975, a working group, the High Order Language Working Group (HOLWG), was formed with the intent to reduce this number by finding or creating a programming language generally suitable for the department's and UK Ministry of Defence requirements. After many iterations beginning with an original Straw man proposal the eventual programming language was named Ada. The total number of high-level programming languages in use for such projects fell from over 450 in 1983 to 37 by 1996.

The HOLWG working group crafted the Steelman language requirements, a series of documents stating the requirements they felt a programming language should satisfy. Many existing languages were formally reviewed, but the team concluded in 1977 that no existing language met the specifications.

Requests for proposals for a new programming language were issued and four contractors were hired to develop their proposals under the names of Red (Intermetrics led by Benjamin Brosgol), Green (CII Honeywell Bull, led by Jean Ichbiah), Blue (SofTech, led by John Goodenough) and Yellow (SRI International, led by Jay Spitzen). In April 1978, after public scrutiny, the Red and Green proposals passed to the next phase. In May 1979, the Green proposal, designed by Jean Ichbiah at CII Honeywell Bull, was chosen and given the name Ada—after Augusta Ada, Countess of Lovelace. This proposal was influenced by the programming language LIS that Ichbiah and his group had developed in the 1970s. The preliminary Ada reference manual was published in ACM SIGPLAN Notices in June 1979. The Military Standard reference manual was approved on December 10, 1980 (Ada Lovelace's birthday), and given the number MIL-STD-1815 in honor of Ada Lovelace's birth year. In 1981, C. A. R. Hoare took advantage of his Turing Award speech to criticize Ada for being overly complex and hence unreliable, but subsequently seemed to recant in the foreword he wrote for an Ada textbook.

Ada attracted much attention from the programming community as a whole during its early days. Its backers and others predicted that it might become a dominant language for general purpose programming and not just defense-related work. Ichbiah publicly stated that within ten years, only two programming languages would remain, Ada and Lisp. Early Ada compilers struggled to implement the large, complex language, and both compile-time and run-time performance tended to be slow and tools primitive. Compiler vendors expended most of their efforts in passing the massive, language-conformance-testing, government-required "ACVC" validation suite that was required in another novel feature of the Ada language effort.

The first validated Ada implementation was the NYU Ada/Ed translator, certified on April 11, 1983. NYU Ada/Ed is implemented in the high-level set language SETL. A number of commercial companies began offering Ada compilers and associated development tools, including Alsys, TeleSoft, DDC-I, Advanced Computer Techniques, Tartan Laboratories, TLD Systems, Verdix, and others.

Augusta Ada King, Countess of Lovelace.

In 1991, the US Department of Defense began to require the use of Ada (the *Ada mandate*) for all software, though exceptions to this rule were often granted. The Department of Defense Ada mandate was effectively removed in 1997, as the DoD began to embrace COTS technology. Similar requirements existed in other NATO countries.

By the late 1980s and early 1990s, Ada compilers had improved in performance, but there were still barriers to full exploitation of Ada's abilities, including a tasking model that was different from what most real-time programmers were used to.

Because of Ada's safety-critical support features, it is now used not only for military applications, but also in commercial projects where a software bug can have severe consequences, e.g., avionics and air traffic control, commercial rockets (e.g., Ariane 4 and 5), satellites and other space systems, railway transport and banking. For example, the Airplane Information Management System, the fly-by-wire system software in the Boeing 777, was written in Ada; developed by Honeywell Air Transport Systems in collaboration with consultants from DDC-I, it became arguably the best-known of any Ada project, civilian or military. The Canadian Automated Air Traffic System was written in 1 million lines of Ada (SLOC count). It featured advanced distributed processing, a distributed Ada database, and object-oriented design. Ada is also used in other air traf-fic systems, e.g., the UK's next-generation Interim Future Area Control Tools Support (iFACTS) air traffic control system is designed and implemented using SPARK Ada. It is also used in the French TVM in-cab signalling system on the TGV high-speed rail sys-tem, and the metro suburban trains in Paris, London, Hong Kong and New York City.

Standardization

The language became an ANSI standard in 1983 (ANSI/MIL-STD 1815A), and without any further changes became an ISO standard in 1987 (ISO-8652:1987). This version of the language is commonly known as Ada 83, from the date of its adoption by ANSI, but is sometimes referred to also as Ada 87, from the date of its adoption by ISO.

Ada 95, the joint ISO/ANSI standard (ISO-8652:1995) was published in February 1995, making Ada 95 the first ISO standard object-oriented programming language. To help with the standard revision and future acceptance, the US Air Force funded the development of the GNAT Compiler. Presently, the GNAT Compiler is part of the GNU Compiler Collection.

Work has continued on improving and updating the technical content of the Ada pro-gramming language. A Technical Corrigendum to Ada 95 was published in October 2001, and a major Amendment, ISO/IEC 8652:1995/Amd 1:2007 was published on March 9, 2007. At the Ada-Europe 2012 conference in Stockholm, the Ada Resource Association (ARA) and Ada-Europe announced the completion of the design of the lat-est version of the Ada programming language and the submission of the reference man-ual to the International Organization for Standardization (ISO) for approval. ISO/IEC 8652:2012 was published in December 2012.

Other related standards include ISO 8651-3:1988 *Information processing systems—Computer graphics—Graphical Kernel System (GKS) language bindings—Part 3: Ada.*

Language Constructs

Ada is an ALGOL-like programming language featuring control structures with re-served words such as *if, then, else, while, for*, and so on. However, Ada also has many data structuring facilities and other abstractions which were not included in the orig-inal ALGOL 60, such as type definitions, records, pointers, enumerations. Such con-structs were in part inherited or inspired from Pascal.

"Hello, World!" in Ada

A common example of a language's syntax is the Hello world program: (hello.adb)

```
with Ada.Text_IO; use Ada.Text_IO;
```

```
procedure Hello is

begin

  Put_Line ("Hello, world!");

end Hello;
```

This program can be compiled by using the freely available open source compiler GNAT, by executing

```
gnatmake hello.adb
```

Data Types

Ada's type system is not based on a set of predefined primitive types but allows users to declare their own types. This declaration in turn is not based on the internal representation of the type but on describing the goal which should be achieved. This allows the compiler to determine a suitable memory size for the type, and to check for violations of the type definition at compile time and run time (i.e., range violations, buffer overruns, type consistency, etc.). Ada supports numerical types defined by a range, modulo types, aggregate types (records and arrays), and enumeration types. Access types define a reference to an instance of a specified type; untyped pointers are not permitted. Special types provided by the language are task types and protected types.

For example, a date might be represented as:

```
type Day_type   is range    1 ..    31;

type Month_type is range    1 ..    12;

type Year_type  is range 1800 .. 2100;

type Hours is mod 24;

type Weekday is (Monday, Tuesday, Wednesday, Thursday, Friday,
Saturday, Sunday);


type Date is

   record

      Day   : Day_type;

      Month : Month_type;

      Year  : Year_type;
```

```
   end record;
```

Types can be refined by declaring subtypes:

```
subtype Working_Hours is Hours range 0 .. 12;              -- at
most 12 Hours to work a day

subtype Working_Day is Weekday range Monday .. Friday;    -- Days
to work


Work_Load: constant array(Working_Day) of Working_Hours   -- im-
plicit type declaration

   := (Friday => 6, Monday => 4, others => 10);            -- look-
up table for working hours with initialization
```

Types can have modifiers such as *limited, abstract, private* etc. Private types can only be accessed and limited types can only be modified or copied within the scope of the package that defines them. Ada 95 adds additional features for object-oriented extension of types.

Control Structures

Ada is a structured programming language, meaning that the flow of control is structured into standard statements. All standard constructs and deep level early exit are supported so the use of the also supported 'go to' commands is seldom needed.

```
-- while a is not equal to b, loop.

while a /= b loop

  Ada.Text_IO.Put_Line ("Waiting");

end loop;


if a > b then

  Ada.Text_IO.Put_Line ("Condition met");

else

  Ada.Text_IO.Put_Line ("Condition not met");

end if;


for i in 1 .. 10 loop
```

```ada
   Ada.Text_IO.Put ("Iteration: ");

   Ada.Text_IO.Put (i);

   Ada.Text_IO.Put_Line;

end loop;


loop

   a := a + 1;

   exit when a = 10;

end loop;


case i is

   when 0 => Ada.Text_IO.Put ("zero");

   when 1 => Ada.Text_IO.Put ("one");

   when 2 => Ada.Text_IO.Put ("two");

   -- case statements have to cover all possible cases:

   when others => Ada.Text_IO.Put ("none of the above");

end case;


for aWeekday in Weekday'Range loop       -- loop over an enumeration

   Put_Line ( Weekday'Image(aWeekday) );          -- output string
representation of an enumeration

   if aWeekday in Working_Day then               -- check of a sub-
type of an enumeration

      Put_Line ( " to work for " &

              Working_Hours'Image (Work_Load(aWeekday)) ); --
access into a lookup table

   end if;

end loop;
```

Packages, Procedures and Functions

Among the parts of an Ada program are packages, procedures and functions.

Example: Package specification (example.ads)

```
package Example is

     type Number is range 1 .. 11;

     procedure Print_and_Increment (j: in out Number);

end Example;
```

Package body (example.adb)

```
with Ada.Text_IO;

package body Example is


  i : Number := Number'First;


  procedure Print_and_Increment (j: in out Number) is


     function Next (k: in Number) return Number is
     begin

        return k + 1;

     end Next;



  begin

     Ada.Text_IO.Put_Line ( "The total is: " & Number'Image(j) );

     j := Next (j);

  end Print_and_Increment;


-- package initialization executed when the package is elaborated

begin

  while i < Number'Last loop

     Print_and_Increment (i);

  end loop;

end Example;
```

This program can be compiled, e.g., by using the freely available open source compiler GNAT, by executing

gnatmake -z example.adb

Packages, procedures and functions can nest to any depth and each can also be the logical outermost block.

Each package, procedure or function can have its own declarations of constants, types, variables, and other procedures, functions and packages, which can be declared in any order.

Concurrency

Ada has language support for task-based concurrency. The fundamental concurrent unit in Ada is a *task* which is a built-in limited type. Tasks are specified in two parts – the task declaration defines the task interface (similar to a type declaration), the task body specifies the implementation of the task. Depending on the implementation, Ada tasks are either mapped to operating system threads or processes, or are scheduled internally by the Ada runtime.

Tasks can have entries for synchronisation (a form of synchronous message passing). Task entries are declared in the task specification. Each task entry can have one or more *accept* statements within the task body. If the control flow of the task reaches an accept statement, the task is blocked until the corresponding entry is called by another task (similarly, a calling task is blocked until the called task reaches the corresponding accept statement). Task entries can have parameters similar to procedures, allowing tasks to synchronously exchange data. In conjunction with *select* statements it is possible to define *guards* on accept statements (similar to Dijkstra's guarded commands).

Ada also offers *protected objects* for mutual exclusion. Protected objects are a monitor-like construct, but use guards instead of conditional variables for signaling (similar to conditional critical regions). Protected objects combine the data encapsulation and safe mutual exclusion from monitors, and entry guards from conditional critical regions. The main advantage over classical monitors is that conditional variables are not required for signaling, avoiding potential deadlocks due to incorrect locking semantics. Like tasks, the protected object is a built-in limited type, and it also has a declaration part and a body.

A protected object consists of encapsulated private data (which can only be accessed from within the protected object), and procedures, functions and entries which are guaranteed to be mutually exclusive (with the only exception of functions, which are required to be side effect free and can therefore run concurrently with other functions). A task calling a protected object is blocked if another task is currently executing inside the same protected object, and released when this other task leaves the protected object. Blocked tasks are queued on the protected object ordered by time of arrival.

Protected object entries are similar to procedures, but additionally have *guards*. If a guard evaluates to false, a calling task is blocked and added to the queue of that entry; now another task can be admitted to the protected object, as no task is currently executing inside the protected object. Guards are re-evaluated whenever a task leaves the protected object, as this is the only time when the evaluation of guards can have changed.

Calls to entries can be *requeued* to other entries with the same signature. A task that is requeued is blocked and added to the queue of the target entry; this means that the protected object is released and allows admission of another task.

The *select* statement in Ada can be used to implement non-blocking entry calls and accepts, non-deterministic selection of entries (also with guards), time-outs and aborts.

The following example illustrates some concepts of concurrent programming in Ada.

```
with Ada.Text_IO; use Ada.Text_IO;


procedure Traffic is


    type Airplane_ID is range 1..10;                  -- 10 airplanes


    task type Airplane (ID: Airplane_ID);             -- task repre-
senting airplanes, with ID as initialisation parameter

    type Airplane_Access is access Airplane;     -- reference type
to Airplane


    protected type Runway is                          -- the shared
runway (protected to allow concurrent access)

        entry Assign_Aircraft (ID: Airplane_ID);   -- all entries
are guaranteed mutually exclusive

        entry Cleared_Runway (ID: Airplane_ID);

        entry Wait_For_Clear;

    private

        Clear: Boolean := True;                        -- protected pri-
vate data - generally more than just a flag...

    end Runway;

    type Runway_Access is access all Runway;
```

```
    -- the air traffic controller task takes requests for takeoff
and landing

    task type Controller (My_Runway: Runway_Access) is

        -- task entries for synchronous message passing

        entry Request_Takeoff (ID: in Airplane_ID; Takeoff: out
Runway_Access);

        entry Request_Approach(ID: in Airplane_ID; Approach: out
Runway_Access);

    end Controller;


    --   allocation of instances

    Runway1     : aliased Runway;                    -- instantiate a
runway

    Controller1: Controller (Runway1'Access); -- and a controller
to manage it


    ------ the implementations of the above types ------

    protected body Runway is

        entry Assign_Aircraft (ID: Airplane_ID)
 when Clear is    -- the entry guard - calling tasks are blocked
until the condition is true

        begin

         Clear := False;

         Put_Line (Airplane_ID'Image (ID) & " on runway ");

        end;


        entry Cleared_Runway (ID: Airplane_ID)
 when not Clear is

        begin
```

```
          Clear := True;

          Put_Line (Airplane_ID' Image (ID) & " cleared runway ");
     end;



     entry Wait_For_Clear
 when Clear is
     begin
          null;        -- no need to do anything here - a task can
only enter if "Clear" is true
     end;

   end Runway;



   task body Controller is
   begin
     loop
          My_Runway.Wait_For_Clear;     -- wait until runway is
available (blocking call)
          select                          -- wait for two types of
requests (whichever is runnable first)
          when Request_Approach' count = 0 =>  -- guard statement
- only accept if there are no tasks queuing on Request_Approach

             accept Request_Takeoff (ID: in Airplane_ID; Takeoff:
out Runway_Access)

                do                               -- start of syn-
chronized part

                My_Runway.Assign_Aircraft (ID);  -- reserve run-
way (potentially blocking call if protected object busy or entry
guard false)

                Takeoff := My_Runway;            -- assign "out"
parameter value to tell airplane which runway

                end Request_Takeoff;                  -- end of the
synchronised part
```

```ada
            or

                accept Request_Approach (ID: in Airplane_ID; Approach:
        out Runway_Access) do

                        My_Runway.Assign_Aircraft (ID);

                        Approach := My_Runway;

                    end Request_Approach;

                or                                      -- terminate if no tasks
        left who could call

                        terminate;

                    end select;

                end loop;

            end;


            task body Airplane is

                Rwy : Runway_Access;

            begin

                Controller1.Request_Takeoff (ID, Rwy); -- This call blocks
        until Controller task accepts and completes the accept block

                Put_Line (Airplane_ID'Image (ID) & "  taking off...");

                delay 2.0;

                Rwy.Cleared_Runway (ID);                    -- call will not
        block as "Clear" in Rwy is now false and no other tasks should
        be inside protected object

                delay 5.0; -- fly around a bit...

                loop

                    select   -- try to request a runway

                        Controller1.Request_Approach (ID, Rwy); -- this is a
        blocking call - will run on controller reaching accept block and
        return on completion

                        exit; -- if call returned we're clear for landing -
        leave select block and proceed...
```

```
            or

                delay 3.0;   -- timeout - if no answer in 3 seconds,
        do something else (everything in following block)

                    Put_Line (Airplane_ID'Image (ID) & "     in holding
        pattern");   -- simply print a message

                end select;

            end loop;

            delay 4.0;   -- do landing approach...

                Put_Line (Airplane_ID'Image (ID) & "           touched
        down!");

                Rwy.Cleared_Runway (ID);   -- notify runway that we're done
        here.

            end;


            New_Airplane: Airplane_Access;


        begin

            for I in Airplane_ID'Range loop  -- create a few airplane tasks

                New_Airplane := new Airplane (I); -- will start running
        directly after creation

                delay 4.0;

            end loop;

        end Traffic;
```

Pragmas

A pragma is a compiler directive that conveys information to the compiler to allow
specific manipulation of compiled output. Certain pragmas are built into the language
while other are implementation-specific.

Examples of common usage of compiler pragmas would be to disable certain features,
such as run-time type checking or array subscript boundary checking, or to instruct
the compiler to insert object code in lieu of a function call (as C/C++ does with inline
functions).

CLU (Programming Language)

CLU is a pioneering programming language created at the Massachusetts Institute of Technology (MIT) by Barbara Liskov and her students between 1974 and 1975. While it did not find extensive use, it introduced many features that are used widely now, and is seen as a step in the development of object-oriented programming (OOP). However, it is not object-oriented, instead being considered an object-based language, as it lacked many features of OOP.

Key contributions include abstract data types, call-by-sharing, iterators, multiple return values (a form of parallel assignment), type-safe parameterized types, and type-safe variant types. It is also notable for its use of classes with constructors and methods, but without inheritance.

Clusters

The syntax of CLU was based on ALGOL, then the starting point for most new language designs. The key addition was the concept of a *cluster*, CLU's type extension system and the root of the language's name (CLUster). Clusters correspond generally to the concept of a "class" in an OO language, and have similar syntax. For instance, here is the CLU syntax for a cluster that implements complex numbers:

```
complex_number = cluster is add, subtract, multiply, ...

    rep = record [ real_part: real, imag_part: real ]

    add = proc ... end add;

    subtract = proc ... end subtract;

    multiply = proc ... end multiply;

    ...

end complex_number;
```

A cluster is a module that encapsulates all of its components except for those explicitly named in the "is" clause. These correspond to the public components of a class in recent OO languages. A cluster also defines a type that can be named outside the cluster (in this case, "complex_number"), but its representation type (rep) is hidden from external clients.

Cluster names are global, and no namespace mechanism was provided to group clusters or allow them to be created "locally" inside other clusters.

CLU does not perform implicit type conversions. In a cluster, the explicit type conversions *up* and *down* change between the abstract type and the representation. There is a universal type *any*, and a procedure force[] to check that an object is a certain type.

Objects may be mutable or immutable, the latter being *base types* such as integers, booleans, characters and strings.

Other Features

Another key feature of the CLU type system are *iterators*, which return objects from a collection serially, one after another. Iterators offer an identical application programming interface (API) no matter what data they are being used with. Thus the iterator for a collection of complex_numbers can be used interchangeably with that for an array of integers. A distinctive feature of CLU iterators is that they are implemented as coroutines, with each value being provided to the caller via a *yield* statement. Iterators like those in CLU are now a common feature of many modern languages, such as C#, Ruby, and Python, though recently they are often referred to as generators.

CLU also includes exception handling, based on various attempts in other languages; exceptions are raised using signal and handled with except. Unlike most other languages with exception handling, exceptions are not implicitly resignaled up the calling chain. Exceptions that are neither caught nor resignaled explicitly are immediately converted into a special failure exception that typically terminates the program.

CLU is often credited as being the first language with type-safe variant types, called *oneofs*, before the language ML had them.

A final distinctive feature in CLU is parallel assignment (multiple assignment), where more than one variable can appear on the left hand side of an assignment operator. For instance, writing x,y = y,x would exchange values of x and y. In the same way, functions could return several values, like x,y,z = f(t). Parallel assignment (though not multiple return values) predates CLU, appearing in CPL (1963), named *simultaneous assignment*, but CLU popularized it and is often credited as the direct influence leading to parallel assignment in later languages.

All objects in a CLU program live in the heap, and memory management is automatic.

CLU supported type parameterized user-defined data abstractions. It was the first language to offer type-safe bounded parameterized types, using structure *where clauses* to express constraints on actual type arguments.

Influence on Other Programming Languages

CLU has influenced many other languages in many ways. In approximate chronological order, these include:

CLU and Ada were major inspirations for C++ templates.

CLU's exception handling mechanisms influenced later languages like C++ and Java.

C++, Sather, Python, and C# include iterators, which first appeared in CLU.

Perl and Lua took multiple assignment and multiple returns from function calls from CLU.

Python and Ruby borrowed several concepts from CLU, such as call by sharing, the *yield* statement, and multiple assignment

ALGOL 68

ALGOL 68 (short for ALGOrithmic Language 1968) is an imperative computer programming language that was conceived as a successor to the ALGOL 60 programming language, designed with the goal of a much wider scope of application and more rigorously defined syntax and semantics.

The contributions of ALGOL 68 to the field of computer science have been deep, wide ranging and enduring, although many of these contributions were only publicly identified when they had reappeared in subsequently developed programming languages.

Overview

ALGOL 68 features include expression-based syntax, user-declared types and structures/tagged-unions, a reference model of variables and reference parameters, string, array and matrix slicing, and also concurrency.

ALGOL 68 was designed by the IFIP Working Group 2.1. On December 20, 1968, the language was formally adopted by Working Group 2.1 and subsequently approved for publication by the General Assembly of IFIP.

ALGOL 68 was defined using a two-level grammar formalism invented by Adriaan van Wijngaarden. Van Wijngaarden grammars use a context-free grammar to generate an infinite set of productions that will recognize a particular ALGOL 68 program; notably, they are able to express the kind of requirements that in many other programming language standards are labelled "semantics" and have to be expressed in ambiguity-prone natural language prose, and then implemented in compilers as *ad hoc* code attached to the formal language parser.

ALGOL 68 has been criticized, most prominently by some members of its design committee such as C. A. R. Hoare and Edsger Dijkstra, for abandoning the simplicity of ALGOL 60, becoming a vehicle for complex or overly general ideas, and doing little to make the compiler writer's task easier, in contrast to deliberately simple contemporaries (and competitors) such as C, S-algol and Pascal.

The main aims and principles of design of ALGOL 68:
 	
1. Completeness and clarity of description
 	
2. Orthogonal design
 	
3. Security
 	
4. Efficiency:
 	
   o Static mode checking
 	
   o Mode-independent parsing
 	
   o Independent compilation
 	
   o Loop optimization
 	
   o Representations – in minimal & larger character sets
	66 ALGOL 68 was the first (and possibly one of the last) major language for which a full formal definition was made before it was implemented.
	
	                   99
	
	              —C.H.A. Koster,

In 1970, ALGOL 68-R became the first working compiler for ALGOL 68.

In the 1973 revision, certain features – such as proceduring, gommas and formal bounds – were omitted. C.f. The language of the unrevised report.

Though European defence agencies (in Britain Royal Signals and Radar Establishment – RSRE) promoted the use of ALGOL 68 for its expected security advantages, the American side of the NATO alliance decided to develop a different project, the Ada programming language, making its use obligatory for US defense contracts.

Algol 68 also had a notable influence within the Soviet Union, details of which can be found in Andrey Ershov's 2014 paper: "ALGOL 68 and Its Impact on the USSR and Russian Programming" and "Алгол 68 и его влияние на программирование в СССР и России" - pages: 336 & 342.

Steve Bourne, who was on the Algol 68 revision committee, took some of its ideas to his Bourne shell (and thereby, to descendant shells such as Bash) and to C (and thereby to descendants such as C++).

The complete history of the project can be found in C.H. Lindsey's *A History of ALGOL 68*.

For a full-length treatment of the language, see Programming Algol 68 Made Easy by Dr. Sian Mountbatten, or Learning Algol 68 Genie by Dr. Marcel van der Veer which includes the Revised Report.

Timeline of ALGOL 68

Year	Event	Contributor
Mar 1959	ALGOL Bulletin Issue 1 (First)	Peter Naur / ACM
Feb 1968	Draft Report Published	IFIP Working Group 2.1
Mar 1968	Algol 68 Final Report Presented at Munich Meeting	IFIP Working Group 2.1
Jun 1968	Meeting in Tirrenia, Italy	IFIP Working Group 2.1
Aug 1968	Meeting in North Berwick, Scotland	IFIP Working Group 2.1
Dec 1968	ALGOL 68 Final Report Presented at Munich Meeting	IFIP Working Group 2.1
Apr 1970	ALGOL 68-R under GEORGE 3 on an ICL 1907F	Royal Signals and Radar Est.
Sep 1973	Algol 68 Revised Report Published	IFIP Working Group 2.1
1975	ALGOL 68C - transportable compiler (zcode VM)	S. Bourne, Andrew Birrell, and Michael Guy
Jun 1977	Strathclyde ALGOL 68 conference, Scotland	ACM
May 1978	Proposals for ALGOL H - A Superlanguage of ALGOL 68	A. P. Black, V. J. Rayward-Smith
1984	Full ALGOL 68S compiler for Sun, SPARC, and PCs	C.H. Lindsey ea, Manchester
Aug 1988	ALGOL Bulletin Issue 52 (last)	Ed. C.H. Lindsey / ACM
May 1997	Algol68 S published on the internet	Charles H. Lindsey
Nov 2001	Algol 68 Genie published on the internet (GNU GPL open source licensing)	Marcel van der Veer

- "A Shorter History of Algol 68"

- ALGOL 68 - 3rd generation ALGOL

The Algorithmic Language ALGOL 68 Reports

- Mar. 1968: Draft Report on the Algorithmic Language ALGOL 68 - Edited by: A. van Wijngaarden, B.J. Mailloux, J.E.L. Peck and C.H.A. Koster.

  > "Van Wijngaarden once characterized the four authors, somewhat tongue-in-cheek, as: Koster: transputter, Peck: syntaxer, Mailloux: implementer, Van Wijngaarden: party ideologist." – Koster.

  Oct. 1968: Penultimate Draft Report on the Algorithmic Language ALGOL 68 – Chapters 1-9 Chapters 10-12 – Edited by: A. van Wijngaarden, B.J. Mailloux, J.E.L. Peck and C.H.A. Koster.

- Dec. 1968: Report on the Algorithmic Language ALGOL 68 – Offprint from Numerische Mathematik, 14, 79-218 (1969); Springer-Verlag. – Edited by: A. van Wijngaarden, B.J. Mailloux, J.E.L. Peck and C.H.A. Koster.

  o WG 2.1 members active in the original design of ALGOL 68: Friedrich L. Bauer • Hans Bekic • Edsger Dijkstra ✳ • Fraser Duncan ✳ • Jan Garwick ✳ • Gerhard Goos • Tony Hoare ✳ • Peter Zilahy Ingerman • Kees

Koster • Peter Landin • Charles Lindsey • Barry Mailloux • John McCarthy • Jack Merner • Peter Naur‡ • Manfred Paul • John Peck • Willem van der Poel • Brian Randell ※ • Doug Ross • Klaus Samelson • Gerhard Seegmüller ※ • Michel Sintzoff • Wlad Turski ※ • Aad van Wijngaarden • Niklaus Wirth‡ • Mike Woodger ※ • Nobuo Yoneda; Key: ※ Signatories to the Minority Report. ‡Resigned after [MR 93].

- Sep. 1973: Revised Report on the Algorithmic Language Algol 68 - Springer-Verlag 1976 - Edited by: A. van Wijngaarden, B.J. Mailloux, J.E.L. Peck, C.H.A. Koster, M. Sintzoff, C.H. Lindsey, L.G.L.T. Meertens and R.G. Fisker.

Timeline of Standardization

1968: On December 20, 1968, the "Final Report" (MR 101) was adopted by the Working Group, then subsequently approved by the General Assembly of UNESCO's IFIP for publication. Translations of the standard were made for Russian, German, French and Bulgarian, and then later Japanese and Chinese. The standard was also made available in Braille.

1984: TC97 considered Algol 68 for standardisation as "New Work Item" TC97/N1642 . West Germany, Belgium, Netherlands, USSR and Czechoslovakia willing to participate in preparing the standard but the USSR and Czechoslovakia "were not the right kinds of member of the right ISO committees" and Algol 68's ISO standardisation stalled.

1988: Subsequently ALGOL 68 became one of the GOST standards in Russia.

- GOST 27974-88 Programming language ALGOL 68 – Язык программирования АЛГОЛ 68

- GOST 27975-88 Programming language ALGOL 68 extended – Язык программирования АЛГОЛ 68 расширенный

Notable Language Elements

Bold Symbols and Reserved Words

There are about 60 such reserved words (some with "brief symbol" equivalents) in the standard language:

```
mode, op, prio, proc,

flex, heap, loc, long, ref, short,

bits, bool, bytes, char, compl, int, real, sema, string, void,

channel, file, format, struct, union,
```

```
at "@", either, is ":=:", isnt  is not ":/=:" ":≠:", of "→",
true, false, empty, nil "o", skip "~",

co "¢", comment "¢", pr, pragmat,

case ~ in ~ ouse ~ in ~ out ~ esac "( ~ | ~ |: ~ | ~ | ~ )",

for ~ from ~ to ~ by ~ while ~ do ~ od,

if ~ then ~ elif ~ then ~ else ~ fi "( ~ | ~ |: ~ | ~ | ~ )",

par begin ~ end "( ~ )", go to, goto, exit ".".
```

Units: Expressions

The basic language construct is the *unit*. A unit may be a *formula*, an *enclosed clause*, a *routine text* or one of several technically needed constructs (assignation, jump, skip, nihil). The technical term *enclosed clause* unifies some of the inherently bracketing constructs known as *block, do statement, switch statement* in other contemporary languages. When keywords are used, generally the reversed character sequence of the introducing keyword is used for terminating the enclosure, e.g. (if ~ then ~ else ~ fi, case ~ in ~ out ~ esac, for ~ while ~ do ~ od). This Guarded Command syntax was reused by Stephen Bourne in the common Unix Bourne shell. An expression may also yield a *multiple value*, which is constructed from other values by a *collateral clause*. This construct just looks like the parameter pack of a procedure call.

Mode: Declarations

The basic data types (called modes in Algol 68 parlance) are real, int, compl (complex number), bool, char, bits and bytes. For example:

```
int n = 2;

co n is fixed as a constant of 2. co

int m := 3;

co m is a newly created local variable whose value is initially
set to 3. co

co    This is short for ref int m = loc int := 3; co

real avogadro = 6.0221415□23; co Avogadro's number co

long long real long long pi = 3.14159 26535 89793 23846 26433
83279 50288 41971 69399 37510;

compl square root of minus one = 0 ⊥ 1;
```

However, the declaration real x; is just syntactic sugar for ref real x = loc real;. That is, x is really the *constant identifier* for a *reference to* a newly generated local real variable.

Furthermore, instead of defining both float and double, or int and long and short, etc., ALGOL 68 provides *modifiers*, so that the presently common double would be written as long real or long long real instead, for example. The *prelude constants* max real and min long int are provided to adapt programs to different implementations.

All variables need to be declared, the declaration does not have to appear prior to the first use.

primitive-declarer: int, real, compl, complex, bool, char, string, bits, bytes, format, file, pipe, channel, sema

- bits - a "packed vector" of bool.

- bytes - a "packed vector" of char.

- string - a flexible array of char.

- sema - a semaphore which can be initialised with the operator level.

Complex types can be created from simpler ones using various type constructors:

- ref *mode* - a reference to a value of type *mode*, similar to & in C/C++ and ref in Pascal

- struct - used to build structures, like struct in C/C++ and record in Pascal

- union - used to build unions, like in C/C++ and Pascal

- proc - used to specify procedures, like functions in C/C++ and procedures/ functions in Pascal

For some examples, see Comparison of ALGOL 68 and C++.

Other declaration symbols include: flex, heap, loc, ref, long, short, events

- flex - declare the array to be flexible, i.e. it can grow in length on demand.

- heap - allocate variable some free space from the global heap.

- loc - allocate variable some free space of the local stack.

- long - declare an int, real or compl to be of a longer size.

- short - declare an int, real or compl to be of a shorter size.

A name for a mode (type) can be declared using a mode declaration, which is similar to typedef in C/C++ and type in Pascal:

```
int max=99;

mode newmode = [0:9][0:max]struct (

    long real a, b, c, short int i, j, k, ref real r

);
```

This is similar to the following C code:

```
const int max=99;

typedef struct {

    double a, b, c; short i, j, k; float *r;

} newmode[9+1][max+1];
```

Note that for ALGOL 68 only the newmode mode-indication appears to the left of the equals symbol, and most notably the construction is made - and can be read - from left to right without regard to priorities. Note also that the lower bound of Algol 68 arrays is one by default, but can be any integer from -*max int* to *max int*.

Mode declarations allow types to be recursive: defined directly or indirectly in terms of themselves. This is subject to some restrictions - for instance, these declarations are illegal:

```
mode A = ref A

mode A = struct (A a, B b)

mode A = proc (A a) A
```

while these are valid:

```
mode A = struct (ref A a, B b)

mode A = proc (ref A a) ref A
```

Coercions: Casting

The coercions produce a coercee from a coercend according to three criteria: the a priori mode of the coercend before the application of any coercion, the a posteriori mode of the coercee required after those coercions, and the syntactic position or "sort" of the coercee. Coercions may be cascaded.

There are six possible coercions, termed "deproceduring", "dereferencing", "uniting", "widening", "rowing" and "voiding". Each coercion, except for "uniting", prescribes a corresponding dynamic effect on the associated values. Hence, a number of primitive actions can be programmed implicitly by coercions.

Context strength – allowed coercions:

- soft – deproceduring

- weak – dereferencing or deproceduring, yielding a name

- meek – dereferencing or deproceduring

- firm – meek, followed by uniting

- strong – firm, followed by widening, rowing or voiding

Coercion Hierarchy with Examples

ALGOL 68 has a hierarchy of contexts which determine which kind of coercions are available at a particular point in the program. These contexts are:

Name	Context location	Coercions available in this context				Coercion examples
		Weak	Meek	Firm	Strong	
Strong	Right hand side of: • Identity-declarations, as "~" in: REAL x = ~ • Initialisations, as "~" in: REAL x := ~ Also: • Actual-parameters of calls, as "~" in:PROC: sin(~) • Enclosed clauses of casts, as "~" in: REAL(~) • Units of routine-texts • Statements yielding VOID • All parts (but one) of a balanced clause • One side of an identity relation, as "~" in: ~ IS ~	All soft then weak dereferencing (deref erencing or deproc eduring, yielding a name)	All weak then derefer encing (deref erenc ing or deproc edur ing)	All meek then uniting	All firm then widen ing, rowing or voiding	Widening occurs if there is no loss of precision. For example: An INT will be coerced to a REAL, and a REAL will be coerced to a LONG REAL. But not vice versa. Examples: INT to LONG INT INT to REAL REAL to COMPL BITS to []BOOL BYTES to STRING A variable can also be coerced (rowed) to an array of length 1. For example: INT to INT REAL to REAL etc.
Firm	• Operands of formulas as "~" in:OP: ~ * ~ • Parameters of transput calls			Example: UNION(INT,REAL) var := 1		
Meek	• Trimscripts (yielding INT) • Enquiries: e.g. as "~" in the following IF ~ THEN ... FI and FROM ~ BY ~ TO ~ WHILE ~ DO ... OD etc • Primaries of calls (e.g. sin in sin(x))		Examples: REF REF BOOL to BOOL REF REF REF INT to INT			
Weak	• Primaries of slices, as in "~" in: ~[1:99] • Secondaries of selections, as "~" in: value OF ~		Examples: REF BOOL to REF BOOL REF REF INT to REF INT REF REF REF REAL to REF REAL REF REF REF REF STRUCT to REF STRUCT			
	The LHS of assignments, as "~" in: ~ := ...					

For more details about Primaries, Secondaries, Tertiary & Quaternaries refer to Operator precedence.

pr & co: Pragmats and Comments

Pragmats are directives in the program, typically hints to the compiler; in newer languages these are called "pragmas" (no 't'). e.g.

```
pragmat heap=32 pragmat
```

```
pr heap=32 pr
```

```
Comments can be inserted in a variety of ways:
```

```
¢ The original way of adding your 2 cents worth to a program ¢
```

```
comment "bold" comment comment
```

```
co Style i comment co
```

```
# Style ii comment #
```

```
£ This is a hash/pound comment for a UK keyboard £
```

Normally, comments cannot be nested in ALGOL 68. This restriction can be circumvented by using different comment delimiters (e.g. use hash only for temporary code deletions).

Expressions and Compound Statements

ALGOL 68 being an expression-oriented programming language, the value returned by an assignment statement is a reference to the destination. Thus, the following is valid ALGOL 68 code:

```
 real half pi, one pi; one pi := 2 * ( half pi := 2 * arc tan(1) )
```

This notion is present in C and Perl, among others. Note that as in earlier languages such as Algol 60 and FORTRAN, spaces are allowed in identifiers, so that half pi is a *single* identifier (thus avoiding the *underscores* versus *camel case* versus *all lower-case* issues).

As another example, to express the mathematical idea of a *sum* of f(i) from i=1 to n, the following ALGOL 68 *integer expression* suffices:

```
 (int sum := 0; for i to n do sum +:= f(i) od; sum)
```

Note that, being an integer expression, the former block of code can be used in *any context where an integer value can be used*. A block of code returns the value of the last expression it evaluated; this idea is present in Lisp, among other languages.

Compound statements are all terminated by distinctive (and somewhat reverent) closing brackets:

- if choice clauses:

```
if condition then statements [ else statements ] fi
```

"brief" form: (condition | statements | statements)

```
if condition1 then statements elif condition2 then statements [
else statements ] fi
```

"brief" form: (condition1 | statements |: condition2 | statements | statements)

This scheme not only avoids the dangling else problem but also avoids having to use begin and end in embedded statement sequences.

- case choice clauses:

```
case switch in statements, statements,... [ out statements ] esac
```

"brief" form: (switch | statements,statements,... | statements)

```
case switch1 in statements, statements,... ouse switch2 in state-
ments, statements,... [ out statements ] esac
```

"brief" form of case statement: (switch1 | statements,statements,... |: switch2 | statements,statements,... | statements)

Choice clause example with *Brief* symbols:

```
proc days in month = (int year, month)int:
   (month|
      31,
      (year÷×4=0 ∧ year÷×100≠0  ∨  year÷×400=0 | 29 | 28 ),
      31, 30, 31, 30, 31, 31, 30, 31, 30, 31
   );
```

Choice clause example with *Bold* symbols:

```
proc days in month = (int year, month)int:
   case month in
      31,
      if year mod 4 eq 0 and year mod 100 ne 0   or   year mod 400
```

```
eq 0 then 29 else 28 fi,

    31, 30, 31, 30, 31, 31, 30, 31, 30, 31

  esac;
```

Choice clause example mixing *Bold* and *Brief* symbols:

```
proc days in month = (int year, month)int:

  case month in

¢Jan¢ 31,

¢Feb¢ ( year mod 4 = 0 and year mod 100 ≠ 0   or   year mod 400 =
0 | 29 | 28 ),

¢Mar¢ 31, 30, 31, 30, 31, 31, 30, 31, 30, 31 ¢ to Dec. ¢

  esac;
```

Algol68 allowed the switch to be of either type int *or* (uniquely) union. The latter allows the enforcing strong typing onto union variables. c.f. union below for example.

- do loop clause:

```
[ for index ] [ from first ] [ by increment ] [ to last ] [ while
condition ] do statements od

 The minimum form of a "loop clause" is thus: do statements od
```

This was considered *the* "universal" loop, the full syntax is:

```
for i from 1 by 1 to 3 while i≠4 do ~ od
```

There are several unusual aspects of the construct:

- only the *do ~ od* portion was compulsory, in which case the loop will iterate indefinitely.

- thus the clause *to 100 do ~ od*, will iterate only 100 times.

- the while "syntactic element" allowed a programmer to break from a for loop early. e.g.

```
int sum sq:=0;

for i

while

  print(("So far:",i,newline));
```

```
  sum sq≤1000
do
  sum sq+:=i↑2
od
```

Subsequent "extensions" to the standard Algol68 allowed the to syntactic element to be replaced with upto and downto to achieve a small optimisation. The same compilers also incorporated:

- until - for late loop termination.

- foreach - for working on arrays in parallel.

Further examples can be found in the code examples below.

Struct, Union & [:]: Structures, Unions and Arrays

ALGOL 68 supports arrays with any number of dimensions, and it allows for the *slicing* of whole or partial rows or columns.

```
  mode vector = [1:3]      real;     # vector mode declaration
(typedef)  #

 mode matrix = [1:3,1:3]real;  # matrix mode declaration (typedef)
#

 vector v1  := (1,2,3);     # array variable initially (1,2,3)  #

 []real v2  = (4,5,6);          # constant array, type equivalent
to vector, bounds are implied  #

 op + = (vector a,b) vector:    # binary operator definition       #

    (vector out; for i from ⌊a to ⌈a do out[i] := a[i]+b[i] od;
out);

 matrix m := (v1, v2, v1+v2);

 print ((m[,2:]));              # a slice of the 2nd and 3rd columns #

Matrices can be sliced either way, e.g.:

 ref vector row = m[2,]; # define a ref (pointer) to the 2nd row #

 ref vector col = m[,2]; # define a ref (pointer) to the 2nd
column #
```

ALGOL 68 supports multiple field structures (struct) and united modes. Reference variables may point to any mode including array slices and structure fields.

For an example of all this, here is the traditional linked list declaration:

```
mode node = union (real, int, compl, string),

    list = struct (node val, ref list next);
```

Usage example for union case of *node*:

Algol68 as in the 1968 Final Report

```
  node n := "1234";

  real r; int i; compl c; string
s

  case r,i,c,s::=n in

    print(("real:", r)),

    print(("int:", i)),

    print(("compl:", c)),

    print(("string:", s))

    out print(("?:", n))

  esac
```

Algol68 as in the 1973 Revised Report

```
node n := "1234";

case n in

    (real r):    print(("re-
al:", r)),

    (int i):    print(("int:",
i)),

    (compl c):  print(("com-
pl:", c)),

                (string    s):
print(("string:", s))

    out       print(("?:", n))

esac
```

Proc: Procedures

Procedure (proc) declarations require type specifications for both the parameters and the result (void if none):

```
proc max of real = (real a, b) real:

    if a > b then a else b fi;
```

or, using the "brief" form of the conditional statement:

```
proc max of real = (real a, b) real: (a>b | a | b);
```

The return value of a proc is the value of the last expression evaluated in the procedure. References to procedures (ref proc) are also permitted. Call-by-reference parameters are provided by specifying references (such as ref real) in the formal argument list. The following example defines a procedure that applies a function (specified as a parameter) to each element of an array:

```
proc apply = (ref [] real a, proc (real) real f):


    for i from lwb a to upb a do a[i] := f(a[i]) od
```

This simplicity of code was unachievable in ALGOL 68's predecessor ALGOL 60.

Op: Operators

The programmer may define new operators and *both* those and the pre-defined ones may be overloaded and their priorities may be changed by the coder. The following example defines operator max with both dyadic and monadic versions (scanning across the elements of an array).

```
prio max = 9;


op max = (int a,b) int: ( a>b | a | b );

op max = (real a,b) real: ( a>b | a | b );

op max = (compl a,b) compl: ( abs a > abs b | a | b );


op max = ([]real a) real:

    (real out := a[lwb a];

    for i from lwb a + 1 to upb a do ( a[i]>out | out:=a[i] ) od;

    out)
```

Array, Procedure, Dereference and Coercion Operations

priority	Operation	+Algol68	+Algol68
Effectively 12 (Primary)	dereferencing, deproceduring(~,~), subscripting[~], rowing[~,], slicing[~:~], size denotations long & short	proceduring	currying(~,,,), diag, trnsp, row, col
Effectively 11 (Secondary)	of (selection), loc & heap (generators)	→ (selection)	new (generators)

These are technically not operators, rather they are considered "units associated with names"

Monadic Operators

priority (Tertiary)	Algol68 "Worthy characters"	+Algol68	+Algol68	+Algol68
10	not ~, up, down, lwb, upb, -, abs, arg, bin, entier, leng, level, odd, repr, round, shorten	¬, ↑, ↓, ⌐, ⌐	norm, trace, t, det, inv	lws, ups, ⌐, ⌐, btb, ctb

Dyadic Operators with Associated Priorities

priority (Tertiary)	Algol68 "Worthy characters"	+Algol68	+Algol68	+Algol68
9	+*, i	+×, ⊥		!
8	shl, shr, **, up, down, lwb, upb	↑, ↓, ⌐, ⌐		××, ^, lws, ups, ⌐, ⌐
7	*, /, %, over, %*, mod, elem	×, ÷, ÷×, ÷*, %×, □		÷:
6	-, +			
5	<, lt, <=, le, >=, ge, >, gt	≤, ≥		
4	eq =, ne ~= /=	≠, ¬=		
3	&, and	∧		/\
2	or	∨		\/
1	minusab, plusab, timesab, divab, overab, modab, plusto, -:=, +:=, *:=, /:=, %:=, %*:=, +=:	×:=, ÷:=, ÷×:=, ÷*:=, %×:=		minus, plus, div, overb, modb, ÷::=, prus

Note: Tertiaries include names nil and ○.

Assignation and Identity Relations Etc

These are technically not operators, rather they are considered "units associated with names"

priority (Quaternaries)	Algol68 "Worthy characters"	+Algol68	+Algol68	+Algol68
Effectively 0	:=, is :=:, isnt :/=: :~=:, at @, ".", "."	:≠: :¬=:	:=:=, =:=	..=, .=, ct, ::, ctab, ::=, .., is not, "..", "."

Note: Quaternaries include names skip and ~.

":=:" (alternatively "is") tests if two pointers are equal; ":/=:" (alternatively "isnt") tests if they are unequal.

Why :=: and :/=: are needed: Consider trying to compare two pointer values, such as the following variables, declared as pointers-to-integer:

```
ref int ip, jp
```

Now consider how to decide whether these two are pointing to the same location, or whether one of them is pointing to nil. The following expression

```
ip = jp
```

will dereference both pointers down to values of type int, and compare those, since the "=" operator is defined for int, but not ref int. It is *not legal* to define "=" for operands of type ref int and int at the same time, because then calls become ambiguous, due to the implicit coercions that can be applied: should the operands be left as ref int and that version of the operator called? Or should they be dereferenced further to int and that version used instead? Therefore the following expression can never be made legal:

```
ip = nil
```

Hence the need for separate constructs not subject to the normal coercion rules for operands to operators. But there is a gotcha. The following expressions:

```
ip :=: jp
```

```
ip :=: nil
```

while legal, will probably not do what might be expected. They will always return false, because they are comparing the *actual addresses of the variables* ip *and* jp, *rather than what they point to.* To achieve the right effect, one would have to write

```
ip :=: ref int(jp)
```

```
ip :=: ref int(nil)
```

Patent application: On 14 May 2003, software patent application No. 20040230959 was filed for the ISNOT operator by employees of Microsoft. This patent was granted on 18 November 2004.

Special Characters

Most of Algol's "special" characters (×, ÷, ≤, ≥, ≠, ¬, ⊃, ≡, ∨, ∧, →, ↓, ↑, ⌐, ⌐, ⌐, ⌐, ⊥, ⌐, ¢, ○ and □) can be found on the IBM 2741 keyboard with the APL "golf-ball" print head inserted, these became available in the mid-1960s while ALGOL 68 was being drafted. These characters are also part of the unicode standard and most of them are available in several popular fonts:

Transput: Input and Output

Transput is the term used to refer to ALGOL 68's input and output facilities. There are pre-defined procedures for unformatted, formatted and binary transput. Files and other transput devices are handled in a consistent and machine-independent manner. The following example prints out some unformatted output to the standard output device:

```
print ((newpage, "Title", newline, "Value of i is ",
   i, "and x[i] is ", x[i], newline))
```

Note the predefined procedures newpage and newline passed as arguments.

Books, Channels and Files

The transput is considered to be of books, channels and files:

- Books are made up of pages, lines and characters, and may be backed up by files.
    - A specific book can be located by name with a call to match.
- channels correspond to physical devices. e.g. card punches and printers.
    - There are three standard channels: stand in channel, stand out channel, stand back channel.
- A file is a means of communicating between a particular program and a book that has been opened via some channel.
    - The mood of a file may be read, write, char, bin, and opened.
    - transput procedures include: establish, create, open, associate, lock, close, scratch.
    - position enquires: char number, line number, page number.
    - layout routines include:
        - space, backspace, newline, newpage.
        - get good line, get good page, get good book, and proc set=(ref file f, int page,line,char)void:
    - A file has event routines. e.g. on logical file end, on physical file end, on page end, on line end, on format end, on value error, on char error.

Formatted Transput

"Formatted transput" in ALGOL 68's transput has its own syntax and patterns (functions), with formats embedded between two $ characters.

Examples:

```
 printf (($21"The sum is:"x, g(0)$, m + n)); ¢ prints the same
as: ¢
```

```
 print ((new line, new line, "The sum is:", space, whole (m + n, 0))
```

Par: Parallel Processing

ALGOL 68 supports programming of parallel processing. Using the keyword par, a *collateral clause* is converted to a *parallel clause*, where the synchronisation of actions is controlled using semaphores. In A68G the parallel actions are mapped to threads when available on the hosting operating system. In A68S a different paradigm of parallel processing was implemented.

```
int initial foot width = 5;

mode foot = struct(

    string name,

    sema width,

    bits toe ¢ packed vector of BOOL ¢

);
```

```
foot left foot:= foot ("Left", level initial foot width, 2r11111),

        right foot:= foot ("Right", level initial foot width,
2r11111);
```

```
¢ 10 round clip in a 1968 Colt Python .357 Magnum ¢

sema rounds = level 10;
```

```
¢ the Magnum needs more barrels to take full advantage of par-
allelism ¢

sema acquire target = level 1;
```

```
prio ∧:= = 1;

op ∧:= = (ref bits lhs, bits rhs) ref bits: lhs := lhs ∧ rhs;
```

```
proc shoot = (ref foot foot)void: (

   ↓ acquire target;

   ↓ rounds;

   print( "BANG! ");

   ↓ width → foot;

   toe → foot ∧:= ¬(bin 1 shl level width → foot);

   printf(($g" : Ouch!! - "5(g)1$, name → foot, []bool(toe → foot)[bits
width - initial foot width + 1:]));

   ↑ acquire target
);



¢ do shooting in parallel to cater for someone hoping to stand on just one foot ¢
par (

   for toe to initial foot width do

      shoot(left foot)

   od, ¢ <= a comma is required ¢

   for toe to initial foot width do

      shoot(right foot)

   od
)
```

Examples of Use

Code Sample

This sample program implements the Sieve of Eratosthenes to find all the prime numbers that are less than 100. nil is the ALGOL 68 analogue of the *null pointer* in other languages. The notation *x* of *y* accesses a member *x* of a struct *y*.

```
begin # Algol-68 prime number sieve, functional style #


   proc error = (string s) void:
```

```
        (print(( newline, " error: ", s, newline)); goto stop);
    proc one to = (int n) list:
        (proc f = (int m,n) list: (m>n | nil | cons(m, f(m+1,n))));
f(1,n));


    mode list = ref node;
    mode node = struct (int h, list t);
    proc cons = (int n, list l) list: heap node := (n,l);
    proc hd   = (list l) int: ( l is nil | error("hd nil"); skip
| h of l );
    proc tl   = (list l) list: ( l is nil | error("tl nil"); skip
| t of l );
    proc show = (list l) void: ( l isnt nil | print(( " ",whole(h-
d(l),0))); show(tl(l)));


    proc filter = (proc (int) bool p, list l) list:
        if l is nil then nil
        elif p(hd(l)) then cons(hd(l), filter(p,tl(l)))
        else filter(p, tl(l))
        fi;


    proc sieve = (list l) list:
        if l is nil then nil
        else
            proc not multiple = (int n) bool: n mod hd(l) ≠ 0;
            cons(hd(l), sieve( filter( not multiple, tl(l) )))
        fi;


    proc primes = (int n) list: sieve( tl( one to(n) ));
```

```
show( primes(100) )
end
```

Operating Systems Written in ALGOL 68

- Cambridge CAP computer – All procedures constituting the operating system were written in ALGOL 68C, although a number of other closely associated protected procedures – such as a paginator – are written in BCPL.

- Eldon 3 - Developed at Leeds University for the ICL 1900 was written in ALGOL 68-R.

- Flex machine – The hardware was custom and microprogrammable, with an operating system, (modular) compiler, editor, garbage collector and filing system all written in ALGOL 68RS. The command shell Curt was designed to access typed data similar to Algol-68 modes.

- VME – S3 was the implementation language of the operating system VME. S3 was based on ALGOL 68 but with data types and operators aligned to those offered by the ICL 2900 Series.

Note: The Soviet Era computers Эльбрус-1 (Elbrus-1) and Эльбрус-2 were created using high-level language Эль-76 (AL-76), rather than the traditional assembly. Эль-76 resembles Algol-68, The main difference is the dynamic binding types in Эль-76 supported at the hardware level. Эль-76 is used for application, job control, system programming.

Applications

Both ALGOL 68C and ALGOL 68-R are written in ALGOL 68, effectively making ALGOL 68 an application of itself. Other applications include:

- ELLA - a hardware description language and support toolset. Developed by the Royal Signals and Radar Establishment during the 1980s and 1990s.

- RAF Strike Command System - "... 400K of error-free ALGOL 68-RT code was produced with three man-years of work. ..."

Libraries and APIs

- NAG Numerical Libraries - a software library of numerical analysis routines. Supplied in ALGOL 68 during the 1980s.

- TORRIX - a programming system for operations on vectors and matrices over arbitrary fields and of variable size by S.G. van der Meulen and M. Veldhorst.

Program Representation

A feature of ALGOL 68, inherited from the ALGOL tradition, is its different representations. There is a *representation language* used to describe algorithms in printed work, a *strict language* (rigorously defined in the Report) and an official *reference language* intended to be used in actual compiler input. In the examples you will observe bold typeface words, this is the strict language. ALGOL 68's reserved words are effectively in a different namespace from identifiers, and spaces are allowed in identifiers, so this next fragment is legal:

```
int a real int = 3 ;
```

The programmer who actually writes code does not always have an option of bold typeface or underlining in the code as this may depend on hardware and cultural issues. So different methods to denote these identifiers have been devised. This is called a *stropping regime*. For example all or some of the following may be available *programming representations*:

```
 int a real int = 3; # the strict language #

'INT'A REAL INT = 3; # QUOTE stropping style #

.INT A REAL INT = 3; # POINT stropping style #

 INT a real int = 3; # UPPER stropping style #

 int a_real_int = 3; # RES stropping style, there are 61 accepted
reserved words #
```

All implementations must recognise at least POINT, UPPER and RES inside PRAGMAT sections. Of these, POINT and UPPER stropping are quite common, while RES stropping is in contradiction to the specification (as there are no reserved words). QUOTE (single apostrophe quoting) was the original recommendation, while matched apostrophe quoting, common in ALGOL 60, is not used much in ALGOL 68.

The following characters were recommended for portability, and termed "worthy characters" in the Report on the Standard Hardware Representation of Algol 68:

- ^ Worthy Characters: ABCDEFGHIJKLMNOPQRSTUVWXYZ0123456789 "#$%'()*+,-./:;<=>@[ ]_|

This reflected a problem in the 1960s where some hardware didn't support lower-case, nor some other non-ASCII characters, indeed in the 1973 report it was written: "Four worthy characters — "|", "_", "[", and "]" — are often coded differently, even at installations which nominally use the same character set."

- Base characters: "Worthy characters" are a subset of "base characters".

Example of Different Program Representations

Algol68 "strict" as typically published	Quote stropping (like wikitext)	For a 7-bit character code compiler	For a 6-bit character code compiler
¢ underline or bold typeface ¢ mode xint = int; xint sum sq:=0; for i while sum sq≠70×70 do sum sq+:=i↑2 od	'pr' quote 'pr' 'mode' 'xint' = 'int'; 'xint' sum sq:=0; 'for' i 'while' sum sq≠70×70 'do' sum sq+:=i↑2 'od'	.PR UPPER .PR MODE XINT = INT; XINT sum sq:=0; FOR i WHILE sum sq/=70*70 DO sum sq+:=i**2 OD	.PR POINT .PR .MODE .XINT = .INT; .XINT SUM SQ:=0; .FOR I .WHILE SUM SQ .NE 70*70 .DO SUM SQ .PLUSAB I .UP 2 .OD

ALGOL 68 allows for every natural language to define its own set of keywords Algol-68. As a result, programmers are able to write programs using keywords from their native language. Below is an example of a simple procedure that calculates "the day following", the code is in two languages: English and German.

```
# Next day date - English variant #

mode date = struct(int day, string month, int year);

proc the day following = (date x) date:
     if day of  x < length of month (month of x, year of x)
     then (day of x + 1, month of x, year of x)
     elif month of x = "December"
     then (1, "January", year of x + 1)
     else (1, successor of month (month of x), year of x)
     fi;

# Nachfolgetag - Deutsche Variante #

menge datum = tupel(ganz tag, wort monat, ganz jahr);

funktion naechster tag nach = (datum x) datum:
         wenn tag von x < monatslaenge(monat von x, jahr von x)
         dann (tag von x + 1, monat von x, jahr von x)
         wennaber monat von x = "Dezember"
         dann (1, "Januar", jahr von x + 1)
         ansonsten (1, nachfolgemonat(monat von x), jahr von x)
         endewenn;
```

Russian/Soviet example: In English Algol68's reverent case statement reads case ~ in ~ out ~ esac, in Cyrillic this reads выб ~ в ~ либо ~ быв.

Some Vanitas

For its technical intricacies, ALGOL 68 needs a cornucopia of methods to deny the existence of something:

```
skip, "~" or "?" - an undefined value always syntactically valid,

empty - the only value admissible to void, needed for selecting
void in a union,

void - syntactically like a mode, but not one,

nil or "o" - a name not denoting anything, of an unspecified ref-
erence mode,

() or specifically [1:0]int - a vacuum is an empty array (here
specifically of mode []int).

undefined - a standards reports procedure raising an exception in
the runtime system.

ℵ - Used in the standards report to inhibit introspection of cer-
tain types. e.g. sema

c.f. below for other examples of ℵ.
```

The term nil is *var* always evaluates to true for any variable (but see above for correct use of is :/=:), whereas it is not known to which value a comparison x < skip evaluates for any integer x.

ALGOL 68 leaves intentionally undefined what happens in case of integer overflow, the integer bit representation, and the degree of numerical accuracy for floating point. In contrast, the language Java has been criticized for over-specifying the latter.

Both official reports included some advanced features that were not part of the standard language. These were indicated with an ⌐ and considered effectively private. Examples include "⌐" and "⌐" for templates, the outtype/intype for crude duck typing, and the straightout and straightin operators for "straightening" nested arrays and structures.

Extract from the 1973 report:

```
§10.3.2.2. Transput modes

a) mode ℵ simplout = union (⟨L int⟩, ⟨L real⟩, ⟨L compl⟩, bool,
⟨L bits⟩,
```

```
                char, [ ] char);
```

b) mode ℵ outtype = ¢ an actual - declarer specifying a mode united

from a sufficient set of modes none of which is 'void' or con-tains 'flexible',

'reference to', 'procedure' or 'union of' ¢;

c) mode ℵ simplin = union (⦉ref L int⦊, ⦉ref L real⦊, ⦉ref L com-pl⦊, ref bool,

⦉ref L bits⦊, ref char, ref [ ] char, ref string);

d) mode ℵ intype = ¢ ... ¢;

§10.3.2.3. Straightening

a) op ℵ straightout = (outtype x) [ ] simplout: ¢ the result of "straightening" 'x' ¢;

b) op ℵ straightin = (intype x) [ ] simplin: ¢ the result of straightening 'x' ¢;

Comparisons with Other Languages

- 1973 – Comparative Notes on Algol 68 and PL/I - S. H. Valentine - February 1973

- 1973 – B. R. Alexander and G. E. Hedrick. A Comparison of PL/1 and ALGOL 68. International Symposium on Computers and Chinese Input/Output Systems. pp. 359–368.

- 1976 – Evaluation of ALGOL 68, JOVIAL J3B, Pascal, Simula 67, and TACPOL Versus TINMAN - Requirements for a Common High Order Programming Language.

- 1976 – A Language Comparison - A Comparison of the Properties of the Programming Languages ALGOL 68, CAMAC-IML, Coral 66, PAS 1, PEARL, PL/1, PROCOL, RTL/2 in Relation to Real Time Programming - R Roessler; K Schenk - Oct 1976

- 1977 – Report to the High Order-Language Working Group (HOLWG) - Executive Summary - Language Evaluation Coordinating Committee - Evaluation of PL/I, Pascal, ALGOL 68, HAL/S, PEARL, SPL/I, PDL/2, LTR, CS-4, LIS, Euclid, ECL, Moral, RTL/2, Fortran, COBOL, ALGOL 60, TACPOL, CMS-2, Simula 67, JOVIAL J3B, JOVIAL J73 & Coral 66.

- 1977 – A comparison of PASCAL and ALGOL 68 - Andrew S. Tanenbaum - June 1977.

- 1980 – A Critical Comparison of Several Programming Language Implementations - Algol 60, FORTRAN, Pascal and Algol 68.

- 1993 – Five Little Languages and How They Grew - BLISS, Pascal, Algol 68, BCPL & C - Dennis M. Ritchie - April 1993.

- 1999 – On Orthogonality: Algol68, Pascal and C

- 2000 – A Comparison of Arrays in ALGOL 68 and BLISS – University of Virginia – Michael Walker – Spring 2000

- 2009 – On Go - oh, go on - How well will Google's Go stand up against Brand X programming language? - David Given – November 2009

- 2010 – Algol and Pascal from "Concepts in Programming Languages - Block-structured procedural languages" – by Dr Marcelo Fiore

- Comparison of ALGOL 68 and C++

Revisions

Except where noted (with a superscript), the language described above is that of the "Revised Report".

The Language of The Unrevised Report

The original language (As per the "Final Report") differs in syntax of the *mode cast*, and it had the feature of *proceduring*, i.e. coercing the value of a term into a procedure which evaluates the term. Proceduring would be intended to make evaluations *lazy*. The most useful application could have been the short-circuited evaluation of boolean operators. In:

```
op andf = (bool a,proc bool b)bool:(a | b | false);

op orf = (bool a,proc bool b)bool:(a | true | b);
```

b is only evaluated if *a* is true.

As defined in ALGOL 68, it did not work as expected, for example in the code:

```
if false andf co proc bool: co ( print ("Should not be execut-
ed"); true)

then ...
```

against the programmers naïve expectations the print *would* be executed as it is only the *value* of the elaborated enclosed-clause after andf that was procedured. Textual insertion of the commented-out proc bool: makes it work.

Some implementations emulate the expected behaviour for this special case by extension of the language.

Before revision, the programmer could decide to have the arguments of a procedure evaluated serially instead of collaterally by using semicolons instead of commas (*gommas*).

For example in:

```
proc test = (real a; real b) :...

...

test (x plus 1, x);
```

The first argument to test is guaranteed to be evaluated before the second, but in the usual:

```
proc test = (real a, b) :...

...

test (x plus 1, x);
```

then the compiler could evaluate the arguments in whatever order it felt like.

Extension Proposals from IFIP WG 2.1

After the revision of the report, some extensions to the language have been proposed to widen the applicability:

- *partial parametrisation* (aka Currying): creation of functions (with fewer parameters) by specification of some, but not all parameters for a call, e.g. a function logarithm of two parameters, base and argument, could be specialised to natural, binary or decadic log,

- *module extension*: for support of external linkage, two mechanisms were proposed, bottom-up *definition modules*, a more powerful version of the facilities from ALGOL 68-R and top-down *holes*, similar to the ENVIRON and USING clauses from ALGOL 68C

- *mode parameters*: for implementation of limited parametrical polymorphism (most operations on data structures like lists, trees or other data containers can be specified without touching the pay load).

So far, only partial parametrisation has been implemented, in Algol 68 Genie.

True ALGOL 68s Specification and Implementation Timeline

⋏	Year	Purpose	State	Description	Target CPU	Licensing	Implementation Language
Generalized ALGOL	1962	Scientific	NL	ALGOL for generalised grammars			
ALGOL Y	1966	Draft proposal	Intl	First version of Algol 68	Specification	ACM	
ALGOL 68	1968	Draft proposal	Intl	IFIP WG 2.1 Draft Report	Specification - March	ACM	
ALGOL 68	1968	Standard	Intl	IFIP WG 2.1 Final Report	Specification - August	ACM	
ALGOL 68-R	1970	Military	UK		ICL 1900		ALGOL 60
EPOS ALGOL	1971	Scientific					
ALGOL 68RS	1972	Military	UK	Portable compiler system	ICL 2900/Series 39, Multics, VMS & C generator (1993)	Crown Copyright	ALGOL 68RS
Algol 68 with areas	1972	Experimental & other	UK	Addition of areas to Algol 68			
Mini ALGOL 68	1973	Research	NL	"An interpreter for simple Algol 68 Programs"	Portable interpreter	Mathematisch Centrum	ALGOL 60
OREGANO	1973	Research	US	"The importance of implementation models."		UCLA	
ALGOL 68C	1975	Scientific	UK	Cambridge Algol 68	ICL, IBM 360, PDP 10 & Unix, Telefunken, Tesla & Z80(1980)	Cambridge	ALGOL 68C
ALGOL 68 Revised Report	1975	Standard	Intl	IFIP WG 2.1 Revised Report	Specification	ACM	
Algol H	1975	Experimental & other	UK	Proposed extensions to the mode system of Algol 68	Specification		ALGOL W
Odra Algol 68	1976	practical uses	USSR/ Poland		Odra 1204/IL	Soviet	ALGOL 60
Oklahoma ALGOL 68	1976	programming instruction	USA	Oklahoma State University implementation	IBM 1130 and System/370/158	Unknown	ANSI Fortran 66.
Berlin ALGOL 68	1977	Research	DE	"The Berlin ALGOL 68 implementation" &	An Abstract ALGOL 68 Machine - machine independent Compiler	Technical University of Berlin	CDL 2
FLACC	1977	Multi-purpose	CA	Revised Report complete implementation with debug features	System/370	lease, Chion Corporation	Assembler
ALGOL 68-RT	1979	Scientific	UK	Parallel ALGOL 68-R			
RS Algol	1979	Scientific	UK				
ALGOL 68+	1980	Scientific	NL	Proposed superlanguage of ALGOL 68			
M-220 ALGOL 68			USSR		M-220	Soviet	EPSILON
Leningrad ALGOL 68	1980	Telecommunications	USSR	Full Language + Modules	IBM, DEC, CAMCOH, PS 1001 & PC	Soviet	

	Year	Purpose	State	Description	Target CPU	Licensing	Implementation Language
Interactive ALGOL 68	1983		UK	Incremental compilation	PC	Noncommercial shareware |	
ALGOL 68S	1985	Scientific	Intl	Sun version of ALGOL 68	Sun-3, Sun SPARC (under SunOS 4.1 & Solaris 2), Atari ST (under GEMDOS), Acorn Archimedes (under RISC OS), VAX-11 under Ultrix-32		
Algol68toC (ctrans)	1985	Electronics	UK	ctrans from ELLA ALGOL 68RS	Portable C generator	Open Sourced & Public Domained 1995	ALGOL 68RS
MK2 Interactive ALGOL 68	1992		UK	Incremental compilation	PC	Noncommercial shareware	
Algol 68 Genie	2001	Full Language	NL	Includes standard collateral clause	Portable interpreter	GPL	C
Algol 68 Genie Version 2.0.0	2010	Full Language	NL		Portable interpreter; optional compilation of selected units	GPL	C

The S3 language that was used to write the ICL VME operating system and much other system software on the ICL 2900 Series was a direct derivative of Algol 68. However, it omitted many of the more complex features, and replaced the basic modes with a set of data types that mapped directly to the 2900 Series hardware architecture.

Implementation Specific Extensions

ALGOL 68R from RRE was the first ALGOL 68 subset implementation, running on the ICL 1900. Based on the original language, the main subset restrictions were *definition before use* and no parallel processing. This compiler was popular in UK universities in the 1970s, where many computer science students learnt ALGOL 68 as their first programming language; the compiler was renowned for good error messages.

ALGOL 68RS from RSRE was a portable compiler system written in ALGOL 68RS (bootstrapped from ALGOL 68R), and implemented on a variety of systems including the ICL 2900/Series 39, Multics and DEC VAX/VMS. The language was based on the Revised Report, but with similar subset restrictions to ALGOL 68R. This compiler survives in the form of an Algol68-to-C compiler.

In ALGOL 68S from Carnegie Mellon University the power of parallel processing was improved by adding an orthogonal extension, *eventing*. Any variable declaration containing keyword event made assignments to this variable eligible for parallel evaluation, i.e. the right hand side was made into a procedure which was moved to one of the processors of the C.mmp multiprocessor system. Accesses to such variables were delayed after termination of the assignment.

Cambridge ALGOL 68C was a portable compiler that implemented a subset of ALGOL 68, restricting operator definitions and omitting garbage collection, flexible rows and formatted transput.

Algol 68 Genie by M. van der Veer is an ALGOL 68 implementation for today's computers and operating systems.

"Despite good intentions, a programmer may violate portability by inadvertently employing a local extension. To guard against this, each implementation should provide a PORTCHECK pragmat option. While this option is in force, the compiler prints a message for each construct that it recognizes as violating some portability constraint."

Quotes

- *... The scheme of type composition adopted by C owes considerable debt to Algol 68, although it did not, perhaps, emerge in a form that Algol's adherents would approve of. The central notion I captured from Algol was a type structure based on atomic types (including structures), composed into arrays, pointers (references), and functions (procedures). Algol 68's concept of unions and casts also had an influence that appeared later.* Dennis Ritchie Apr 1993.

- *... C does not descend from Algol 68 is true, yet there was influence, much of it so subtle that it is hard to recover even when I think hard. In particular, the union type (a late addition to C) does owe to A68, not in any details, but in the idea of having such a type at all. More deeply, the type structure in general and even, in some strange way, the declaration syntax (the type-constructor part) was inspired by A68. And yes, of course, "long".* Dennis Ritchie, 18 June 1988

- "Congratulations, your Master has done it" - Niklaus Wirth

- *The more I see of it, the more unhappy I become* - E.W. Dijkstra, 1968

- *[...] it was said that A68's popularity was inversely proportional to [...] the distance from Amsterdam* - Guido van Rossum

- *[...] The best we could do was to send with it a minority report, stating our considered view that, "... as a tool for the reliable creation of sophisticated programs, the language was a failure." [...]* - C. A. R. Hoare in his Oct 1980 Turing Award Lecture

  - Their actual minority report quote from 1970: *"[...] More than ever it will be required from an adequate programming tool that it assists, by structure, the programmer in the most difficult aspects of his job, viz. in the reliable creation of sophisticated programs. In this respect we fail to see how the language proposed here [Algol68] is a significant step forward: on the contrary, we feel that its implicit view of the programmer's task is very much the same as, say, ten years ago. This forces upon us the conclusion that, regarded as a programming tool, the language must be regarded as obsolete. [...]"* Signed by: Dijkstra, Duncan, Garwick, Hoare, Randell, Seegmueller, Turski, Woodger. And then on Dec. 23, 1968, Jan V. Garwick

References

- Ulf Bilting & Jan Skansholm "Vägen till C" (Swedish) meaning "The Road to C", third edition, Studentlitteratur, year 2000, page 3. ISBN 91-44-01468-6.

- Kernighan, Brian W.; Ritchie, Dennis M. (March 1988). The C Programming Language (2nd ed.). Englewood Cliffs, NJ: Prentice Hall. ISBN 0-13-110362-8.

- Harbison, Samuel P.; Steele, Guy L. (2002). C: A Reference Manual (5th ed.). Englewood Cliffs, NJ: Prentice Hall. ISBN 0-13-089592-X.

- Schultz, Thomas (2004). C and the 8051 (3rd ed.). Otsego, MI: PageFree Publishing Inc. p. 20. ISBN 1-58961-237-X. Retrieved 10 February 2012.

- Raymond, Eric S. (11 October 1996). The New Hacker's Dictionary (3rd ed.). MIT Press. p. 432. ISBN 978-0-262-68092-9. Retrieved 5 August 2012.

- "Consolidated Ada 2012 Language Reference Manual". Ada Conformity Assessment Authority. Archived from the original on 2016-03-03. Retrieved 2016-02-23.

- "Technical Corrigendum 1 for Ada 2012". Ada Conformity Assessment Authority. Archived from the original on 2016-03-02. Retrieved 2016-02-23.

- Ganssle, Jack (2013-05-29). "Ada Resource Association – News and resource for the Ada programming language". Adaic.org. Retrieved 2013-06-14.

- Applications, libraries, and test suites — Software Preservation Group. Softwarepreservation.org. Retrieved on 2013-07-21.

- An abstract ALGOL 68 machine and its application in a machine independent compiler - Springer. Springerlink.com. Retrieved on 2013-07-21.

- For example, gcc provides _FORTIFY_SOURCE. "Security Features: Compile Time Buffer Checks (FORTIFY_SOURCE)". fedoraproject.org. Retrieved 2012-08-05.

- "ISO/IEC 8652:2012 Information technology -- Programming languages -- Ada". International Organization for Standardization. Retrieved 2012-12-23.

- Lu Hu-quan (1971). "The Translation of Algol 68 into Chinese." (PDF). Institute of Mathematics, Academia Sinica - Peking, China. Retrieved August 17, 2012.

- Lindsey, C.H.; Boom, H.J. (Dec 1978). "A Modules and Separate Compilation facility for ALGOL 68". ALGOL Bulletin (43). doi:10.1145/1061719.1061724. Retrieved 2011-05-05.

- Oliver, J. R.; Newton, R.S. (1979). "Practical experience with ALGOL 68-RT" (PDF). The Computer Journal. 22 (2): 114–118. doi:10.1093/comjnl/22.2.114. Retrieved 2011-04-09.

- SofTech Inc., Waltham, MA (1983-04-11). "Ada Compiler Validation Summary Report: NYU Ada/ED, Version 19.7 V-001". Retrieved 2010-12-16. CS1 maint: Uses authors parameter (link)

- S. Tucker Taft; Florence Olsen (1999-06-30). "Ada helps churn out less-buggy code". Government Computer News. pp. 2–3. Retrieved 2010-09-14.

Types of C++ Programming Language

C++ has a number of programming languages; some of these languages are C++03, C++11, C++14 and C++17. C++03 is the standard version of C++ globally whereas C++11 is the standard version of C++. The following chapter helps the reader in understanding all the types of C++.

C++03

C++03 is a version of an international standard for the programming language C++. It is defined by two standards organizations, the International Standards Organization (ISO) and the International Electrotechnical Commission (IEC), in standard ISO/IEC 14882:2003.

C++03 replaced the prior revision of the C++ standard, called C++98, and was later replaced by C++11. C++03 was primarily a bug fix release for the implementers to ensure greater consistency and portability. This revision addressed 92 core language defect reports, 125 library defect reports, and included only one new language feature: value initialization

Among the more noteworthy defect reports addressed by C++03 was the library defect report 69, whose resolution added the requirement that elements in a vector are stored contiguously. This codifies the common expectation that a C++ std::vector object uses a memory layout similar to an array. While most implementations satisfied this expectation, it was not required by C++98.

C++11

C++11 is a version of the standard for the programming language C++. It was approved by International Organization for Standardization (ISO) on 12 August 2011, replacing C++03, and superseded by C++14 on 18 August 2014. The name follows the tradition of naming language versions by the publication year of the specification, though it was formerly named *C++0x* because it was expected to be published before 2010.

Although one of the design goals was to prefer changes to the libraries over changes to the core language, C++11 does make several additions to the core language. Areas of the core language that were significantly improved include multithreading support, generic programming support, uniform initialization, and performance. Significant changes were also made to the C++ Standard Library, incorporating most of the C++ Technical Report 1 (TR1) libraries, except the library of mathematical special functions.

C++11 was published as *ISO/IEC 14882:2011* in September 2011 and is available for a fee. The working draft most similar to the published C++11 standard is N3337, dated 16 January 2012; it has only editorial corrections from the C++11 standard.

Design Goals

The design committee attempted to stick to a number of goals in designing C++11:

- Maintain stability and compatibility with C++98 and possibly with C

- Prefer introducing new features via the standard library, rather than extending the core language

- Prefer changes that can evolve programming technique

- Improve C++ to facilitate systems and library design, rather than introduce new features useful only to specific applications

- Increase type safety by providing safer alternatives to earlier unsafe techniques

- Increase performance and the ability to work directly with hardware

- Provide proper solutions for real-world problems

- Implement *zero-overhead* principle (further support needed by some utilities must be used only if the utility is used)

- Make C++ easy to teach and to learn without removing any utility needed by expert programmers

Attention to beginners is considered important, because most computer programmers will always be such, and because many beginners never widen their knowledge, limiting themselves to work in aspects of the language in which they specialize.

Extensions to The C++ Core Language

One function of the C++ committee is the development of the language core. Areas of the core language that were significantly improved include multithreading support, generic programming support, uniform initialization, and performance.

For the purposes of this article, core language features and changes are grouped into four general sections: run-time performance enhancements, build-time performance enhancements, usability enhancements, and new functionality. Some features could fall into multiple groups, but they are mentioned only in the group that primarily represents that feature.

Core Language Runtime Performance Enhancements

These language features primarily exist to provide some kind of performance benefit, either of memory or of computational speed.

Rvalue References and Move Constructors

In C++03 (and before), temporaries (termed "rvalues", as they often lie on the right side of an assignment) were intended to never be modifiable — just as in C — and were considered to be indistinguishable from const T& types; nevertheless, in some cases, temporaries could have been modified, a behavior that was even considered to be a useful loophole. C++11 adds a new non-const reference type called an rvalue reference, identified by T&&. This refers to temporaries that are permitted to be modified after they are initialized, for the purpose of allowing "move semantics".

A chronic performance problem with C++03 is the costly and unneeded deep copies that can happen implicitly when objects are passed by value. To illustrate the issue, consider that a std::vector<T> is, internally, a wrapper around a C-style array with a size. If a std::vector<T> temporary is created or returned from a function, it can be stored only by creating a new std::vector<T> and copying all the rvalue's data into it. Then the temporary and all its memory is destroyed. (For simplicity, this discussion neglects the return value optimization.)

In C++11, a move constructor of std::vector<T> that takes an rvalue reference to a std::vector<T> can copy the pointer to the internal C-style array out of the rvalue into the new std::vector<T>, then set the pointer inside the rvalue to null. Since the temporary will never again be used, no code will try to access the null pointer, and because the pointer is null, its memory is not deleted when it goes out of scope. Hence, the operation not only forgoes the expense of a deep copy, but is safe and invisible.

Rvalue references can provide performance benefits to existing code without needing to make any changes outside the standard library. The type of the returned value of a function returning a std::vector<T> temporary does not need to be changed explicitly to std::vector<T> && to invoke the move constructor, as temporaries are considered rvalues automatically. (However, if std::vector<T> is a C++03 version without a move constructor, then the copy constructor will be invoked with a const std::vector<T>&, incurring a significant memory allocation.)

For safety reasons, some restrictions are imposed. A named variable will never be considered to be an rvalue even if it is declared as such. To get an rvalue, the function template std::move() should be used. Rvalue references can also be modified only under certain circumstances, being intended to be used primarily with move constructors.

Due to the nature of the wording of rvalue references, and to some modification to the wording for lvalue references (regular references), rvalue references allow developers to provide perfect function forwarding. When combined with variadic templates, this ability allows for function templates that can perfectly forward arguments to another function that takes those particular arguments. This is most useful for forwarding constructor parameters, to create factory functions that will automatically call the correct constructor for those particular arguments. This is seen in the emplace_back set of the C++ standard library methods.

Constexpr – Generalized Constant Expressions

C++ has always had the concept of constant expressions. These are expressions such as 3+4 that will always yield the same results, at compile time and at run time. Constant expressions are optimization opportunities for compilers, and compilers frequently execute them at compile time and hardcode the results in the program. Also, in several places, the C++ specification requires using constant expressions. Defining an array requires a constant expression, and enumerator values must be constant expressions.

However, a constant expression has never been allowed to contain a function call or object constructor. So a piece of code as simple as this is illegal:

```
int get_five() {return 5;}

int some_value[get_five() + 7]; // Create an array of 12 inte-
gers. Ill-formed C++
```

This was not legal in C++03, because get_five() + 7 is not a constant expression. A C++03 compiler has no way of knowing if get_five() actually is constant at runtime. In theory, this function could affect a global variable, call other non-runtime constant functions, etc.

C++11 introduced the keyword constexpr, which allows the user to guarantee that a function or object constructor is a compile-time constant. The above example can be rewritten as follows:

```
constexpr int get_five() {return 5;}

int some_value[get_five() + 7]; // Create an array of 12 inte-
gers. Legal C++11
```

This allows the compiler to understand, and verify, that get_five() is a compile-time constant.

Using constexpr on a function imposes some limits on what that function can do. First, the function must have a non-void return type. Second, the function body cannot declare variables or define new types. Third, the body may contain only declarations, null statements and a single return statement. There must exist argument values such that, after argument substitution, the expression in the return statement produces a constant expression.

Before C++11, the values of variables could be used in constant expressions only if the variables are declared const, have an initializer which is a constant expression, and are of integral or enumeration type. C++11 removes the restriction that the variables must be of integral or enumeration type if they are defined with the constexpr keyword:

```
constexpr double earth_gravitational_acceleration = 9.8;

constexpr double moon_gravitational_acceleration = earth_gravi-
tational_acceleration / 6.0;
```

Such data variables are implicitly const, and must have an initializer which must be a constant expression.

To construct constant expression data values from user-defined types, constructors can also be declared with constexpr. A constexpr constructor's function body can contain only declarations and null statements, and cannot declare variables or define types, as with a constexpr function. There must exist argument values such that, after argument substitution, it initializes the class's members with constant expressions. The destructors for such types must be trivial.

The copy constructor for a type with any constexpr constructors should usually also be defined as a constexpr constructor, to allow objects of the type to be returned by value from a constexpr function. Any member function of a class, such as copy constructors, operator overloads, etc., can be declared as constexpr, so long as they meet the requirements for constexpr functions. This allows the compiler to copy objects at compile time, perform operations on them, etc.

If a constexpr function or constructor is called with arguments which aren't constant expressions, the call behaves as if the function were not constexpr, and the resulting value is not a constant expression. Likewise, if the expression in the return statement of a constexpr function does not evaluate to a constant expression for a given invocation, the result is not a constant expression.

Modification to The Definition of Plain Old Data

In C++03, a class or struct must follow a number of rules for it to be considered a plain old data (POD) type. Types that fit this definition produce object layouts that are compatible with C, and they could also be initialized statically. The C++03 standard has restrictions on what types are compatible with C or can be statically initialized despite no technical reason a compiler couldn't accept the program; if someone were to create a C++03 POD type and add a non-virtual member function, this type would no longer be a POD type, could not be statically initialized, and would be incompatible with C despite no change to the memory layout.

C++11 relaxed several of the POD rules, by dividing the POD concept into two separate concepts: *trivial* and *standard-layout*.

A type that is *trivial* can be statically initialized. It also means that it is legal to copy data around via memcpy, rather than having to use a copy constructor. The lifetime of a *trivial* type begins when its storage is defined, not when a constructor completes.

A trivial class or struct is defined as one that:

1. Has a trivial default constructor. This may use the default constructor syntax (SomeConstructor() = default;).

2. Has trivial copy and move constructors, which may use the default syntax.

3. Has trivial copy and move assignment operators, which may use the default syntax.

4. Has a trivial destructor, which must not be virtual.

Constructors are trivial only if there are no virtual member functions of the class and no virtual base classes. Copy/move operations also require all non-static data members to be trivial.

A type that is *standard-layout* means that it orders and packs its members in a way that is compatible with C. A class or struct is standard-layout, by definition, provided:

1. It has no virtual functions

2. It has no virtual base classes

3. All its non-static data members have the same access control (public, private, protected)

4. All its non-static data members, including any in its base classes, are in the same one class in the hierarchy

5. The above rules also apply to all the base classes and to all non-static data members in the class hierarchy

6. It has no base classes of the same type as the first defined non-static data member

A class/struct/union is considered POD if it is trivial, standard-layout, and all of its non-static data members and base classes are PODs.

By separating these concepts, it becomes possible to give up one without losing the other. A class with complex move and copy constructors may not be trivial, but it could be standard-layout and thus interop with C. Similarly, a class with public and private non-static data members would not be standard-layout, but it could be trivial and thus memcpy-able.

Core Language Build-time Performance Enhancements

Extern Template

In C++03, the compiler must instantiate a template whenever a fully specified template is encountered in a translation unit. If the template is instantiated with the same types in many translation units, this can dramatically increase compile times. There is no way to prevent this in C++03, so C++11 introduced extern template declarations, analogous to extern data declarations.

C++03 has this syntax to oblige the compiler to instantiate a template:

```
template class std::vector<MyClass>;
```

C++11 now provides this syntax:

```
extern template class std::vector<MyClass>;
```

which tells the compiler *not* to instantiate the template in this translation unit.

Core Language Usability Enhancements

These features exist for the primary purpose of making the language easier to use. These can improve type safety, minimize code repetition, make erroneous code less likely, etc.

Initializer Lists

C++03 inherited the initializer-list feature from C. A struct or array is given a list of arguments in braces, in the order of the members' definitions in the struct. These initializer-lists are recursive, so an array of structs or struct containing other structs can use them.

```
struct Object {
    float first;
    int second;
};

Object scalar = {0.43f, 10}; //One Object, with first=0.43f and
second=10

Object anArray[] = {{13.4f, 3}, {43.28f, 29}, {5.934f, 17}}; //
```

```
An array of three Objects
```

This is very useful for static lists, or initializing a struct to some value. C++ also provides constructors to initialize an object, but they are often not as convenient as the initializer list. However, C++03 allows initializer-lists only on structs and classes that conform to the Plain Old Data (POD) definition; C++11 extends initializer-lists, so they can be used for all classes including standard containers like std::vector.

C++11 binds the concept to a template, called std::initializer_list. This allows constructors and other functions to take initializer-lists as parameters. For example:

```
class SequenceClass {

public:

    SequenceClass(std::initializer_list<int> list);

};
```

This allows SequenceClass to be constructed from a sequence of integers, such as:

```
SequenceClass some_var = {1, 4, 5, 6};
```

This constructor is a special kind of constructor, called an initializer-list-constructor. Classes with such a constructor are treated specially during uniform initialization.

The class std::initializer_list<> is a first-class C++11 standard library type. However, they can be initially constructed statically by the C++11 compiler only via use of the {} syntax. The list can be copied once constructed, though this is only a copy-by-reference. An initializer list is constant; its members cannot be changed once the initializer list is created, nor can the data in those members be changed.

Because initializer_list is a real type, it can be used in other places besides class constructors. Regular functions can take typed initializer lists as arguments. For example:

```
void function_name(std::initializer_list<float> list);


function_name({1.0f, -3.45f, -0.4f});
```

Standard containers can also be initialized in these ways:

```
std::vector<std::string> v = { "xyzzy", "plugh", "abracadabra" };

std::vector<std::string> v({ "xyzzy", "plugh", "abracadabra" });
```

```
std::vector<std::string> v{ "xyzzy", "plugh", "abracadabra" };
// see "Uniform initialization" below
```

Uniform Initialization

C++03 has a number of problems with initializing types. Several ways to do this exist, and some produce different results when interchanged. The traditional constructor syntax, for example, can look like a function declaration, and steps must be taken to ensure that the compiler's most vexing parse rule will not mistake it for such. Only aggregates and POD types can be initialized with aggregate initializers (using SomeType var = {/*stuff*/};).

C++11 provides a syntax that allows for fully uniform type initialization that works on any object. It expands on the initializer list syntax:

```
struct BasicStruct {

    int x;

    double y;

};


struct AltStruct {

    AltStruct(int x, double y) : x_{x}, y_{y} {}


    private:

        int x_;

        double y_;

};


BasicStruct var1{5, 3.2};

AltStruct var2{2, 4.3};
```

The initialization of var1 behaves exactly as though it were aggregate-initialization. That is, each data member of an object, in turn, will be copy-initialized with the corresponding value from the initializer-list. Implicit type conversion will be used where needed. If no conversion exists, or only a narrowing conversion exists, the program is ill-formed. The initialization of var2 invokes the constructor.

One can also do this:

```
struct IdString {

    std::string name;

    int identifier;

};


IdString get_string() {

    return {"foo", 42}; //Note the lack of explicit type.

}
```

Uniform initialization does not replace constructor syntax, which is still needed at times. If a class has an initializer list constructor (TypeName(initializer_list<SomeType>);), then it takes priority over other forms of construction, provided that the initializer list conforms to the sequence constructor's type. The C++11 version of std::vector has an initializer list constructor for its template type. Thus this code:

```
std::vector<int> the_vec{4};
```

will call the initializer list constructor, not the constructor of std::vector that takes a single size parameter and creates the vector with that size. To access the latter constructor, the user will need to use the standard constructor syntax directly.

Type Inference

In C++03 (and C), to use a variable, its type must be specified explicitly. However, with the advent of template types and template metaprogramming techniques, the type of something, particularly the well-defined return value of a function, may not be easily expressed. Thus, storing intermediates in variables is difficult, possibly needing knowledge of the internals of a given metaprogramming library.

C++11 allows this to be mitigated in two ways. First, the definition of a variable with an explicit initialization can use the auto keyword. This creates a variable of the specific type of the initializer:

```
auto some_strange_callable_type = std::bind(&some_function, _2,
_1, some_object);

auto other_variable = 5;
```

The type of some_strange_callable_type is simply whatever the particular template function override of std::bind returns for those particular arguments. This type is easily determined procedurally by the compiler as part of its semantic analysis duties, but is not easy for the user to determine upon inspection.

The type of other_variable is also well-defined, but it is easier for the user to determine. It is an int, which is the same type as the integer literal.

Further, the keyword decltype can be used to determine the type of expression at compile-time. For example:

```
int some_int;

decltype(some_int) other_integer_variable = 5;
```

This is more useful in conjunction with auto, since the type of auto variable is known only to the compiler. However, decltype can also be very useful for expressions in code that makes heavy use of operator overloading and specialized types.

```
auto is also useful for reducing the verbosity of the code. For
instance, instead of writing

for (std::vector<int>::const_iterator itr = myvec.cbegin(); itr
!= myvec.cend(); ++itr)
```

the programmer can use the shorter

```
for (auto itr = myvec.cbegin(); itr != myvec.cend(); ++itr)
```

which can be further compacted since "myvec" implements begin/end iterators:

```
for (auto& x : myvec)
```

This difference grows as the programmer begins to nest containers, though in such cases typedefs are a good way to decrease the amount of code.

The type denoted by decltype can be different from the type deduced by auto.

```
#include <vector>

int main() {

    const std::vector<int> v(1);

    auto a = v;          // a has type int

    decltype(v) b = 1; // b has type const int&, the return
type of

                        //    std::vector<int>::operator[]
```

```
(size_type) const

    auto c = 0;              // c has type int

    auto d = c;              // d has type int

    decltype(c) e;           // e has type int, the type of the
entity named by c

    decltype((c)) f = c;     // f has type int&, because (c) is an
lvalue

    decltype(0) g;           // g has type int, because 0 is an
rvalue

}
```

Range-based for Loop

C++11 extends the syntax of the for statement to allow for easy iteration over a range of elements:

```
int my_array = {1, 2, 3, 4, 5};

// double the value of each element in my_array:

for (int& x : my_array) {

    x *= 2;

}

// similar but also using type inference for array elements

for (auto& x : my_array) {

    x *= 2;

}
```

This form of for, called the "range-based for", will iterate over each element in the list. It will work for C-style arrays, initializer lists, and any type that has begin() and end() functions defined for it that return iterators. All the standard library containers that have begin/end pairs will work with the range-based for statement.

Lambda Functions and Expressions

C++11 provides the ability to create anonymous functions, called lambda functions. These are defined as follows:

```
[](int x, int y) -> int { return x + y; }
```

The return type is implicit; it returns the type of the return expression (decltype(x+y)). The return type of lambda can be omitted as long as all return expressions return the same type. A lambda can optionally be a closure.

Alternative Function Syntax

Standard C function declaration syntax was perfectly adequate for the feature set of the C language. As C++ evolved from C, it kept the basic syntax and extended it where needed. However, as C++ grew more complex, it exposed several limits, especially regarding template function declarations. For example, in C++03 this is disallowed:

```
template<class Lhs, class Rhs>
  Ret adding_func(const Lhs &lhs, const Rhs &rhs) {return lhs +
rhs;} //Ret must be the type of lhs+rhs
```

The type Ret is whatever the addition of types Lhs and Rhs will produce. Even with the aforementioned C++11 functionality of decltype, this is not possible:

```
template<class Lhs, class Rhs>
  decltype(lhs+rhs) adding_func(const Lhs &lhs, const Rhs &rhs)
{return lhs + rhs;} //Not legal C++11
```

This is not legal C++ because lhs and rhs have not yet been defined; they will not be valid identifiers until after the parser has parsed the rest of the function prototype.

To work around this, C++11 introduced a new function declaration syntax, with a *trailing-return-type*:

```
template<class Lhs, class Rhs>
  auto adding_func(const Lhs &lhs, const Rhs &rhs) -> decl-
type(lhs+rhs) {return lhs + rhs;}
```

This syntax can be used for more mundane function declarations and definitions:

```
struct SomeStruct  {
    auto func_name(int x, int y) -> int;
};

auto SomeStruct::func_name(int x, int y) -> int {
    return x + y;
}
```

Use of the keyword "auto" in this case is only part of the syntax and doesn't perform automatic type deduction.

Object Construction Improvement

In C++03, constructors of a class are not allowed to call other constructors of that class. Each constructor must construct all of its class members itself or call a common member function, like these,

```
class SomeType   {

    int number;

private:

    void Construct(int new_number) { number = new_number; }

public:

    SomeType(int new_number) { Construct(new_number); }

    SomeType() { Construct(42); }

};
```

Constructors for base classes cannot be directly exposed to derived classes; each derived class must implement constructors even if a base class constructor would be appropriate. Non-constant data members of classes cannot be initialized at the site of the declaration of those members. They can be initialized only in a constructor.

C++11 provides solutions to all of these problems.

C++11 allows constructors to call other peer constructors (termed delegation). This allows constructors to utilize another constructor's behavior with a minimum of added code. Delegation has been used in other languages e.g., Java, Objective-C.

This syntax is as follows:

```
class SomeType   {

    int number;

public:

    SomeType(int new_number) : number(new_number) {}

    SomeType() : SomeType(42) {}

};
```

Notice that, in this case, the same effect could have been achieved by making new_ number a defaulting parameter. The new syntax, however, allows the default value (42) to be expressed in the implementation rather than the interface — a benefit to maintainers of library code since default values for function parameters are "baked in" to call sites, whereas constructor delegation allows the value to be changed without recompilation of the code using the library.

This comes with a caveat: C++03 considers an object to be constructed when its constructor finishes executing, but C++11 considers an object constructed once *any* constructor finishes execution. Since multiple constructors will be allowed to execute, this will mean that each delegating constructor will be executing on a fully constructed object of its own type. Derived class constructors will execute after all delegation in their base classes is complete.

For base-class constructors, C++11 allows a class to specify that base class constructors will be inherited. Thus, the C++11 compiler will generate code to perform the inheritance, the forwarding of the derived class to the base class. This is an all-or-nothing feature: either all of that base class's constructors are forwarded or none of them are. Also, restrictions exist for multiple inheritance, such that class constructors cannot be inherited from two classes that use constructors with the same signature. Nor can a constructor in the derived class exist that matches a signature in the inherited base class.

The syntax is as follows:

```
class BaseClass {

public:

    BaseClass(int value);

};

class DerivedClass : public BaseClass {

public:

    using BaseClass::BaseClass;

};
```

For member initialization, C++11 allows this syntax:

```
class SomeClass {

public:

    SomeClass() {}

    explicit SomeClass(int new_value) : value(new_value) {}
```

```
private:

    int value = 5;

};
```

Any constructor of the class will initialize value with 5, if the constructor does not override the initialization with its own. So the above empty constructor will initialize value as the class definition states, but the constructor that takes an int will initialize it to the given parameter.

It can also use constructor or uniform initialization, instead of the assignment initialization shown above.

Explicit Overrides and Final

In C++03, it is possible to accidentally create a new virtual function, when one intended to override a base class function. For example:

```
struct Base {

    virtual void some_func(float);

};

struct Derived : Base {

    virtual void some_func(int);

};
```

Suppose the Derived::some_func is intended to replace the base class version. But instead, because it has a different signature, it creates a second virtual function. This is a common problem, particularly when a user goes to modify the base class.

C++11 provides syntax to solve this problem.

```
struct Base {

    virtual void some_func(float);

};

struct Derived : Base {

    virtual void some_func(int) override; // ill-formed -
doesn't override a base class method

};
```

The override special identifier means that the compiler will check the base class(es) to see if there is a virtual function with this exact signature. And if there is not, the compiler will indicate an error.

C++11 also adds the ability to prevent inheriting from classes or simply preventing overriding methods in derived classes. This is done with the special identifier final. For example:

```
struct Base1 final { };

struct Derived1 : Base1 { }; // ill-formed because the class
Base1 has been marked final

struct Base2 {

    virtual void f() final;

};

struct Derived2 : Base2 {

    void f(); // ill-formed because the virtual function
Base2::f has been marked final

};
```

In this example, the virtual void f() final; statement declares a new virtual function, but it also prevents derived classes from overriding it. It also has the effect of preventing derived classes from using that particular function name and parameter combination.

Note that neither override nor final are language keywords. They are technically identifiers for declarator attributes:

- they gain special meaning as attributes only when used in those specific trailing contexts (after all type specifiers, access specifiers, member declarations (for struct, class and enum types) and declarator specifiers, but before initialization or code implementation of each declarator in a comma-separated list of declarators);

- they do not alter the declared type signature and do not declare or override any new identifier in any scope;

- the recognized and accepted declarator attributes may be extended in future versions of C++ (some compiler-specific extensions already recognize added declarator attributes, to provide code generation options or optimization hints to the compiler, or to generate added data into the compiled code, intended for debuggers, linkers, and deployment of the compiled code, or to provide added system-specific security attributes, or to enhance reflection abilities at runtime, or to provide added binding information for interoperability with other programming languages and runtime systems; these extensions may take parameters between parentheses after the declarator attribute identifier; for ANSI conformance, these compiler-specific extensions should use the double underscore prefix convention).

- In any other location, they can be valid identifiers for new declarations (and later use if they are accessible).

Null Pointer Constant

For the purposes of this section and this section alone, every occurrence of "0" is meant as "a constant expression which evaluates to 0, which is of type int". In reality, the constant expression can be of any integral type.

Since the dawn of C in 1972, the constant 0 has had the double role of constant integer and null pointer constant. The ambiguity inherent in the double meaning of 0 was dealt with in C by using the preprocessor macro NULL, which commonly expands to either ((void*)0) or 0. C++ didn't adopt the same behavior, allowing only 0 as a null pointer constant. This interacts poorly with function overloading:

```
void foo(char *);

void foo(int);
```

If NULL is defined as 0 (which is usually the case in C++), the statement foo(NULL); will call foo(int), which is almost certainly not what the programmer intended, and not what a superficial reading of the code suggests.

C++11 corrects this by introducing a new keyword to serve as a distinguished null pointer constant: nullptr. It is of type nullptr_t, which is implicitly convertible and comparable to any pointer type or pointer-to-member type. It is not implicitly convertible or comparable to integral types, except for bool. While the original proposal specified that an rvalue of type nullptr should not be convertible to bool, the core language working group decided that such a conversion would be desirable, for consistency with regular pointer types. The proposed wording changes were unanimously voted into the Working Paper in June 2008.

For backwards compatibility reasons, 0 remains a valid null pointer constant.

```
char *pc = nullptr;      // OK

int  *pi = nullptr;      // OK

bool   b = nullptr;      // OK. b is false.

int    i = nullptr;      // error

foo(nullptr);            // calls foo(nullptr_t), not foo(int);
```

```
/*

   Note that foo(nullptr_t) will actually call foo(char *) in
the example above using an implicit conversion,

   only if no other functions are overloading with compatible
pointer types in scope.

   If multiple overloadings exist, the resolution will fail as
it is ambiguous,

   unless there is an explicit declaration of foo(nullptr_t).


   In standard types headers for C++11, the nullptr_t  type
should be declared as:

      typedef decltype(nullptr) nullptr_t;

   but not as:

      typedef int nullptr_t; // prior versions of C++ which
need NULL to be defined as 0

      typedef void *nullptr_t; // ANSI C which defines NULL as
((void*)0)

*/
```

Strongly Typed Enumerations

In C++03, enumerations are not type-safe. They are effectively integers, even when the enumeration types are distinct. This allows the comparison between two enum values of different enumeration types. The only safety that C++03 provides is that an integer or a value of one enum type does not convert implicitly to another enum type. Further, the underlying integral type is implementation-defined; code that depends on the size of the enumeration is thus non-portable. Lastly, enumeration values are scoped to the enclosing scope. Thus, it is not possible for two separate enumerations to have matching member names.

C++11 allows a special classification of enumeration that has none of these issues. This is expressed using the enum class (enum struct is also accepted as a synonym) declaration:

enum class Enumeration {

```
    Val1,

    Val2,
```

```
    Val3 = 100,

    Val4 // = 101

};
```

This enumeration is type-safe. Enum class values are not implicitly converted to integers. Thus, they cannot be compared to integers either (the expression Enumeration::Val4 == 101 gives a compile error).

The underlying type of enum classes is always known. The default type is int; this can be overridden to a different integral type as can be seen in this example:

```
enum class Enum2 : unsigned int {Val1, Val2};
```

With old-style enumerations the values are placed in the outer scope. With new-style enumerations they are placed within the scope of the enum class name. So in the above example, Val1 is undefined, but Enum2::Val1 is defined.

There is also a transitional syntax to allow old-style enumerations to provide explicit scoping, and the definition of the underlying type:

```
enum Enum3 : unsigned long {Val1 = 1, Val2};
```

In this case the enumerator names are defined in the enumeration's scope (Enum3::Val1), but for backwards compatibility they are also placed in the enclosing scope.

Forward-declaring enums are also possible in C++11. Formerly, enum types could not be forward-declared because the size of the enumeration depends on the definition of its members. As long as the size of the enumeration is specified either implicitly or explicitly, it can be forward-declared:

```
enum Enum1;                      // Illegal in C++03 and C++11;
the underlying type cannot be determined.
```

```
enum Enum2 : unsigned int;       // Legal in C++11, the under-
lying type is specified explicitly.
```

```
enum class Enum3;                // Legal in C++11, the under-
lying type is int.
```

```
enum class Enum4 : unsigned int; // Legal in C++11.
```

```
enum Enum2 : unsigned short;     // Illegal in C++11, because
Enum2 was formerly declared with a different underlying type.
```

Right Angle Bracket

C++03's parser defines ">>" as the right shift operator or stream extraction operator in all cases. However, with nested template declarations, there is a tendency for the pro-grammer to neglect to place a space between the two right angle brackets, thus causing a compiler syntax error.

C++11 improves the specification of the parser so that multiple right angle brackets will be interpreted as closing the template argument list where it is reasonable. This can be overridden by using parentheses around parameter expressions using the ">", ">=" or ">>" binary operators:

```
template<bool Test> class SomeType;

std::vector<SomeType<1>2>> x1;    // Interpreted as a std::vector
of SomeType<true>,

    // followed by "2 >> x1", which is not legal syntax for a
declarator. 1 is true.

std::vector<SomeType<(1>2)>> x1;   // Interpreted as std::vector
of SomeType<false>,

    // followed by the declarator "x1", which is legal C++11
syntax. (1>2) is false.
```

Explicit Conversion Operators

C++98 added the explicit keyword as a modifier on constructors to prevent single-ar-gument constructors from being used as implicit type conversion operators. However, this does nothing for actual conversion operators. For example, a smart pointer class may have an operator bool() to allow it to act more like a primitive pointer: if it includes this conversion, it can be tested with if (smart_ptr_variable) (which would be true if the pointer was non-null and false otherwise). However, this allows other, unintended conversions as well. Because C++ bool is defined as an arithmetic type, it can be implic-itly converted to integral or even floating-point types, which allows for mathematical operations that are not intended by the user.

In C++11, the explicit keyword can now be applied to conversion operators. As with constructors, it prevents using those conversion functions in implicit conversions. However, language contexts that specifically need a boolean value (the conditions of if-statements and loops, and operands to the logical operators) count as explicit con-versions and can thus use a bool conversion operator.

For example, this feature solves cleanly the safe bool issue.

Template Aliases

In C++03, it is possible to define a typedef only as a synonym for another type, includ-

ing a synonym for a template specialization with all actual template arguments specified. It is not possible to create a typedef template. For example:

```
template <typename First, typename Second, int Third>

class SomeType;


template <typename Second>

typedef SomeType<OtherType, Second, 5> TypedefName; // Illegal
in C++03
```

This will not compile.

C++11 adds this ability with this syntax:

```
template <typename First, typename Second, int Third>

class SomeType;


template <typename Second>

using TypedefName = SomeType<OtherType, Second, 5>;
```

The using syntax can be also used as type aliasing in C++11:

```
typedef void (*FunctionType)(double);        // Old style

using FunctionType = void (*)(double); // New introduced syntax
```

Unrestricted Unions

In C++03, there are restrictions on what types of objects can be members of a union.
For example, unions cannot contain any objects that define a non-trivial constructor or
destructor. C++11 lifts some of these restrictions.

If a union member has a non trivial special member function, the compiler will not generate the equivalent member function for the union and it must be manually defined.

This is a simple example of a union permitted in C++11:

```
#include <new> // Needed for placement 'new'.


struct Point {
```

```
    Point() {}

    Point(int x, int y): x_(x), y_(y) {}

    int x_, y_;
};


union U {

    int z;

    double w;

    Point p; // Illegal in C++03; legal in C++11.

    U() {} // Due to the Point member, a constructor definition
is now needed.

    U(const Point& pt) : p(pt) {} // Construct Point object us-
ing initializer list.

    U& operator=(const Point& pt) { new(&p) Point(pt); return
*this; } // Assign Point object using placement 'new'.
};
```

The changes will not break any existing code since they only relax current rules.

Core Language Functionality Improvements

These features allow the language to do things that were formerly impossible, exceedingly verbose, or needed non-portable libraries.

Variadic Templates

In C++11, templates can take variable numbers of template parameters. This also allows the definition of type-safe variadic functions.

New String Literals

C++03 offers two kinds of string literals. The first kind, contained within double quotes, produces a null-terminated array of type const char. The second kind, defined as L"", produces a null-terminated array of type const wchar_t, where wchar_t is a wide-character of undefined size and semantics. Neither literal type offers support for string literals with UTF-8, UTF-16, or any other kind of Unicode encodings.

The definition of the type char has been modified to explicitly express that it's at least the size needed to store an eight-bit coding of UTF-8, and large enough to contain any member of the compiler's basic execution character set. It was formerly defined as only the latter in the C++ standard itself, then relying on the C standard to guarantee at least 8 bits.

C++11 supports three Unicode encodings: UTF-8, UTF-16, and UTF-32. Along with the formerly noted changes to the definition of char, C++11 adds two new character types: char16_t and char32_t. These are designed to store UTF-16 and UTF-32 respectively.

Creating string literals for each of these encodings can be done thusly:

```
u8"I'm a UTF-8 string."
```

```
u"This is a UTF-16 string."
```

```
U"This is a UTF-32 string."
```

The type of the first string is the usual const char[]. The type of the second string is const char16_t[] (note lower case 'u' prefix). The type of the third string is const char32_t[] (upper case 'U' prefix).

When building Unicode string literals, it is often useful to insert Unicode codepoints directly into the string. To do this, C++11 allows this syntax:

```
u8"This is a Unicode Character: \u2018."
```

```
u"This is a bigger Unicode Character: \u2018."
```

```
U"This is a Unicode Character: \U00002018."
```

The number after the \u is a hexadecimal number; it does not need the usual 0x prefix. The identifier \u represents a 16-bit Unicode codepoint; to enter a 32-bit codepoint, use \U and a 32-bit hexadecimal number. Only valid Unicode codepoints can be entered. For example, codepoints on the range U+D800–U+DFFF are forbidden, as they are reserved for surrogate pairs in UTF-16 encodings.

It is also sometimes useful to avoid escaping strings manually, particularly for using literals of XML files, scripting languages, or regular expressions. C++11 provides a raw string literal:

```
R"(The String Data \ Stuff " )"
```

```
R"delimiter(The String Data \ Stuff " )delimiter"
```

In the first case, everything between the "(and the)" is part of the string. The " and \ characters do not need to be escaped. In the second case, the "delimiter(starts the string, and it ends only when)delimiter" is reached. The string delimiter can be any string up to 16 characters in length, including the empty string. This string cannot contain spaces, control characters, '(', ')', or the '\' character. Using this delimiter string allows the user to have ")" characters within raw string literals. For example, R"delimiter((a-z))delimiter" is equivalent to "(a-z)".

Raw string literals can be combined with the wide literal or any of the Unicode literal prefixes:

```
u8R"XXX(I'm a "raw UTF-8" string.)XXX"

uR"*(This is a "raw UTF-16" string.)*"

UR"(This is a "raw UTF-32" string.)"
```

User-defined Literals

C++03 provides a number of literals. The characters 12.5 are a literal that is resolved by the compiler as a type double with the value of 12.5. However, the addition of the suffix f, as in 12.5f, creates a value of type float that contains the value 12.5. The suffix modifiers for literals are fixed by the C++ specification, and C++ code cannot create new literal modifiers.

C++11 also includes the ability for the user to define new kinds of literal modifiers that will construct objects based on the string of characters that the literal modifies.

Literals transformation is redefined into two distinct phases: raw and cooked. A raw literal is a sequence of characters of some specific type, while the cooked literal is of a separate type. The C++ literal 1234, as a raw literal, is this sequence of characters '1', '2', '3', '4'. As a cooked literal, it is the integer 1234. The C++ literal 0xA in raw form is '0', 'x', 'A', while in cooked form it is the integer 10.

Literals can be extended in both raw and cooked forms, with the exception of string literals, which can be processed only in cooked form. This exception is due to the fact that strings have prefixes that affect the specific meaning and type of the characters in question.

All user-defined literals are suffixes; defining prefix literals is not possible. All suffixes starting with any character except underscore (_) are reserved by the standard. Thus, all user-defined literals have suffixes starting with an underscore (_).

User-defined literals processing the raw form of the literal are defined as follows:

```
OutputType operator "" _suffix(const char * literal_string);


OutputType some_variable = 1234_suffix;
```

The second statement executes the code defined by the user-defined literal function. This function is passed "1234" as a C-style string, so it has a null terminator.

An alternative mechanism for processing integer and floating point raw literals is via a variadic template:

```
template<char...> OutputType operator "" _tuffix();
```

```
OutputType some_variable = 1234_tuffix;
```

```
OutputType another_variable = 2.17_tuffix;
```

This instantiates the literal processing function as operator "" _tuffix<'1', '2', '3', '4'>(). In this form, there is no terminating null character to the string. The main purpose for doing this is to use C++11's constexpr keyword and the compiler to allow the literal to be transformed entirely at compile time, assuming OutputType is a constexpr-constructible and copyable type, and the literal processing function is a constexpr function.

For numeric literals, the type of the cooked literal is either unsigned long long for integral literals or long double for floating point literals. (Note: There is no need for signed integral types because a sign-prefixed literal is parsed as an expression containing the sign as a unary prefix operator and the unsigned number.) There is no alternative template form:

```
OutputType operator "" _suffix(unsigned long long);
```

```
OutputType operator "" _suffix(long double);
```

```
OutputType some_variable = 1234_suffix; // Uses the 'unsigned
long long' overload.
```

```
OutputType another_variable = 3.1416_suffix; // Uses the 'long
double' overload.
```

In accord with the formerly mentioned new string prefixes, for string literals, these are used:

```
OutputType operator "" _ssuffix(const char    * string_values,
size_t num_chars);
```

```
OutputType operator "" _ssuffix(const wchar_t  * string_values,
size_t num_chars);
```

```
OutputType operator "" _ssuffix(const char16_t * string_values,
size_t num_chars);
```

```
OutputType operator "" _ssuffix(const char32_t * string_values,
size_t num_chars);
```

```
OutputType some_variable =    "1234"_ssuffix; // Uses the 'const
char *' overload.

OutputType some_variable = u8"1234"_ssuffix; // Uses the 'const
char *' overload.

OutputType some_variable =  L"1234"_ssuffix; // Uses the 'const
wchar_t *'  overload.

OutputType some_variable =  u"1234"_ssuffix; // Uses the 'const
char16_t *' overload.

OutputType some_variable =  U"1234"_ssuffix; // Uses the 'const
char32_t *' overload.
```

There is no alternative template form. Character literals are defined similarly.

Multithreading Memory Model

C++11 standardizes support for multithreaded programming.

There are two parts involved: a memory model which allows multiple threads to co-exist in a program and library support for interaction between threads.

The memory model defines when multiple threads may access the same memory location, and specifies when updates by one thread become visible to other threads.

Thread-local Storage

In a multi-threaded environment, it is common for every thread to have some unique variables. This already happens for the local variables of a function, but it does not happen for global and static variables.

A new *thread-local* storage duration (in addition to the existing *static, dynamic* and *automatic*) is indicated by the storage specifier thread_local.

Any object which could have static storage duration (i.e., lifetime spanning the entire execution of the program) may be given thread-local duration instead. The intent is that like any other static-duration variable, a thread-local object can be initialized using a constructor and destroyed using a destructor.

Explicitly Defaulted and Deleted Special Member Functions

In C++03, the compiler provides, for classes that do not provide them for themselves, a default constructor, a copy constructor, a copy assignment operator (operator=), and a destructor. The programmer can override these defaults by defining custom versions.

C++ also defines several global operators (such as operator new) that work on all classes, which the programmer can override.

However, there is very little control over creating these defaults. Making a class inherently non-copyable, for example, requires declaring a private copy constructor and copy assignment operator and not defining them. Attempting to use these functions is a violation of the One Definition Rule (ODR). While a diagnostic message is not required, violations may result in a linker error.

In the case of the default constructor, the compiler will not generate a default constructor if a class is defined with *any* constructors. This is useful in many cases, but it is also useful to be able to have both specialized constructors and the compiler-generated default.

C++11 allows the explicit defaulting and deleting of these special member functions. For example, this type explicitly declares that it is using the default constructor:

```
struct SomeType {

    SomeType() = default; //The default constructor is explic-
itly stated.

    SomeType(OtherType value);

};
```

Alternatively, certain features can be explicitly disabled. For example, this type is non-copyable:

```
struct NonCopyable {

    NonCopyable() = default;

    NonCopyable(const NonCopyable&) = delete;

    NonCopyable& operator=(const NonCopyable&) = delete;

};
```

The = delete specifier can be used to prohibit calling any function, which can be used to disallow calling a member function with particular parameters. For example:

```
struct NoInt {

    void f(double i);

    void f(int) = delete;

};
```

An attempt to call f() with an int will be rejected by the compiler, instead of performing a silent conversion to double. This can be generalized to disallow calling the function with any type other than double as follows:

```
struct OnlyDouble {

    void f(double d);

    template<class T> void f(T) = delete;

};
```

Type Long Long Int

In C++03, the largest integer type is long int. It is guaranteed to have at least as many usable bits as int. This resulted in long int having size of 64 bits on some popular implementations and 32 bits on others. C++11 adds a new integer type long long int to address this issue. It is guaranteed to be at least as large as a long int, and have no fewer than 64 bits. The type was originally introduced by C99 to the standard C, and most C++ compilers supported it as an extension already.

Static Assertions

C++03 provides two methods to test assertions: the macro assert and the preprocessor directive #error. However, neither is appropriate for use in templates: the macro tests the assertion at execution-time, while the preprocessor directive tests the assertion during preprocessing, which happens before instantiation of templates. Neither is appropriate for testing properties that are dependent on template parameters.

The new utility introduces a new way to test assertions at compile-time, using the new keyword static_assert. The declaration assumes this form:

```
static_assert (constant-expression, error-message);
```

Here are some examples of how static_assert can be used:

```
static_assert((GREEKPI > 3.14) && (GREEKPI < 3.15), "GREEKPI is
inaccurate!");

template<class T>

struct Check {

    static_assert(sizeof(int) <= sizeof(T), "T is not big
enough!");

};
```

```
template<class Integral>

Integral foo(Integral x, Integral y) {

    static_assert(std::is_integral<Integral>::value, "foo() pa-
rameter must be an integral type.");

}
```

When the constant expression is false the compiler produces an error message. The first example is similar to the preprocessor directive #error, although the preprocessor does only support integral types. In contrast, in the second example the assertion is checked at every instantiation of the template class Check.

Static assertions are useful outside of templates also. For instance, a given implementation of an algorithm might depend on the size of a long long being larger than an int, something the standard does not guarantee. Such an assumption is valid on most systems and compilers, but not all.

Allow Sizeof to Work on Members of Classes without an Explicit Object

In C++03, the sizeof operator can be used on types and objects. But it cannot be used to do this:

```
struct SomeType { OtherType member; };
```

```
sizeof(SomeType::member); // Does not work with C++03. Okay
with C++11
```

This should return the size of OtherType. C++03 disallows this, so it is a compile error. C++11 allows it. It is also allowed for the alignof operator introduced in C++11.

Control and Query Object Alignment

C++11 allows variable alignment to be queried and controlled with alignof and alignas.

The alignof operator takes the type and returns the power of 2 byte boundary on which the type instances must be allocated (as a std::size_t). When given a reference type alignof returns the referenced type's alignment; for arrays it returns the element type's alignment.

The alignas specifier controls the memory alignment for a variable. The specifier takes a constant or a type; when supplied a type alignas(T) is shorthand for alignas(alignof(T)). For example, to specify that a char array should be properly aligned to hold a float:

```
alignas(float) unsigned char c[sizeof(float)]
```

Allow Garbage Collected Implementations

Prior C++ standards provided for programmer-driven garbage collection via set_new_handler, but gave no definition of object reachability for the purpose of automatic garbage collection. C++11 defines conditions under which pointer values are "safely derived" from other values. An implementation may specify that it operates under *strict pointer safety*, in which case pointers that are not derived according to these rules can become invalid.

Attributes

C++11 provides a standardized syntax for compiler/tool extensions to the language. Such extensions were traditionally specified using #pragma directive or vendor-specific keywords (like __attribute__ for GNU and __declspec for Microsoft). With the new syntax, added information can be specified in a form of an attribute enclosed in double square brackets. An attribute can be applied to various elements of source code:

```
int [[attr1]] i [[attr2, attr3]];
```

```
[[attr4(arg1, arg2)]] if (cond)

{

    [[vendor::attr5]] return i;

}
```

In the example above, attribute attr1 applies to the type of variable i, attr2 and attr3 apply to the variable itself, attr4 applies to the if statement and vendor::attr5 applies to the return statement. In general (but with some exceptions), an attribute specified for a named entity is placed after the name, and before the entity otherwise. As shown above, several attributes may be listed inside one pair of double square brackets, added arguments may be provided for an attribute, and attributes may be scoped by vendor-specific attribute namespaces.

It is recommended that attributes have no language semantic meaning and do not change the sense of a program when ignored. Attributes can be useful for providing information that, for example, helps the compiler to issue better diagnostics or optimize the generated code.

C++11 provides two standard attributes itself: noreturn to specify that a function does not return, and carries_dependency to help optimizing multi-threaded code by indicating that function arguments or return value carry a dependency.

C++ Standard Library Changes

A number of new features were introduced in the C++11 standard library. Many of these could have been implemented under the old standard, but some rely (to a greater or lesser extent) on new C++11 core features.

A large part of the new libraries was defined in the document *C++ Standards Committee's Library Technical Report* (called TR1), which was published in 2005. Various full and partial implementations of TR1 are currently available using the namespace std::tr1. For C++11 they were moved to namespace std. However, as TR1 features were brought into the C++11 standard library, they were upgraded where appropriate with C++11 language features that were not available in the initial TR1 version. Also, they may have been enhanced with features that were possible under C++03, but were not part of the original TR1 specification.

The committee intends to create a second technical report (called TR2) now that standardization of C++11 is complete. Library proposals which were not ready in time for C++11 will be put into TR2 or further technical reports.

Upgrades to Standard Library Components

C++11 offers a number of new language features that the currently existing standard library components can benefit from. For example, most standard library containers can benefit from Rvalue reference based move constructor support, both for quickly moving heavy containers around and for moving the contents of those containers to new memory locations. The standard library components were upgraded with new C++11 language features where appropriate. These include, but are not necessarily limited to:

- Rvalue references and the associated move support
- Support for the UTF-16 encoding unit, and UTF-32 encoding unit Unicode character types
- Variadic templates (coupled with Rvalue references to allow for perfect forwarding)
- Compile-time constant expressions
- decltype
- explicit conversion operators
- default/deleted functions

Further, much time has passed since the prior C++ standard. Much code using the standard library has been written. This has revealed parts of the standard libraries that could use some improving. Among the many areas of improvement considered were standard library allocators. A new scope-based model of allocators was included in C++11 to supplement the prior model.

Threading Facilities

While the C++03 language provides a memory model that supports threading, the primary support for actually using threading comes with the C++11 standard library.

A thread class (std::thread) is provided, which takes a function object (and an optional series of arguments to pass to it) to run in the new thread. It is possible to cause a thread to halt until another executing thread completes, providing thread joining support via the std::thread::join() member function. Access is provided, where feasible, to the underlying native thread object(s) for platform-specific operations by the std::-thread::native_handle() member function.

For synchronization between threads, appropriate mutexes (std::mutex, std::recursive_mutex, etc.) and condition variables (std::condition_variable and std::condition_variable_any) are added to the library. These are accessible via Resource Acquisition Is Initialization (RAII) locks (std::lock_guard and std::unique_lock) and locking algorithms for easy use.

For high-performance, low-level work, communicating between threads is sometimes needed without the overhead of mutexes. This is done using atomic operations on memory locations. These can optionally specify the minimum memory visibility constraints needed for an operation. Explicit memory barriers may also be used for this purpose.

The C++11 thread library also includes futures and promises for passing asynchronous results between threads, and std::packaged_task for wrapping up a function call that can generate such an asynchronous result. The futures proposal was criticized because it lacks a way to combine futures and check for the completion of one promise inside a set of promises.

Further high-level threading facilities such as thread pools have been remanded to a future C++ technical report. They are not part of C++11, but their eventual implementation is expected to be built entirely on top of the thread library features.

The new std::async facility provides a convenient method of running tasks and tying them to a std::future. The user can choose whether the task is to be run asynchronously on a separate thread or synchronously on a thread that waits for the value. By default, the implementation can choose, which provides an easy way to take advantage of hardware concurrency without oversubscription, and provides some of the advantages of a thread pool for simple usages.

Tuple Types

Tuples are collections composed of heterogeneous objects of pre-arranged dimensions. A tuple can be considered a generalization of a struct's member variables.

The C++11 version of the TR1 tuple type benefited from C++11 features like variadic templates. To implement reasonably, the TR1 version required an implementation-defined maximum number of contained types, and substantial macro trickery. By contrast, the implementation of the C++11 version requires no explicit implementation-defined maximum number of types. Though compilers will have an internal maximum recursion depth for template instantiation (which is normal), the C++11 version of tuples will not expose this value to the user.

Using variadic templates, the declaration of the tuple class looks as follows:

```
template <class ...Types> class tuple;
```

An example of definition and use of the tuple type:

```
typedef std::tuple <int, double, long &, const char *> test_tuple;

long lengthy = 12;

test_tuple proof (18, 6.5, lengthy, "Ciao!");


lengthy = std::get<0>(proof);   // Assign to 'lengthy' the value
18.

std::get<3>(proof) = " Beautiful!";   // Modify the tuple's
fourth element.
```

It's possible to create the tuple proof without defining its contents, but only if the tuple elements' types possess default constructors. Moreover, it's possible to assign a tuple to another tuple: if the two tuples' types are the same, each element type must possess a copy constructor; otherwise, each element type of the right-side tuple must be convertible to that of the corresponding element type of the left-side tuple or that the corresponding element type of the left-side tuple has a suitable constructor.

```
typedef std::tuple <int , double, string      > tuple_1 t1;

typedef std::tuple <char, short , const char * > tuple_2 t2
('X', 2, "Hola!");

t1 = t2; // Ok, first two elements can be converted,

        // the third one can be constructed from a 'const char
*'.
```

Just like std::make_pair for std::pair, there exists std::make_tuple to automatically create std::tuples using type deduction and auto helps to declare such a tuple. std::tie creates tuples of lvalue references to help unpack tuples. std::ignore also helps here. See the example:

```
auto record = std::make_tuple("Hari Ram", "New Delhi", 3.5, 'A');

std::string name ; float gpa ; char grade ;

std::tie(name, std::ignore, gpa, grade) = record ; // st-
d::ignore helps drop the place name

std::cout << name << ' ' << gpa << ' ' << grade << std::endl ;
```

Relational operators are available (among tuples with the same number of elements), and two expressions are available to check a tuple's characteristics (only during compilation):

- std::tuple_size<T>::value returns the number of elements in the tuple T,

- std::tuple_element<I, T>::type returns the type of the object number I of the tuple T.

Hash Tables

Including hash tables (unordered associative containers) in the C++ standard library is one of the most recurring requests. It was not adopted in C++03 due to time constraints only. Although hash tables are less efficient than a balanced tree in the worst case (in the presence of many collisions), they perform better in many real applications.

Collisions are managed only via *linear chaining* because the committee didn't consider it to be opportune to standardize solutions of *open addressing* that introduce quite a lot of intrinsic problems (above all when erasure of elements is admitted). To avoid name clashes with non-standard libraries that developed their own hash table implementations, the prefix "unordered" was used instead of "hash".

The new library has four types of hash tables, differentiated by whether or not they accept elements with the same key (unique keys or equivalent keys), and whether they map each key to an associated value. They correspond to the four existing binary-search-tree-based associative containers, with an unordered_ prefix.

Type of hash table	Associated values	Equivalent keys
std::unordered_set	No	No
std::unordered_multiset	No	Yes
std::unordered_map	Yes	No
std::unordered_multimap	Yes	Yes

The new classes fulfill all the requirements of a container class, and have all the methods needed to access elements: insert, erase, begin, end.

This new feature didn't need any C++ language core extensions (though implementations will take advantage of various C++11 language features), only a small extension of the header <functional> and the introduction of headers <unordered_set> and <unordered_map>. No other changes to any existing standard classes were needed, and it doesn't depend on any other extensions of the standard library.

Regular Expressions

The new library, defined in the new header <regex>, is made of a couple of new classes:

- regular expressions are represented by instance of the template class std::regex;

- occurrences are represented by instance of the template class std::match_results.

The function std::regex_search is used for searching, while for 'search and replace' the function std::regex_replace is used which returns a new string. The algorithms std::regex_search and std::regex_replace take a regular expression and a string and write the occurrences found in the struct std::match_results.

Here is an example of the use of std::match_results:

```
const char *reg_esp = "[ ,.\\t\\n;:]"; // List of separator
characters.


// this can be done using raw string literals:
// const char *reg_esp = R"([ ,.\t\n;:])";


std::regex rgx(reg_esp); // 'regex' is an instance of the tem-
plate class

                        // 'basic_regex' with argument of type
'char'.
std::cmatch match; // 'cmatch' is an instance of the template
class

                    // 'match_results' with argument of type
'const char *'.
const char *target = "Unseen University - Ankh-Morpork";
```

```
// Identifies all words of 'target' separated by characters of
'reg_esp'.
if (std::regex_search(target, match, rgx)) {
    // If words separated by specified characters are present.


    const size_t n = match.size();
    for (size_t a = 0; a < n; a++) {
        std::string str (match[a].first, match[a].second);
        std::cout << str << "\n";
    }
}
```

Note the use of double backslashes, because C++ uses backslash as an escape character. The C++11 raw string feature could be used to avoid the problem.

The library <regex> requires neither alteration of any existing header (though it will use them where appropriate) nor an extension of the core language. In POSIX C, regular expressions are also available the C POSIX library#regex.h.

General-purpose Smart Pointers

C++11 provides std::unique_ptr, and improvements to std::shared_ptr and std::weak_ptr from TR1. std::auto_ptr is deprecated.

Extensible Random Number Facility

The C standard library provides the ability to generate pseudorandom numbers via the function rand. However, the algorithm is delegated entirely to the library vendor. C++ inherited this functionality with no changes, but C++11 provides a new method for generating pseudorandom numbers.

C++11's random number functionality is split into two parts: a generator engine that contains the random number generator's state and produces the pseudorandom numbers; and a distribution, which determines the range and mathematical distribution of the outcome. These two are combined to form a random number generator object.

Unlike the C standard rand, the C++11 mechanism will come with three base generator engine algorithms:

- linear_congruential_engine,
- subtract_with_carry_engine, and
- mersenne_twister_engine.

C++11 also provides a number of standard distributions:

- uniform_int_distribution,
- uniform_real_distribution,
- bernoulli_distribution,
- binomial_distribution,
- geometric_distribution,
- negative_binomial_distribution,
- poisson_distribution,
- exponential_distribution,
- gamma_distribution,
- weibull_distribution,
- extreme_value_distribution,
- normal_distribution,
- lognormal_distribution,
- chi_squared_distribution,
- cauchy_distribution,
- fisher_f_distribution,
- student_t_distribution,
- discrete_distribution,
- piecewise_constant_distribution and
- piecewise_linear_distribution.

The generator and distributions are combined as in this example:

```
#include <random>
```

```
#include <functional>


std::uniform_int_distribution<int> distribution(0, 99);

std::mt19937 engine; // Mersenne twister MT19937

auto generator = std::bind(distribution, engine);

int random = generator(); // Generate a uniform integral vari-
ate between 0 and 99.

int random2 = distribution(engine); // Generate another sample
directly using the distribution and the engine objects.
```

Wrapper Reference

A wrapper reference is obtained from an instance of the template class reference_wrapper. Wrapper references are similar to normal references ('&') of the C++ language. To obtain a wrapper reference from any object the function template ref is used (for a constant reference cref is used).

Wrapper references are useful above all for function templates, where references to parameters rather than copies are needed:

```
// This function will obtain a reference to the parameter 'r'
and increment it.

void func (int &r)   { r++; }


// Template function.

template<class F, class P> void g (F f, P t)   { f(t); }


int main()

{

    int i = 0;

    g (func, i); // 'g<void (int &r), int>' is instantiated

                 // then 'i' will not be modified.

    std::cout << i << std::endl; // Output -> 0
```

```
    g (func, std::ref(i)); // 'g<void(int &r),reference_wrap-
per<int>>' is instantiated

                          // then 'i' will be modified.

    std::cout << i << std::endl; // Output -> 1

}
```

This new utility was added to the existing <utility> header and didn't need further extensions of the C++ language.

Polymorphic Wrappers for Function Objects

Polymorphic wrappers for function objects are similar to function pointers in semantics and syntax, but are less tightly bound and can indiscriminately refer to anything which can be called (function pointers, member function pointers, or functors) whose arguments are compatible with those of the wrapper.

An example can clarify its characteristics:

```
std::function<int (int, int)> func; // Wrapper creation using

                          // template class 'func-
tion'.
std::plus<int> add; // 'plus' is declared as 'template<class T>
T plus( T, T ) ;'

                          // then 'add' is type 'int add( int x, int
y )'.
func = add;   // OK - Parameters and return types are the same.


int a = func (1, 2); // NOTE: if the wrapper 'func' does not
refer to any function,

                          // the exception 'std::bad_function_call'
is thrown.


std::function<bool (short, short)> func2 ;

if (!func2) { // True because 'func2' has not yet been assigned
a function.
```

```
    bool adjacent(long x, long y);

    func2 = &adjacent; // OK - Parameters and return types are
convertible.


    struct Test {

        bool operator()(short x, short y);

    };

    Test car;

    func = std::ref(car); // 'std::ref' is a template function
that returns the wrapper

                            // of member function 'operator()' of
struct 'car'.

}

func = func2; // OK - Parameters and return types are convert-
ible.
```

The template class function was defined inside the header <functional>, without needing any change to the C++ language.

Type Traits for Metaprogramming

Metaprogramming consists of creating a program that creates or modifies another program (or itself). This can happen during compilation or during execution. The C++ Standards Committee has decided to introduce a library that allows metaprogramming during compiling via templates.

Here is an example of a meta-program, using the C++03 standard: a recursion of template instances for calculating integer exponents:

```
template<int B, int N>

struct Pow {

    // recursive call and recombination.

    enum{ value = B*Pow<B, N-1>::value };

};
```

```
template< int B >

struct Pow<B, 0> {

    // ''N == 0'' condition of termination.

    enum{ value = 1 };

};

int quartic_of_three = Pow<3, 4>::value;
```

Many algorithms can operate on different types of data; C++'s templates support generic programming and make code more compact and useful. Nevertheless, it is common for algorithms to need information on the data types being used. This information can be extracted during instantiation of a template class using *type traits*.

Type traits can identify the category of an object and all the characteristics of a class (or of a struct). They are defined in the new header <type_traits>.

In the next example there is the template function 'elaborate' that, depending on the given data types, will instantiate one of the two proposed algorithms (algorithm.do_it).

```
// First way of operating.

template< bool B > struct Algorithm {

    template<class T1, class T2> static int do_it (T1 &, T2 &)
{ /*...*/ }

};



// Second way of operating.

template<> struct Algorithm<true> {

    template<class T1, class T2> static int do_it (T1, T2)    {
/*...*/ }

};



// Instantiating 'elaborate' will automatically instantiate the
correct way to operate.
```

```
template<class T1, class T2>

int elaborate (T1 A, T2 B)

{

    // Use the second way only if 'T1' is an integer and if
'T2' is

    // in floating point, otherwise use the first way.

    return Algorithm<std::is_integral<T1>::value && std::is_
floating_point<T2>::value>::do_it( A, B ) ;

}
```

Via *type traits*, defined in header <type_traits>, it's also possible to create type transformation operations (static_cast and const_cast are insufficient inside a template).

This type of programming produces elegant and concise code; however the weak point of these techniques is the debugging: uncomfortable during compilation and very difficult during program execution.

Uniform Method for Computing The Return Type of Function Objects

Determining the return type of a template function object at compile-time is not intuitive, particularly if the return value depends on the parameters of the function. As an example:

```
struct Clear {

    int    operator()(int) const;    // The parameter type is

    double operator()(double) const; // equal to the return
type.

};


template <class Obj>

class Calculus {

public:

    template<class Arg> Arg operator()(Arg& a) const {
```

```
        return member(a);

    }

private:

    Obj member;

};
```

Instantiating the class template Calculus<Clear>, the function object of calculus will have always the same return type as the function object of Clear. However, given class Confused below:

```
struct Confused {

    double operator()(int) const;      // The parameter type is not

    int    operator()(double) const;   // equal to the return type.

};
```

Attempting to instantiate Calculus<Confused> will cause the return type of Calculus to not be the same as that of class Confused. The compiler may generate warnings about the conversion from int to double and vice versa.

TR1 introduces, and C++11 adopts, the template class std::result_of that allows one to determine and use the return type of a function object for every declaration. The object CalculusVer2 uses the std::result_of object to derive the return type of the function object:

```
template< class Obj >

class CalculusVer2 {

public:

    template<class Arg>

    typename std::result_of<Obj(Arg)>::type operator()(Arg& a) const {

        return member(a);

    }

private:
```

```
    Obj member;

};
```

In this way in instances of function object of CalculusVer2<Confused> there are no conversions, warnings, or errors.

The only change from the TR1 version of std::result_of is that the TR1 version allowed an implementation to fail to be able to determine the result type of a function call. Due to changes to C++ for supporting decltype, the C++11 version of std::result_of no longer needs these special cases; implementations are required to compute a type in all cases.

Improved C Compatibility

For compatibility with C, from C99, these were added:

- Preprocessor:
    - variadic macros,
    - concatenation of adjacent narrow/wide string literals,
    - _Pragma() – equivalent of #pragma.
- long long – integer type that is at least 64 bits long.
- ___func___ – macro evaluating to the name of the function it is in.
- Headers:
    - cstdbool (stdbool.h),
    - cstdint (stdint.h),
    - cinttypes (inttypes.h).

Features Originally Planned but Removed or not Included

Heading for a separate TR:

- Modules
- Decimal types
- Math special functions

Postponed:

- Concepts

- More complete or required garbage collection support

- Reflection

- Macro scopes

Features Removed or Deprecated

The term sequence point was removed, being replaced by specifying that either one operation is sequenced before another, or that two operations are unsequenced.

The former use of the keyword export was removed. The keyword itself remains, being reserved for potential future use.

Dynamic exception specifications are deprecated. Compile-time specification of non-exception-throwing functions is available with the noexcept keyword, which is useful for optimization.

std::auto_ptr is deprecated, having been superseded by std::unique_ptr.

Function object base classes (std::unary_function, std::binary_function), adapters to pointers to functions and adapters to pointers to members, and binder classes are all deprecated.

C++14

C++14 is a version of the standard for the programming language C++, it is intended to be a small extension over C++11, featuring mainly bug fixes and small improvements. Its approval was announced on August 18, 2014. C++14 was released on December 15, 2014.

Because earlier C++ standard revisions were noticeably late, the name "C++1y" was sometimes used instead until its approval, similarly to how the C++11 standard used to be termed "C++0x" with the expectation of its release before 2010 (although in fact it slipped into 2010 and finally 2011).

New Language Features

These are the features added to the core language of C++14.

Function Return Type Deduction

C++11 allowed lambda functions to deduce the return type based on the type of the expression given to the return statement. C++14 provides this ability to all functions.

It also extends these facilities to lambda functions, allowing return type deduction for functions that are not of the form return expression;.

In order to induce return type deduction, the function must be declared with auto as the return type, but without the trailing return type specifier in C++11:

```
auto DeduceReturnType();    // Return type to be determined.
```

If multiple return expressions are used in the function's implementation, then they must all deduce the same type.

Functions that deduce their return types can be forward declared, but they cannot be used until they have been defined. Their definitions must be available to the translation unit that uses them.

Recursion can be used with a function of this type, but the recursive call must happen after at least one return statement in the definition of the function:

```
auto Correct(int i) {

  if (i == 1)

    return i;                 // return type deduced as int

  else

    return Correct(i-1)+i;  // ok to call it now

}



auto Wrong(int i) {

  if (i != 1)

    return Wrong(i-1)+i;  // Too soon to call this. No prior
return statement.

  else

    return i;                 // return type deduced as int

}
```

Alternate Type Deduction on Declaration

In C++11, two methods of type deduction were added. auto was a way to create a variable of the appropriate type, based on a given expression. decltype was a way to compute the type of a given expression. However, the way decltype and auto deduce types are different. In particular, auto always deduces a non-reference type, as though by using std::decay, while auto&& always deduces a reference type. However, decltype can be prodded into deducing a reference or non-reference type, based on the value category of the expression and the nature of the expression it is deducing:

```
int i;

int&& f();

auto x3a = i;                 // decltype(x3a) is int

decltype(i) x3d = i;          // decltype(x3d) is int

auto x4a = (i);               // decltype(x4a) is int

decltype((i)) x4d = (i);      // decltype(x4d) is int&

auto x5a = f();               // decltype(x5a) is int

decltype(f()) x5d = f();      // decltype(x5d) is int&&
```

C++14 adds the decltype(auto) syntax. This allows auto declarations to use the decltype rules on the given expression.

The decltype(auto) syntax can also be used with return type deduction, by using decltype(auto) syntax instead of auto for the function's return type deduction.

Relaxed Constexpr Restrictions

C++11 introduced the concept of a constexpr-declared function; a function which could be executed at compile time. Their return values could be consumed by operations that require constant expressions, such as an integer template argument. However, C++11 constexpr functions could only contain a single expression that is returned (as well as static_asserts and a small number of other declarations).

C++14 relaxes these restrictions. Constexpr-declared functions may now contain the following:

- Any declarations except:
  - static or thread_local variables.
  - Variable declarations without initializers.
- The conditional branching statements if and switch.
- Any looping statement, including range-based for.
- Expressions which change the value of an object if the lifetime of that object

began within the constant expression function. This includes calls to any non-const constexpr-declared non-static member functions.

goto statements are forbidden in C++14 relaxed constexpr-declared functions.

Also, C++11 stated that all non-static member functions that were declared constexpr were also implicitly declared const, with respect to this. That has since been removed; non-static member functions may be non-const. However, per the above restrictions, a non-const constexpr member function can only modify a class member if that object's lifetime began within the constant expression evaluation.

Variable Templates

In prior versions of C++, only functions, classes or type aliases could be templated. C++14 now allows the creation of variables that are templated. An example given in the proposal is a variable pi that can be read to get the value of pi for various types (e.g., 3 when read as an integral type; the closest value possible with float, double or long double precision when read as float, double or long double, respectively; etc.).

The usual rules of templates apply to such declarations and definitions, including specialization.

```
template<typename T>

constexpr T pi = T(3.1415926535897932384626643383);


// Usual specialization rules apply:

template<>

constexpr const char* pi<const char*> = "pi";
```

Aggregate Member Initialization

C++11 added member initializers, expressions to be applied to members at class scope if a constructor did not initialize the member itself. The definition of aggregates was changed to explicitly exclude any class with member initializers; therefore, they are not allowed to use aggregate initialization.

C++14 relaxes this restriction, allowing aggregate initialization on such types. If the braced init list does not provide a value for that argument, the member initializer takes care of it.

Binary Literals

Numeric literals in C++14 can be specified in binary form. The syntax uses the prefixes

0b or 0B. The syntax is also used in other languages e.g. Java, C#, Swift, Go, Scala, Ruby, Python, OCaml, and as an unofficial extension in some C compilers since at least 2007.

Digit Separators

In C++14, the single-quote character may be used arbitrarily as a digit separator in numeric literals, both integer literals and floating point literals. This can make it easier for human readers to parse large numbers through subitizing.

```
auto integer_literal = 1'000'000;
auto floating_point_literal = 0.000'015'3;
auto binary_literal = 0b0100'1100'0110;
auto silly_example = 1'0'0'000'00;
```

Generic Lambdas

In C++11, lambda function parameters need to be declared with concrete types. C++14 relaxes this requirement, allowing lambda function parameters to be declared with the auto type specifier.

```
auto lambda = [](auto x, auto y) {return x + y;};
```

As for auto type deduction, generic lambdas follow the rules of template argument deduction (which are similar, but not identical in all respects). The above code is equivalent to this:

```
struct unnamed_lambda

{

  template<typename T, typename U>

    auto operator()(T x, U y) const {return x + y;}

};

auto lambda = unnamed_lambda{};
```

Lambda Capture Expressions

C++11 lambda functions capture variables declared in their outer scope by value-copy or by reference. This means that value members of a lambda cannot be move-only types. C++14 allows captured members to be initialized with arbitrary expressions. This allows both capture by value-move and declaring arbitrary members of the lambda, without having a correspondingly named variable in an outer scope.

This is done via the use of an initializer expression:

```
auto lambda = [value = 1] {return value;};
```

The lambda function lambda returns 1, which is what value was initialized with. The declared capture deduces the type from the initializer expression as if by auto.

This can be used to capture by move, via the use of the standard std::move function:

```
std::unique_ptr<int> ptr(new int(10));

auto lambda = [value = std::move(ptr)] {return *value;};
```

The Attribute [[Deprecated]]

The deprecated attribute allows marking an entity deprecated, which makes it still legal to use but puts users on notice that use is discouraged and may cause a warning message to be printed during compilation. An optional string literal can appear as the argument of deprecated, to explain the rationale for deprecation and/or to suggest a replacement.

```
[[deprecated]] int f();


[[deprecated("g() is thread-unsafe. Use h() instead")]]

void g( int& x );


void h( int& x );


void test() {

  int a = f(); // warning: 'f' is deprecated

  g(a); // warning: 'g' is deprecated: g() is thread-unsafe.
Use h() instead

}
```

New Standard Library Features

Shared Mutexes and Locking

C++14 adds a shared timed mutex and a companion shared lock type.

Heterogeneous Lookup in Associative Containers

The C++ Standard Library defines four associative container classes. These classes allow the user to look up a value based on a value of that type. The map containers allow the user to specify a key and a value, where lookup is done by key and returns a value. However, the lookup is always done by the specific key type, whether it is the key as in maps or the value itself as in sets.

C++14 allows the lookup to be done via an arbitrary type, so long as the comparison operator can compare that type with the actual key type. This would allow a map from std::string to some value to compare against a const char* or any other type for which an operator< overload is available.

To preserve backwards compatibility, heterogeneous lookup is only allowed when the comparator given to the associative container allows it. The standard library classes std::less<> and std::greater<> are augmented to allow heterogeneous lookup.

Standard User-defined Literals

C++11 defined the syntax for user-defined literal suffixes, but the standard library did not use any of them. C++14 adds the following standard literals:

- "s", for creating the various std::basic_string types.

- "h", "min", "s", "ms", "us", "ns", for creating the corresponding std::chrono::duration time intervals.

- "if", "i", "il", for creating the corresponding std::complex<float>, std::complex<double> and std::complex<long double> imaginary numbers.

```
auto str = "hello world"s;  // auto deduces string

auto dur = 60s;             // auto deduces chrono::seconds

auto z   = 1i;              // auto deduces complex<double>
```

The two "s" literals do not interact, as the string one only operates on string literals, and the one for seconds operates only on numbers.

Tuple Addressing Via Type

The std::tuple type introduced in C++11 allows an aggregate of typed values to be indexed by a compile-time constant integer. C++14 extends this to allow fetching from a tuple by type instead of by index. If the tuple has more than one element of the type, a compile-time error results:

```
tuple<string, string, int> t("foo", "bar", 7);
```

```
int i = get<int>(t);          // i == 7

int j = get<2>(t);            // Same as before: j == 7

string s = get<string>(t);   // Compile-time error due to ambi-
guity
```

Smaller Library Features

```
std::make_unique can be used like std::make_shared for st-
d::unique_ptr objects.
```

```
std::integral_constant gained an operator() overload to return
the constant value.
```

The class template std::integer_sequence and related alias templates were added for representing compile-time integer sequences, such as the indices of elements in a parameter pack.

The global std::begin/std::end functions were augmented with std::cbegin/std::cend functions, which return constant iterators, and std::rbegin/std::rend and std::crbegin/std::crend which return reverse iterators.

The std::exchange function template to assign a new value to a variable and return the old value.

New overloads of std::equal, std::mismatch, and std::is_permutation that take a pair of iterators for the second range, so that the caller does not need to separately check that the two ranges are of the same length.

The std::is_final type trait which detects if a class is marked final.

The std::quoted stream I/O manipulator allows inserting and extracting strings with embedded spaces, by placing delimiters (defaulting to double-quotes) on output and stripping them on input, and escaping any embedded delimiters.

Compiler Support

Clang finished support for C++14 in 3.4 though under the standard name c++1y. GCC finished support for C++14 in GCC 5, and made C++14 the default C++ standard in GCC 6 Microsoft Visual Studio 2015 has support for some but not all C++14 features.

C++17

C++17 (also called C++1z) is the informal name for the future revision of the C++ ISO/

IEC standard. The specification for the C++17 revision is under development and "nearly feature-complete" to be finished in 2017.

Expected Features

- Addition of a default text message for static_assert
- Addition of std::string_view, a non-owning reference to a character sequence or string-slice
- Removal of trigraphs
- Allow typename in a template template parameter
- New rules for auto deduction from braced-init-list
- std::uncaught_exceptions, as a replacement of std::uncaught_exception
- Nested namespace definition
- Attributes for namespaces and enumerators
- UTF-8 character literals
- Constant evaluation for all non-type template arguments
- Folding expressions
- New insertion functions for std::map and std::unordered_map
- Uniform container access
- Definition of "contiguous iterators"
- Removal of some deprecated types and functions like std::auto_ptr, std::random_shuffle or old function adaptors
- A file system library based on boost::filesystem
- Parallel versions of STL algorithms
- Additional mathematical special functions
- Most of Library Fundamentals TS I (e.g. std::optional, std::any)
- std::variant, a type-safe union container
- A compile-time static if with the form if constexpr(expression)
- Structured bindings, allowing auto [a, b] = getTwoReturnValues();
- Initializers in if and switch statements

- Guaranteed copy elision by compilers in some cases

- Some extensions on aligned memory allocation

- Template deduction of constructors, allowing pair(5.0, false) instead of pair<double,bool>(5.0, false)

- Inline variables, which allows the declaration of variables in header files

References

- Herb, Sutter (2002). More Exceptional C++: 40 New Engineering Puzzles, Programming Problems, and Solutions. Boston: Pearson Education, Inc. p. 48. ISBN 0-201-70434-X.

- Wong, Michael (30 April 2013). "The View from the C++ Standard meeting April 2013 Part 1". C/C++ Cafe. Retrieved 27 January 2016.

- Spertus, Mike; Pall, Attila (19 April 2013). "N3671 Making non-modifying sequence operations more robust: Revision 2". Retrieved 5 January 2016.

- Sutter, Herb (20 April 2013). "Trip Report: ISO C++ Spring 2013 Meeting". isocpp.org. Retrieved 14 June 2013.

- Merrill, Jason (17 April 2013). "N3638 Return type deduction for normal functions (Revision 5)". Retrieved 14 June 2013.

Language Extensions of C++

CLI is a programing language, which was created by Microsoft. It was created with the intention of replacing the managed extensions for C++. Some other extensions of C++, like Cilk was created with the purpose of programming languages for multithreaded parallel computing. This section also focuses on some aspects of C++, aspect C++, CLI.

Managed Extensions for C++

Managed Extensions for C++ or just Managed C++ is a now deprecated Microsoft set of deviations from C++, including grammatical and syntactic extensions, keywords and attributes, to bring the C++ syntax and language to the .NET Framework. These extensions allowed C++ code to be targeted to the Common Language Runtime (CLR) in the form of managed code as well as continue to interoperate with native code. Managed C++ was not a complete standalone, or full-fledged programming language.

In 2004, the Managed C++ extensions were significantly revised to clarify and simplify syntax and expand functionality to include managed generics. These new extensions were designated C++/CLI and included in Microsoft Visual Studio 2005. The term Managed C++ and the extensions it refers to are thus deprecated and superseded by the new extensions.

Design

"Managed" refers to managed code that it is run in, or *managed* by, the .NET virtual machine that functions as a sandbox for enhanced security in the form of more runtime checks, such as buffer overrun checks. Additionally, applications written in Managed C++ compile to CIL — Common Intermediate Language — and not directly to native CPU instructions like regular C++ applications do.

Managed C++ code could inter-operate with any other language also targeted for the CLR such as C# and Visual Basic .NET as well as make use of features provided by the CLR such as garbage collection. This means Managed C++ occupies a unique position in the gallery of .NET languages. It is the only language that can communicate directly with .NET languages (such as C#, VB.NET) *and* native C++. The other .NET languages can only communicate with C++ code via PInvoke or COM. But since Managed C++ can communicate directly in both managed and standard C++ contexts, it is often used as a "bridge".

Additional or Amended Functionality Provided in Managed C++

Programs coded in Managed C++ provide additional functionality of the .NET Framework and the CLR. Most notable of these is garbage collection, which relieves the programmer of manual memory management. The garbage collector (or GC) is handled by the CLR. Memory management is executed quite quickly, but for more performance critical applications, native, unmanaged code is most likely the preferred option.

Also, C++ has evolved much over time and most software written in the language is object oriented. Managed C++ and the use of classes and class based objects remains prevalent like in Visual C++. The only major change to this in Managed C++ is that the capabilities of multiple inheritance are not supported. This is because of a limitation of the CLR. A class managed under the CLR's garbage collector cannot inherit more than one class. This is explained further in other sections.

Advantages Over Native Code

- Managed and unmanaged code can be mixed together in the same CLI assembly seamlessly. This allows the programmer to keep unmanaged code that cannot be ported over to the .NET Framework without re-writing it completely. Some ramifications of using this hybrid convention are present though.

- Managed C++ is the only language that can contain unmanaged code and natively communicate with all other .NET languages. Managed C++ is thus very convenient for interoperability between programmers who use different languages, including those in the .NET theater and those who use standard C++.

Disadvantages Compared to Unmanaged Code

- Managed C++ introduces a lot of new keywords and syntactic conventions that can impair the readability of code, especially if C++ code is included directly and interacts directly with Managed C++ code in the same assembly.

- Managed C++ is superseded by C++/CLI and thus obsolete as C++/CLI has been standardized.

Disadvantages to Fully Managed Code (C#, Visual Basic, Etc)

- Managed C++ requires a slightly longer development time than other .NET languages that could be applied to projects that still produce the same result, since the implications of pointers in C++ are still required, even in managed C++ code.

- Managed C++ does not support ASP.NET web applications, which is a capability supported by all other languages targeting the .NET Framework, including other third party languages.

- Managed C++ includes no support for generic programming (aka templates). C++/CLI has this support.

Main Programmatic Changes in Managed C++

The following list of changes pertain to the differences in Object Oriented Programming compared to programming with standard C++.

- (Global change) Existing C++ to be ported over the CLR must be appended with the following:

```
//hello.cpp


//new using directive

#using <mscorlib.dll>


//another using namespace directive.

using namespace System;


int main()

{

  Console::WriteLine("Hello, world!");

  return 0;

}
```

A new preprocessor directive

```
#using <mscorlib.dll>
```

is required. In addition to that, more #using directives are required to import more libraries to use more namespaces in the Base Class Library, such as

```
#using <System.Windows.Forms.dll>
```

and

```
using namespace System::Windows::Forms;
```

to utilize Windows Forms.

- To compile code to target the CLR, a new compiler option must be introduced.

```
cl.exe hello.cpp /clr
```

/clr enables any code referencing the .NET Framework to be compiled as CIL.

- A class can be designated to be garbage collected via the __gc extension keyword.

```
//gc.cpp


#using <mscorlib.dll>


  __gc class gc
{
   int* i;
   char* g;
   float* j;
};


int main()
{
   while(true)
   {
      gc^ _gc = gcnew gc();
   }
   return 0;
}
```

The preceding code can be compiled and executed without any fear of memory leaks. Because class gc is managed under the garbage collector, there is no need to call the delete operator. To achieve the same with unmanaged code, the delete keyword is required:

```
//nogc.cpp


class gc
```

```
{
  int* i;
  char* g;
  float* j;
};


int main()
{
  while(true)
  {
    gc* _gc = new gc();
    delete _gc;
  }
  return 0;
}
```

Notes:

- A __gc designated class can have a constructor declared.

- A __gc designated class can have a destructor declared.

- A __gc designated class cannot inherit more than one class. (This is a limitation of the CLR)

- A __gc designated class cannot inherit another class that is not __gc designated.

- A __gc designated class cannot be inherited by another class that is not __gc designated.

- A __gc designated class can implement any number of __gc interfaces.

- A __gc designated class cannot implement an unmanaged interface.

- A __gc designated class is by default not made visible outside of its own assembly. Use

```
public __gc class hey { };
```

the public keyword to modify the access of the a __gc designated class.

A __gc designated class can be destroyed manually using the delete keyword, but only if the __gc designated class has a user-defined destructor.

- An interface can be declared with the __gc extension keyword preceding it. Such as:

```
//interface.cpp

#using <mscorlib.dll>


__gc __interface ClassBase
{
    void Init();

    int Common();

}
```

The preceding code must be compiled with /clr and /LD to produce a simple DLL file.

Notes:

- A __gc __interface cannot contain any data members, static members, nested class declarations and no access specifiers.

- A __gc __interface can only inherit from another __gc __interface interface or the System::Object. Inheritance from System::Object is the default behavior.

- A __gc __interface cannot contain any implementation (body code) of its declared function prototypes.

Comparing Managed C++

The following contains main points and programmatic standards that differ between Managed C++ and other well known programming languages that are similar in concept.

...to Java

Differences

- Running Java code requires an appropriate virtual machine, while running Managed C++ code requires an appropriate implementation of the .NET Framework.

Disadvantages

- Java provides a documentation on the source code, while Managed C++ does not. *(C++/CLI now supports this feature in Visual C++ .NET 2005 and later)*

- Java has many other development tools and solutions available for Java programmers to use, while Managed C++ is only available under Visual Studio .NET. *Managed C++ applications can be compiled using the Visual C++ Toolkit 2003 however, which is provided free of charge.*

Advantages

- Managed C++ can access the computer system on a low level interface much more efficiently than Java. Java programmers must use the JNI (Java Native Interface) to utilise low level services of the host operating system.

...to C#

Differences

- While C# supports pointers just as in C++, this feature is turned off by default.

Disadvantages

- Like Java, C# is syntactically simpler when dealing with managed code. And C# supports the .NET Framework natively.

- C# can achieve basically the same result when applied to the same solution as one used with Managed C++, as all syntactic and structural conventions remain strikingly similar.

- Managed C++, though it is a strongly typed language due to its introduction into the CLR, can be prone to errors if unmanaged compiled code is introduced in the same solution, while C# is pure MSIL.

Advantages

- C# must use the .NET Framework and provided class libraries to access the computer system on a low level.

- Porting over applications to the .NET Framework from C or C++ is much easier to do using Managed C++.

- The Microsoft Visual C++ .NET compiler, which compiles Managed C++ to target the .NET Framework, produces a much more matured set of instructions in its resultant assembly, thus improving performance. Performance will vary depending on the code, but in general, Managed C++ code (MSIL) is slightly faster or more efficient than code (MSIL) compiled using the C# compiler.

...to C++

Disadvantages

- native C++ code may be faster at runtime.

- C++ does not require an installation of an associated compiler and managed runtime environment on the target system

- C++ supports generic programming. Until the final release of C++/CLI however, Managed C++ programmers must revert for workarounds for using generics in their solutions.

- C++ supports the keyword "const" and const correctness. Managed C++, like Java and C#, does not contain this feature. [Making a managed class immutable, or restricting set accessors on public interfaces enables managed code to have the same protection, to a degree.]

- C++ code is not constricted by the CLR's restrictions. For example, the CLR does not allow classes to inherit other classes privately, thus

```
public __gc class one { int i; };

public __gc class two: private one { int h; i = h; }; //error
```

will produce a compiler error.

[Though this is not necessarily a redeeming feature, as the point of making a class private is to prevent inheritance or access outside the class library.]

Also, __gc classes cannot inherit from more than one class, as such

```
__gc class a {};

__gc class b {};

__gc class c: public a, public b {}; //will produce an error
```

the preceding will produce a compile error.

[This is an advantage when multiple inheritance leads to problems. It could be interpreted as an advantage of managed code to prohibit poor technique. Conversely, multiple inheritance is often a very natural fit to some software modeling scenarios, and greater complexity can result in trying to avoid its use.]

Advantages

- Managed C++ supports a greater degree of reflection than regular C++, which is generally much more convenient depending on the function of the code, or what the code is intended for.

- Managed C++ can inter-operate with all other .NET capable languages, including other third party languages.

- Managed C++ is garbage collected. In standard C++, memory management and allocation is the responsibility of the programmer.

AspectC++

AspectC++ is an aspect-oriented extension of C and C++ languages. It has a source-to-source compiler, which translates AspectC++ source code into compilable C++. The compiler is available under the GNU GPL, though some extensions specific to Microsoft Windows are only available through pure-systems GmbH.

Aspect-oriented programming allows modularizing cross-cutting concerns in a single module, an aspect. Aspects can modify existing classes, but most commonly they provide 'advice' that runs before, after, or around existing functionality.

Example

All calls to a specific function can be traced using an aspect, rather than inserting 'cerr' or print statements in many places:

```
aspect Tracer

{

    advice call("% %Iter::Reset(...)") : before()

    {

        cerr << "about to call Iter::Reset for " << Join-
Point::signature() << endl;

    }

};
```

The Tracer aspect will print out a message before any call to %Iter::Reset. The %Iter syntax means that it will match all classes that end in Iter.

Each 'matched' location in the source code is called a join point—the advice is joined to (or advises) that code. AspectC++ provides a join point API to provide and access to information about the join point. For example, the function:

```
JoinPoint::signature()
```

returns the name of the function (that matched %Iter::Reset) that is about to be called.

The join point API also provides compile-time type information that can be used within an aspect to access the type or the value of the arguments and the return type and return value of a method or function.

C++/CLI

C++/CLI (C++ modified for Common Language Infrastructure) is a language specification created by Microsoft and intended to supersede Managed Extensions for C++. It is a complete revision that aims to simplify the older Managed C++ syntax, which is now deprecated. C++/CLI was standardized by Ecma as ECMA-372. It is currently available in Visual Studio 2005, 2008, 2010, 2012, 2013 and 2015, including the Express editions.

Syntax Changes

C++/CLI should be thought of as a language of its own (with a new set of keywords, for example), instead of the C++ superset-oriented Managed C++ (MC++) (whose non-standard keywords were styled like __gc or__value). Because of this, there are some major syntactic changes, especially related to the elimination of ambiguous identifiers and the addition of .NET-specific features.

Many conflicting syntaxes, such as the multiple versions of operator new() in MC++, have been split: in C++/CLI, .NET reference types are created with the new keyword gcnew (i.e. garbage collected new()). Also, C++/CLI has introduced the concept of generics from .NET (similar, for the most common purposes, to standard C++ templates, but quite different in their implementation).

Handles

In MC++, there were two different types of pointers: __nogc pointers were normal C++ pointers, while __gc pointers worked on .NET reference types. In C++/CLI, however, the only type of pointer is the normal C++ pointer, while the .NET reference types are accessed through a "handle", with the new syntax ClassName^ (instead of ClassName*). This new construct is especially helpful when managed and standard C++ code is mixed; it clarifies which objects are under .NET automatic garbage collection and which objects the programmer must remember to explicitly destroy.

Tracking References

A tracking reference in C++/CLI is a handle of a passed-by-reference variable. It is similar in concept to using "*&" (reference to a pointer) in Standard C++, and (in function declarations) corresponds to the "ref" keyword applied to types in C#, or "ByRef" in Visual Basic .NET. C++/CLI uses a "^%" syntax to indicate a tracking reference to a handle.

The following code shows an example of the use of tracking references. Replacing the tracking reference with a regular handle variable would leave the resulting string array with 10 uninitialized string handles, as only copies of the string handles in the array would be set, due to their being passed by value rather than by reference.

```
int main()

{

    array<String^> ^arr = gcnew array<String^>(10);

    int i = 0;


    for each(String^% s in arr) {

        s = i++.ToString();

    }


    return 0;

}
```

Note that this would be illegal in C#, which does not allow foreach loops to pass values by reference. Hence, a workaround would be required.

Finalizers and Automatic Variables

Another change in C++/CLI is the introduction of the finalizer syntax !ClassName(), a special type of nondeterministic destructor that is run as a part of the garbage collection routine. The C++ destructor syntax ~ClassName() also exists for managed objects, and better reflects the "traditional" C++ semantics of deterministic destruction (that is, destructors that can be called by user code with delete).

In the raw .NET paradigm, the nondeterministic destruction model overrides the protected Finalize method of the root Object class, while the deterministic model is implemented through the IDisposable interface method Dispose (which the C++/CLI compiler turns the destructor into). Objects from C# or VB.NET code that override the Dispose method can be disposed of manually in C++/CLI with delete just as .NET classes in C++/CLI can.

```
// C++/CLI

ref class MyClass

{

public:

    MyClass();   // constructor

    ~MyClass(); // (deterministic) destructor (implemented as
IDisposable.Dispose())

protected:

    !MyClass(); // finalizer (non-deterministic destructor) (im-
plemented as Finalize())


public:

    static void Test()

    {

        MyClass automatic; // Not a handle, no initialization:
compiler calls constructor here


        MyClass ^user = gcnew MyClass();

        delete user;


        // Compiler calls automatic's destructor when automatic
goes out of scope

    }

};
```

Operator Overloading

Operator overloading works analogously to standard C++. Every * becomes a ^, every & becomes an %, but the rest of the syntax is unchanged, except for an important addition: for .NET classes, operator overloading is possible not only for classes themselves, but also for references to those classes. This feature is necessary to give a ref class the semantics for operator overloading expected from .NET ref classes. (In reverse, this also means that for .NET framework ref classes, reference operator overloading often is implicitly implemented in C++/CLI.)

For example, comparing two distinct String references (String^) via the operator ==
will give true whenever the two strings are equal. The operator overloading is static,
however. Thus, casting to Object^ will remove the overloading semantics.

```
//effects of reference operator overloading

String ^s1 = "abc";

String ^s2 = "ab" + "c";

Object ^o1 = s1;

Object ^o2 = s2;

s1 == s2; // true

o1 == o2; // false
```

C++/CX

The new C++/CX targeting WinRT, although it produces entirely unmanaged code,
borrows the ref and ^ syntax for the reference-counted components that WinRT, which
are similar to COM "objects".

C++/CX

C++/CX *(component extensions)* is a language extension for C++ compilers from Microsoft that enables C++ programmers to write programs for the new Windows Runtime
platform, or *WinRT*.

The language extensions borrow syntax from C++/CLI but target the Windows Run-
time and native code instead of the Common Language Runtime and managed code. It
brings a set of syntax and library abstractions that interface with the COM-based Win-
RT programming model in a way that is natural to native C++ programmers.

It is possible to call the Windows Runtime from Standard C++ via the Windows Run-
time C++ Template Library (WRL).

Extension Syntax

C++/CX introduces syntax extensions for programming for the Windows Runtime. The
overall non platform-specific syntax is compatible with the C++11 standard.

Objects

WinRT objects are created, or *activated*, using ref new and assigned to variables declared with the ^ (hat) notation inherited from C++/CLI.

```
Foo^ foo = ref new Foo();
```

A WinRT variable is simply a pair of a pointer to virtual method table and pointer to the object's internal data.

Reference Counting

A WinRT object is reference counted and thus handles similarly to ordinary C++ objects enclosed in shared_ptrs. An object will be deleted when there are no remaining references that lead to it.

There is no garbage collection involved. Nevertheless, the keyword gcnew has been reserved for possible future use.

Classes

Runtime Classes

There are special kinds of *runtime classes* that may contain component extension constructs. These are simply referred to as *ref classes* because they are declared using ref class.

```
public ref class MyClass

{


};
```

Partial Classes

C++/CX introduces the concept of partial classes. The feature allows a single class to be split across multiple files, mainly to enable the XAML graphical user interface design tools to auto-generate code in a separate file in order not to break the logic written by the developer. The parts are later merged at compilation.

.NET languages like C# have had this feature for many years. Partial classes have not yet made it into the C++ standard and cannot therefore be used in pure C++11.

A file that is generated and updated by the GUI-designer, and thus should not be modified by the programmer. Note the keyword partial.

```
// foo.private.h

#pragma once
```

```
partial ref class foo

{

private:

    int id_;

    Platform::String^ name_;

};
```

The file where the programmer writes user-interface logic. The header in which the compiler-generated part of the class is defined is imported. Note that the keyword partial is not necessary.

```
// foo.public.h

#pragma once

#include "foo.private.h"


ref class foo

{

public:

    int GetId();

    Platform::String^ GetName();

};
```

This is the file in which the members of the partial class are implemented.

```
// foo.cpp

#include "pch.h"

#include "foo.public.h"


int foo::GetId() {return id_;}

Platform::String^ foo::GetName {return name_;}
```

Generics

Windows Runtime and thus C++/CX supports runtime-based generics. Generic type information is contained in the metadata and instantiated at runtime, unlike C++ templates which are compile-time constructs. Both are supported by the compiler and can be combined.

```
generic<typename T>

public ref class bag

{

    property T Item;

};
```

Metadata

All WinRT programs expose their declared classes and members through metadata. The format is the same that was standardized as part of the Common Language Infrastructure (CLI), the standard created from the .NET Framework. Because of this, code can be shared across C++/CX, CLI languages and Javascript that target Windows Runtime.

Runtime Library

The C++/CX has a set of libraries that target the Windows Runtime. These help bridge the functionality of the C++ Standard Library and WinRT.

Preprocessor-based Detection

You can detect if C++/CX extension is turned on by testing existence of __cplusplus_ winrt preprocessor symbol.

```
#ifdef __cplusplus_winrt

// C++/CX specific code goes here...

#endif
```

Cilk

Cilk, Cilk++ and Cilk Plus are general-purpose programming languages designed for multithreaded parallel computing. They are based on the C and C++ programming languages, which they extend with constructs to express parallel loops and the fork–join idiom.

Originally developed in the 1990s at the Massachusetts Institute of Technology (MIT) in the group of Charles E. Leiserson, Cilk was later commercialized as Cilk++ by a spinoff company, Cilk Arts. That company was subsequently acquired by Intel, which increased compatibility with existing C and C++ code, calling the result Cilk Plus.

History

MIT Cilk

The Cilk programming language grew out of three separate projects at the MIT Laboratory for Computer Science:

- Theoretical work on scheduling multi-threaded applications.

- StarTech – a parallel chess program built to run on the Thinking Machines Corporation's Connection Machine model CM-5.

- PCM/Threaded-C – a C-based package for scheduling continuation-passing-style threads on the CM-5

In April 1994 the three projects were combined and christened "Cilk". The name Cilk is not an acronym, but an allusion to "nice threads" (silk) and the C programming language. The Cilk-1 compiler was released in September 1994.

The original Cilk language was based on ANSI C, with the addition of Cilk-specific keywords to signal parallelism. When the Cilk keywords are removed from Cilk source code, the result should always be a valid C program, called the *serial elision* (or *C elision*) of the full Cilk program, with the same semantics as the Cilk program running on a single processor. Despite several similarities, Cilk is not directly related to AT&T Bell Labs' Concurrent C.

Cilk was implemented as a translator to C, targeting the GNU C Compiler (GCC). The last version, Cilk 5.4.6, is available from the MIT Computer Science and Artificial Intelligence Laboratory (CSAIL), but is no longer supported.

A showcase for Cilk's capabilities was the Cilkchess parallel chess-playing program, which won several computer chess prizes in the 1990s, including the 1996 Open Dutch Computer Chess Championship.

Cilk Arts and Cilk++

Prior to c. 2006, the market for Cilk was restricted to high-performance computing. The emergence of multicore processors in mainstream computing means that hundreds of millions of new parallel computers are now being shipped every year. Cilk Arts was formed to capitalize on that opportunity: in 2006, Leiserson launched Cilk Arts to create and bring to market a modern version of Cilk that supports the commercial needs of an upcoming generation of programmers. The company closed a Series A venture financing round in October 2007, and its product, Cilk++ 1.0, shipped in December, 2008.

Cilk++ differs from Cilk in several ways: support for C++, support for loops, and hyperobjects – a new construct designed to solve data race problems created by parallel accesses to global variables. Cilk++ was proprietary software. Like its predecessor, it was implemented as a Cilk-to-C++ compiler. It supported the Microsoft and GNU compilers.

Intel Cilk Plus

On July 31, 2009, Cilk Arts announced on its web site that its products and engineering team were now part of Intel Corp. Intel and Cilk Arts integrated and advanced the technology further resulting in a September 2010 release of Intel Cilk Plus. Cilk Plus adopts simplifications, proposed by Cilk Arts in Cilk++, to eliminate the need for several of the original Cilk keywords while adding the ability to spawn functions and to deal with variables involved in reduction operations. Cilk Plus differs from Cilk and Cilk++ by adding array extensions, being incorporated in a commercial compiler (from Intel), and compatibility with existing debuggers.

Cilk Plus was first implemented in the Intel C++ Compiler with the release of the Intel compiler in Intel Composer XE 2010. An open source (BSD-licensed) implementation was contributed by Intel to the GNU Compiler Collection (GCC), which shipped Cilk Plus support in version 4.9, except for the _Cilk_for keyword, which was added in GCC 5.0. In February 2013, Intel announced a Clang fork with Cilk Plus support. The Intel Compiler, but not the open source implementations, comes with a race detector and a performance analyzer.

Intel has stated its desire to refine Cilk Plus and to enable it to be implemented by other compilers to gain industry wide adoption. It has also released a specification to enable other compatible implementations, and has said the trademark will be usable by compliant implementations.

Differences Between Versions

In the original MIT Cilk implementation, the first Cilk keyword is in fact cilk, which identifies a function which is written in Cilk. Since Cilk procedures can call C procedures directly, but C procedures cannot directly call or spawn Cilk procedures, this keyword is needed to distinguish Cilk code from C code. Cilk Plus removes this restriction, as well as the cilk keyword, so C and C++ functions can call into Cilk Plus code and vice versa.

Language Features

The principle behind the design of the Cilk language is that the programmer should be responsible for *exposing* the parallelism, identifying elements that can safely be executed in parallel; it should then be left to the run-time environment, particularly the scheduler, to decide during execution how to actually divide the work between processors. It is because these responsibilities are separated that a Cilk program can run without rewriting on any number of processors, including one.

Task Parallelism: Spawn and Sync

Cilk's main addition to C are two keywords that together allow writing task-parallel programs.

- The spawn keyword, when preceding a function call (spawn f(x)), indicates that the function call (f(x)) can safely run in parallel with the statements following it in the calling function. Note that the scheduler is not *obligated* to run this procedure in parallel; the keyword merely alerts the scheduler that it can do so.

- A sync statement indicates that execution of the current function cannot proceed until all previously spawned function calls have completed. This is an example of a barrier method.

(In Cilk Plus, the keywords are spelled _Cilk_spawn and _Cilk_sync, or cilk_spawn and cilk_sync if the Cilk Plus headers are included.)

Below is a recursive implementation of the Fibonacci function in Cilk, with parallel recursive calls, which demonstrates the spawn, and sync keywords. The original Cilk required any function using these to be annotated with the cilk keyword, which is gone as of Cilk Plus. (Cilk program code is not numbered; the numbers have been added only to make the discussion easier to follow.)

```
1  cilk int fib(int n) {

2      if (n < 2) {

3          return n;

4      }

5      else {

6          int x, y;

7

8          x = spawn fib(n - 1);

9          y = spawn fib(n - 2);

10

11         sync;

12
```

```
13          return x + y;

14      }

15  }
```

If this code was executed by a *single* processor to determine the value of fib(2), that processor would create a frame for fib(2), and execute lines 1 through 5. On line 6, it would create spaces in the frame to hold the values of x and y. On line 8, the processor would have to suspend the current frame, create a new frame to execute the procedure fib(1), execute the code of that frame until reaching a return statement, and then resume the fib(2) frame with the value of fib(1) placed into fib(2)'s x variable. On the next line, it would need to suspend again to execute fib(0) and place the result in fib(2)'s y variable.

When the code is executed on a *multiprocessor* machine, however, execution proceeds differently. One processor starts the execution of fib(2); when it reaches line 8, however, the spawn keyword modifying the call to fib(n-1) tells the processor that it can safely give the job to a second processor: this second processor can create a frame for fib(1), execute its code, and store its result in fib(2)'s frame when it finishes; the first processor continues executing the code of fib(2) at the same time. A processor is not obligated to assign a spawned procedure elsewhere; if the machine only has two processors and the second is still busy on fib(1) when the processor executing fib(2) gets to the procedure call, the first processor will suspend fib(2) and execute fib(0) itself, as it would if it were the only processor. Of course, if another processor is available, then it will be called into service, and all three processors would be executing separate frames simultaneously.

(The preceding description is not entirely accurate. Even though the common terminology for discussing Cilk refers to processors making the decision to spawn off work to other processors, it is actually the scheduler which assigns procedures to processors for execution, using a policy called *work-stealing*, described later.)

If the processor executing fib(2) were to execute line 13 before both of the other processors had completed their frames, it would generate an incorrect result or an error; fib(2) would be trying to add the values stored in x and y, but one or both of those values would be missing. This is the purpose of the sync keyword, which we see in line 11: it tells the processor executing a frame that it must suspend its own execution until all the procedure calls it has spawned off have returned. When fib(2) is allowed to proceed past the sync statement in line 11, it can only be because fib(1) and fib(0) have completed and placed their results in x and y, making it safe to perform calculations on those results.

The code example above uses the syntax of Cilk-5. The original Cilk (Cilk-1) used a rather different syntax that required programming in an explicit continuation-passing style, and the Fibonacci examples looks as follows:

```
thread fib(cont int k, int n)

{

    if (n < 2) {

        send_argument(k, n);

    }

    else {

        cont int x, y;

        spawn_next sum(k, ?x, ?y);

        spawn fib(x, n - 1);

        spawn fib(y, n - 2);

    }

}


thread sum(cont int k, int x, int y)

{

    send_argument(k, x + y);

}
```

Inside fib's recursive case, the spawn_next keyword indicates the creation of a *successor* thread (as opposed to the *child* threads created by spawn), which executes the sum subroutine after waiting for the *continuation variables* x and y to be filled in by the recursive calls. The base case and sum use a send_argument(k, n) operation to set their continuation variable k to the value of n, effectively "returning" the value to the successor thread.

Inlets

The two remaining Cilk keywords are slightly more advanced, and concern the use of *inlets*. Ordinarily, when a Cilk procedure is spawned, it can return its results to the parent procedure only by putting those results in a variable in the parent's frame, as we assigned the results of our spawned procedure calls in the example to x and y.

The alternative is to use an inlet. An inlet is a function internal to a Cilk procedure which handles the results of a spawned procedure call as they return. One major reason to use inlets is that all the inlets of a procedure are guaranteed to operate atomically with regards to each other and to the parent procedure, thus avoiding the bugs that could occur if the multiple returning procedures tried to update the same variables in the parent frame at the same time.

- The inlet keyword identifies a function defined within the procedure as an inlet.

- The abort keyword can only be used inside an inlet; it tells the scheduler that any other procedures that have been spawned off by the parent procedure can safely be aborted.

Inlets were removed when Cilk became Cilk++, and are not present in Cilk Plus.

Parallel Loops

Cilk++ added an additional construct, the parallel loop, denoted cilk_for in Cilk Plus. These loops look like

```
1 void loop(int *a, int n)

2 {

3      #pragma cilk grainsize = 100  // optional

4      cilk_for (int i = 0; i < n; i++) {

5            a[i] = f(a[i]);

6      }

7 }
```

This implements the parallel map idiom: the body of the loop, here a call to f followed by an assignment to the array a, is executed for each value of i from zero to n in an indeterminate order. The optional "grain size" pragma determines the coarsening: any sub-array of one hundred or fewer elements is processed sequentially. Although the Cilk specification does not specify the exact behavior of the construct, the typical implementation is a divide-and-conquer recursion, as if the programmer had written

```
static void recursion(int *a, int start, int end)

{

    if (end - start <= 100) {  // The 100 here is the grain-
size.

        for (int i = start; i < end; i++) {
```

```
            a[i] = f(a[i]);

        }

    }

    else {

        int midpoint = start + (end - start) / 2;

        cilk_spawn recursion(a, start, midpoint);

        recursion(a, midpoint, end);

        cilk_sync;

    }

}


void loop(int *a, int n)

{

    recursion(a, 0, n);

}
```

The reasons for generating a divide-and-conquer program rather than the obvious alternative, a loop that spawn-calls the loop body as a function, lie in both the grainsize handling and in efficiency: doing all the spawning in a single task makes load balancing a bottleneck.

A review of various parallel loop constructs on HPCwire found the cilk_for construct to be quite general, but noted that the Cilk Plus specification did not stipulate that its iterations need to be data-independent, so a compiler cannot automatically vectorize a cilk_for loop. The review also noted the fact that reductions (e.g., sums over arrays) need additional code.

Reducers and Hyperobjects

Cilk++ added a kind of objects called *hyperobjects*, that allow multiple strands to share state without race conditions and without using explicit locks. Each strand has a view on the hyperobject that it can use and update; when the strands synchronize, the views are combined in a way specified by the programmer.

The most common type of hyperobject is a reducer, which corresponds to the reduction clause in OpenMP or to the algebraic notion of a monoid. Each reducer has an identity element and an associative operation that combines two values. The archetypal reducer is summation of numbers: the identity element is zero, and the associative *reduce* operation computes a sum. This reducer is built into Cilk++ and Cilk Plus:

```
// Compute ∑ foo(i) for i from 0 to N, in parallel.
cilk::reducer_opadd<float> result(0);
cilk_for (int i = 0; i < N; i++)
    result += foo(i);
```

Other reducers can be used to construct linked lists or strings, and programmers can define custom reducers.

A limitation of hyperobjects is that they provide only limited determinacy. Burckhardt *et al.* point out that even the sum reducer can result in non-deterministic behavior, showing a program that may produce either 1 or 2 depending on the scheduling order:

```
void add1(cilk::reducer_opadd<int> &r) { r++; }
// ...
cilk::reducer_opadd<int> r(0);
cilk_spawn add1(r);
if (r == 0) { r++; }
cilk_sync;
output(r.get_value());
```

Array Notation

Intel Cilk Plus adds notation to express high-level operations on entire arrays or sections of arrays; e.g., an axpy-style function that is ordinarily written

```
// y ← α x + y
void axpy(int n, float alpha, const float *x, float *y)
{
    for (int i = 0; i < n; i++) {
        y[i] += alpha * x[i];
    }
}
```

can in Cilk Plus be expressed as

```
y[0:n] += alpha * x[0:n];
```

This notation helps the compiler to effectively vectorize the application. Intel Cilk Plus allows C/C++ operations to be applied to multiple array elements in parallel, and also provides a set of built-in functions that can be used to perform vectorized shifts, rotates, and reductions. Similar functionality exists in Fortran 90; Cilk Plus differs in that it never allocates temporary arrays, so memory usage is easier to predict.

Elemental Functions

In Cilk Plus, an elemental function is a regular function which can be invoked either on scalar arguments or on array elements in parallel. They are similar to the kernel functions of OpenCL.

#Pragma Simd

This pragma gives the compiler permission to vectorize a loop even in cases where auto-vectorization might fail. It is the simplest way to manually apply vectorization.

Work-stealing

The Cilk scheduler uses a policy called "work-stealing" to divide procedure execution efficiently among multiple processors. Again, it is easiest to understand if we look first at how Cilk code is executed on a single-processor machine.

The processor maintains a stack on which it places each frame that it has to suspend in order to handle a procedure call. If it is executing *fib(2)*, and encounters a recursive call to *fib(1)*, it will save *fib(2)*'s state, including its variables and where the code suspended execution, and put that state on the stack. It will not take a suspended state off the stack and resume execution until the procedure call that caused the suspension, and any procedures called in turn by that procedure, have all been fully executed.

With multiple processors, things of course change. Each processor still has a stack for storing frames whose execution has been suspended; however, these stacks are more like deques, in that suspended states can be removed from either end. A processor can still only remove states from its *own* stack from the same end that it puts them on; however, any processor which is not currently working (having finished its own work, or not yet having been assigned any) will pick another processor at random, through the scheduler, and try to "steal" work from the opposite end of their stack – suspended states, which the stealing processor can then begin to execute. The states which get stolen are the states that the processor stolen from would get around to executing last.

References

- "Charm++ Programming Language Manual" (PDF). http://cs.illinois.edu/: University of Illinois at Urbana-Champaign, Department of Computer Science. Retrieved 2011-08-12.

- "Array "Hello World": A Slightly More Advanced "Hello World" Program: Array "Hello World" Code". http://charm.cs.uiuc.edu/: PPL - UIUC PARALLEL PROGRAMMING LABORATORY. Retrieved 2011-08-12.

- "Parallel Studio 2011: Now We Know What Happened to Ct, Cilk++, and RapidMind", Dr. Dobbs Journal (2010-09-02). Retrieved on 2010-09-14.

- "Intel Cilk Plus: A quick, easy and reliable way to improve threaded performance", Intel. Retrieved on 2010-09-14.

- "Cilk Plus specification and runtime ABI freely available for download", James Reinders. Retrieved on 2010-11-03.

Techniques and Features of C++

Computer programming has a feature called copy elision. Copy elision is a method which is essential to eliminate the unnecessary coping of objects. Templates (C++) and decltypes are other prominent techniques used in C++. The text elucidates all the tools and methods of C++.

Copy Elision

In C++ computer programming, copy elision refers to a compiler optimization technique that eliminates unnecessary copying of objects. The C++ language standard generally allows implementations to perform any optimization, provided the resulting program's observable behavior is the same *as if*, i.e. pretending, the program was executed exactly as mandated by the standard.

The standard also describes a few situations where copying can be eliminated even if this would alter the program's behavior, the most common being the return value optimization. Another widely implemented optimization, described in the C++ standard, is when a temporary object of class type is copied to an object of the same type. As a result, *copy-initialization* is usually equivalent to *direct-initialization* in terms of performance, but not in semantics; *copy-initialization* still requires an accessible copy constructor. The optimization can not be applied to a temporary object that has been bound to a reference. Example:

```
#include <iostream>


int n = 0;

struct C {

  explicit C(int) {}

  C(const C&) { ++n; } // the copy constructor has a visible
side effect

};                     // it modifies an object with static
storage duration
```

```
int main() {

  C c1(42); // direct-initialization, calls C::C(42)

  C c2 = C(42); // copy-initialization, calls C::C( C(42) )


  std::cout << n << std::endl; // prints 0 if the copy was
elided, 1 otherwise

  return 0;

}
```

According to the standard a similar optimization may be applied to objects being thrown and caught, but it is unclear whether the optimization applies to both the copy from the thrown object to the *exception object*, and the copy from the *exception object* to the object declared in the *exception-declaration* of the *catch clause*. It is also unclear whether this optimization only applies to temporary objects, or named objects as well. Given the following source code:

```
#include <iostream>


struct C {

  C() {}

  C(const C&) { std::cout << "Hello World!\n"; }

};


void f() {

  C c;

  throw c; // copying the named object c into the exception ob-
ject.

}            // It is unclear whether this copy may be elided.


int main() {

  try {
```

```
    f();

  }

  catch(C c) {   // copying the exception object into the tempo-
rary in the exception declaration.

  }                    // It is also unclear whether this copy may be
elided.

}
```

A conforming compiler should therefore produce a program which prints "Hello World!" twice. In the current revision of the C++ standard (C++11), the issues have been addressed, essentially allowing both the copy from the named object to the exception object, and the copy into the object declared in the exception handler to be elided.

GCC provides the -fno-elide-constructors option to disable copy-elision. This option is useful to observe (or not observe!) the effects of Return Value Optimization or other optimizations where copies are elided. It is generally not recommended to disable this important optimization.

Template (C++)

Templates are a feature of the C++ programming language that allows functions and classes to operate with generic types. This allows a function or class to work on many different data types without being rewritten for each one.

Templates are of great utility to programmers in C++, especially when combined with multiple inheritance and operator overloading. The C++ Standard Library provides many useful functions within a framework of connected templates.

Major inspirations for C++ templates were the parameterized modules provided by CLU and the generics provided by Ada.

Technical Overview

There are three kinds of templates: *function templates*, *class templates* and, since C++14, *variable templates*. Since C++11, templates may be either variadic or non-variadic; in earlier versions of C++ they are always non-variadic.

Function Templates

A *function template* behaves like a function except that the template can have arguments of many different types. In other words, a function template represents a family of functions. The format for declaring function templates with type parameters is:

```
template <class identifier> function_declaration;

template <typename identifier> function_declaration;
```

Both expressions have the same meaning and behave in exactly the same way. The latter form was introduced to avoid confusion, since a type parameter need not be a class. (it can also be a basic type such as int or double.)

For example, the C++ Standard Library contains the function template max(x, y) which returns the larger of x and y. That function template could be defined like this:

```
template <typename T>

inline T max(T a, T b) {

    return a > b ? a : b;

}
```

This single function definition works with many data types. The usage of a function template saves space in the source code file in addition to limiting changes to one function description and making the code easier to read.

A template does not produce smaller object code, though, compared to writing separate functions for all the different data types used in a specific program. For example, if a program uses both an int and a double version of the max() function template shown above, the compiler will create an object code version of max() that operates on int arguments and another object code version that operates on double arguments. The compiler output will be identical to what would have been produced if the source code had contained two separate non-templated versions of max(), one written to handle int and one written to handle double.

Here is how the function template could be used:

```
#include <iostream>


int main()

{

    // This will call max<int> by implicit argument deduction.

    std::cout << max(3, 7) << std::endl;


    // This will call max<double> by implicit argument deduc-
```

tion.

```
    std::cout << max(3.0, 7.0) << std::endl;



    // This depends on the compiler. Some compilers handle this
by defining a template

    // function like double max <double> ( double a, double
b);;, while in some compilers

    // we need to explicitly cast it, like std::cout << max-
<double>(3,7.0);

    std::cout << max(3, 7.0) << std::endl;

    std::cout << max<double>(3, 7.0) << std::endl;

    return 0;

}
```

In the first two cases, the template argument Type is automatically deduced by the compiler to be int and double, respectively. In the third case automatic deduction of max(3, 7.0) would fail because the type of the parameters must in general match the template arguments exactly. Therefore, we explicitly instantiate the double version with max<double>().

This function template can be instantiated with any copy-constructible type for which the expression y > x is valid. For user-defined types, this implies that the greater-than operator (>) must be overloaded in the type.

Class Templates

A class template provides a specification for generating classes based on parameters. Class templates are generally used to implement containers. A class template is instantiated by passing a given set of types to it as template arguments. The C++ Standard Library contains many class templates, in particular the containers adapted from the Standard Template Library, such as vector.

Variable Templates

In C++14, templates can be also used for variables, as in the following example:

```
template<typename T> constexpr T pi = T(3.14159265358979323846263383L);
```

Template Specialization

When a function or class is instantiated from a template, a specialization of that template is created by the compiler for the set of arguments used, and the specialization is referred to as being a generated specialization.

Explicit Template Specialization

Sometimes, the programmer may decide to implement a special version of a function (or class) for a given set of template type arguments which is called an explicit specialization. In this way certain template types can have a specialized implementation that is optimized for the type or more meaningful implementation than the generic implementation.

- If a class template is specialized by a subset of its parameters it is called partial template specialization (function templates cannot be partially specialized).

- If all of the parameters are specialized it is a *full specialization*.

Explicit specialization is used when the behavior of a function or class for particular choices of the template parameters must deviate from the generic behavior: that is, from the code generated by the main template, or templates. For example, the template definition below defines a specific implementation of max() for arguments of type bool:

```
template <>
bool max<bool>(bool a, bool b) {

    return a || b;

}
```

Variadic Templates

C++11 introduced variadic templates, which can take a variable number of arguments in a manner somewhat similar to variadic functions such as std::printf. Both function templates and class templates can be variadic.

Advantages and Disadvantages of Templates Over Macros

Some uses of templates, such as the max() function mentioned above, were previously fulfilled by function-like preprocessor macros. For example, the following is a C++ max() macro that evaluates to the maximum of its two arguments as defined by the < operator:

```
#define max(a,b) ((a) < (b) ? (b) : (a))
```

Both macros and templates are expanded at compile time. Macros are always expanded inline, while templates are only expanded inline when the compiler deems it appropriate. When expanded inline, macro functions and function templates have no extraneous runtime overhead. Template functions with many lines of code will incur runtime overhead when they are not expanded inline, but the reduction in code size may help the code to load from disk more quickly or fit within RAM caches.

Macro arguments are not evaluated prior to expansion. The expression using the macro defined above

```
max(0, std::rand() - 100)
```

may evaluate to a negative number (because std::rand() will be called twice as specified in the macro, using different random numbers for comparison and output respectively), while the call to template function

```
std::max(0, std::rand() - 100)
```

will always evaluate to a non-negative number.

As opposed to macros, templates are considered type-safe; that is, they require type-checking at compile time. Hence, the compiler can determine at compile time whether the type associated with a template definition can perform all of the functions required by that template definition.

By design, templates can be utilized in very complex problem spaces, whereas macros are substantially more limited.

There are fundamental drawbacks to the use of templates:

1. Historically, some compilers exhibited poor support for templates. So, the use of templates could decrease code portability.

2. Many compilers lack clear instructions when they detect a template definition error. This can increase the effort of developing templates, and has prompted the development of Concepts for possible inclusion in a future C++ standard.

3. Since the compiler generates additional code for each template type, indiscriminate use of templates can lead to code bloat, resulting in larger executables.

4. Because a template by its nature exposes its implementation, injudicious use in large systems can lead to longer build times.

5. It can be difficult to debug code that is developed using templates. Since the compiler replaces the templates, it becomes difficult for the debugger to locate the code at runtime.

6. Templates of templates (nested templates) are not supported by all compilers, or might have a limit on the nesting level.

7. Templates are in the headers, which require a complete rebuild of all project pieces when changes are made.

8. No information hiding. All code is exposed in the header file. No one library can solely contain the code.

Additionally, the use of the "less than" and "greater than" signs as delimiters is problematic for tools (such as text editors) which analyze source code syntactically. It is difficult for such tools to determine whether a use of these tokens is as comparison operators or template delimiters. For example, this line of code:

```
foo (a < b, c > d) ;
```

may be a function call with two parameters, each the result of a comparison expression, or possibly a function call with one parameter, utilizing the C++ comma operator (whose end result would depend on possible side effects of a, b, c, and/or d). Alternatively, it could be a declaration of a constructor for class foo taking a parameter d whose type is the parameterized a < b, c >.

Generic Programming Features in Other Languages

Initially, the concept of templates was not included in some languages, such as Java and C# 1.0. Java's adoption of generics mimics the behaviour of templates, but is technically different. C# added generics (parameterized types) in .NET 2.0. The generics in Ada predate C++ templates.

Although C++ templates, Java generics, and .NET generics are often considered similar, generics only mimic the basic behavior of C++ templates. Some of the advanced template features utilized by libraries such as Boost and STLSoft, and implementations of the STL itself, for template metaprogramming (explicit or partial specialization, default template arguments, template non-type arguments, template template arguments, ...) are not available with generics.

In C++ templates, compile-time cases were historically performed by pattern matching over the template arguments, so e.g. the below Factorial template's base case is implemented by matching 0 rather than with an inequality test, which was hitherto unavailable. However, the arrival in C++11 of standard library features such as std::conditional has provided another, more flexible way to handle conditional template instantiation.

```
// Induction


template <int N>
```

```
struct Factorial {

  static const int value = N * Factorial<N - 1>::value;

};



// Base case via template specialization:



template <>

struct Factorial<0> {

  static const int value = 1;

};
```

With these definitions, one can compute, say 6! at compile time using the expression Factorial<6>::value. Alternatively, constexpr in C++11 can be used to calculate such values directly using a function at compile-time.

Input/Output (C++)

In the C++ programming language, Input/output library refers to a family of class templates and supporting functions in the C++ Standard Library that implement stream-based input/output capabilities. It is an object-oriented alternative to C's FILE-based streams from the C standard library.

Overview

Most of the classes in the library are actually very generalized class templates. Each template can operate on various character types, and even the operations themselves, such as how two characters are compared for equality, can be customized. However, the majority of code needs to do input and output operations using only one or two character types, thus most of the time the functionality is accessed through several typedefs, which specify names for commonly used combinations of template and character type.

For example, basic_fstream<CharT,Traits> refers to the generic class template that implements input/output operations on file streams. It is usually used as fstream which is an alias for basic_fstream<char,char_traits<char>>, or, in other words, basic_fstream working on characters of type char with the default character operation set.

The classes in the library could be divided into roughly two categories: abstractions and implementations. Classes, that fall into abstractions category, provide an interface which is sufficient for working with any type of a stream. The code using such classes doesn't depend on the exact location the data is read from or is written to. For example, such code could write data to a file, a memory buffer or a web socket without a recompilation. The implementation classes inherit the abstraction classes and provide an implementation for concrete type of data source or sink. The library provides implementations only for file-based streams and memory buffer-based streams.

The classes in the library could also be divided into two groups by whether it implements low-level or high-level operations. The classes that deal with low-level stuff are called stream buffers. They operate on characters without providing any formatting functionality. These classes are very rarely used directly. The high-level classes are called streams and provide various formatting capabilities. They are built on top of stream buffers.

The following table lists and categorizes all classes provided by the input-output library.

Class	Explanation	Typedefs
Stream buffers (low level functionality)		
basic_streambuf	provides abstract low level input/output interface, that can be implemented for concrete data sources or sinks. Rarely used directly.	• streambuf - operates on characters of type char • wstreambuf - operates on characters of type wchar_t
basic_filebuf	implements low level input/output interface for file-based streams. Rarely used directly.	• filebuf - operates on characters of type char • wfilebuf - operates on characters of type wchar_t
basic_stringbuf	implements low level input/output interface for string-based streams. Rarely used directly.	• stringbuf - operates on characters of type char • wstringbuf - operates on characters of type wchar_t
Support classes		
ios_base	manages formatting information and exception state	N/A
basic_ios	manages a stream buffer	• ios - operates on characters of type char • wios - operates on characters of type wchar_t
Input streams buffers (high level functionality)		
basic_istream	wraps an abstract stream buffer and provides high level input interface, such as formatting capabilities.	• istream - operates on characters of type char • wistream - operates on characters of type wchar_t

basic_ifstream	an input stream that wraps a file stream buffer. Provides functions to open or close a file in addition to those of generic input stream	• ifstream - operates on characters of type char • wifstream - operates on characters of type wchar_t
basic_ istringstream	an input stream that wraps a string stream buffer. Provides functions to access the underlying string in addition to those of generic input stream	• istringstream - operates on characters of type char • wistringstream - operates on characters of type wchar_t
Output streams buffers (high level functionality)		
basic_ostream	wraps an abstract stream buffer and provides high level output interface, such as formatting capabilities.	• ostream - operates on characters of type char • wostream - operates on characters of type wchar_t
basic_ ofstream	an output stream that wraps a file stream buffer. Provides functions to open or close a file in addition to those of generic output stream	• ofstream - operates on characters of type char • wofstream - operates on characters of type wchar_t
basic_ ostringstream	an output stream that wraps a string stream buffer. Provides functions to access the underlying string in addition to those of generic output stream	• ostringstream - operates on characters of type char • wostringstream - operates on characters of type wchar_t
Input/output streams buffers (high level functionality)		
basic_iostream	wraps an abstract stream buffer and provides high level input/output interface, such as formatting capabilities.	• iostream - operates on characters of type char • wiostream - operates on characters of type wchar_t
basic_fstream	an input/output stream that wraps a file stream buffer. Provides functions to open or close a file in addition to those of generic input/output stream	• fstream - operates on characters of type char • wfstream - operates on characters of type wchar_t
basic_ stringstream	an input/output stream that wraps a string stream buffer. Provides functions to access the underlying string in addition to those of generic input/output stream	• stringstream - operates on characters of type char • wstringstream - operates on characters of type wchar_t

Header Files

The classes of the input/output library reside in several headers.

- <ios> contains the definitions of ios_base and basic_ios classes, that manage formatting information and the associated streambuffer.

- <istream> contains the definition of basic_istream class template, which implements formatted input

- <ostream> contains the definition of basic_ostream class template, which implements formatted output

- <iostream> contains the definition of basic_iostream class template, which implements formatted input and output

- <fstream> contains the definitions of basic_ifstream, basic_ofstream and basic_fstream class templates which implement formatted input, output and input/output on file streams.

- <sstream> contains the definitions of basic_istringstream, basic_ostringstream and basic_stringstream class templates which implement formatted input, output and input/output on string-based streams.

- <iomanip> contains formatting manipulators.

- <iosfwd> contains forward declarations of all classes in the input/output library.

Stream Buffers

Support Classes

ios_base and basic_ios are two classes that manage the lower-level bits of a stream. ios_base stores formatting information and the state of the stream. basic_ios manages the associated stream-buffer. basic_ios is commonly known as simply ios or wios, which are two typedefs for basic_ios with a specific character type. basic_ios and ios_base are very rarely used directly by programmers. Usually, their functionality is accessed through other classes such as iostream which inherit them.

Typedefs

Name	description
ios	convenience typedef for a basic_ios working with characters of type char
wios	convenience typedef for a basic_ios working with characters of type wchar_t
streamoff	supports internal operations.

streampos	holds the current position of the buffer pointer or file pointer.
wstreampos	holds the current position of the buffer pointer or file pointer.
streamsize	specifies the size of the stream.

Formatting Manipulators

Name	Description
boolalpha / noboolalpha	specifies whether variables of type bool appear as true and false or as 0 and 1 in the stream.
skipws / noskipws	specifies whether the white space is skipped in input operations
showbase / noshowbase	specifies whether the notational base of the number is displayed
showpoint / noshowpoint	specifies whether to display the fractional part of a floating point number, when the fractional part is zero
showpos / noshowpos	specifies whether to display + for positive numbers
unitbuf / nounitbuf	specifies whether the output should be buffered
uppercase / nouppercase	specifies whether uppercase characters should be used in hexadecimal integer and floating-point output
left / right / internal	specifies how a number should be justified
dec / oct/ hex	specifies the notation an integer number should be displayed in
fixed / scientific/ hexfloat(C++11) / defaultfloat(C++11)	specifies the notation a floating-point number should be displayed in

Input/Output Streams

C++ input/output streams are primarily defined by iostream, a header file that is part of the C++ standard library (the name stands for Input/Output Stream). In C++ and its predecessor, the C programming language, there is no special syntax for streaming data input or output. Instead, these are combined as a library of functions. Like the cstdio header inherited from C's stdio.h, iostream provides basic input and output services for C++ programs. iostream uses the objects cin, cout, cerr, and clog for sending data to and from the standard streams input, output, error (unbuffered), and log (buffered) respectively. As part of the C++ standard library, these objects are a part of the std namespace.

The cout object is of type ostream, which overloads the left bit-shift operator to make it perform an operation completely unrelated to bitwise operations, and notably evaluate to the value of the left argument, allowing multiple operations on the same ostream object, essentially as a different syntax for method cascading, exposing a fluent interface. The cerr and clog objects are also of type ostream, so they overload that operator as well. The cin object is of type istream, which overloads the right bit-shift operator. The directions of the bit-shift operators make it seem as though data is flowing towards the output stream or flowing away from the input stream.

Output Formatting

Methods

width(int x)	minimum number of characters for next output
fill(char x)	character used to fill with in the case that the width needs to be elongated to fill the minimum.
precision(int x)	sets the number of significant digits for floating-point numbers

Manipulators

Manipulators are objects that can modify a stream using the << or >> operators.

"end line": inserts a newline into the stream and calls flush.
"end string": inserts a null character into the stream and calls flush.
forces an output stream to write any buffered characters
causes an inputstream to 'eat' whitespace
tells the stream to show the decimal point and some zeros with whole numbers

Other manipulators can be found using the header iomanip.

Criticism

Some environments do not provide a shared implementation of the C++ library. These include embedded systems and Windows systems running programs built with MinGW. Under these systems, the C++ standard library must be statically linked to a program, which increases the size of the program, or distributed as a shared library alongside the program. Some implementations of the C++ standard library have significant amounts of dead code. For example, GNU libstdc++ automatically constructs a locale when building an ostream even if a program never uses any types (date, time or money) that a locale affects, and a statically linked hello world program that uses <iostream> of GNU libstdc++ produces an executable an order of magnitude larger than an equivalent program that uses <cstdio>. There exist partial implementations of the C++ standard library designed for space-constrained environments; their <iostream> may leave out features that programs in such environments may not need, such as locale support.

Naming Conventions

Please refer to Standard streams.

Examples

The canonical Hello world program can be expressed as follows:

```
#include <iostream>
```

```
int main()

{

    std::cout << "Hello, world!\n";

}
```

This program would output "Hello, world!" followed by a newline and standard output stream buffer flush.

The following example creates a file called 'file.txt' and puts the text 'Hello World' followed by a newline into it.

```
#include <fstream>

int main()

{

    std::ofstream file("file.txt");

    file << "Hello world!\n";

}
```

Decltype

In the C++ programming language, decltype is a keyword used to query the type of an expression. Introduced in C++11, its primary intended use is in generic programming, where it is often difficult, or even impossible, to express types that depend on template parameters.

As generic programming techniques became increasingly popular throughout the 1990s, the need for a type-deduction mechanism was recognized. Many compiler vendors implemented their own versions of the operator, typically called typeof, and some portable implementations with limited functionality, based on existing language features were developed. In 2002, Bjarne Stroustrup proposed that a standardized version of the operator be added to the C++ language, and suggested the name "decltype", to reflect that the operator would yield the "declared type" of an expression.

decltype's semantics were designed to cater to both generic library writers and novice programmers. In general, the deduced type matches the type of the object or function exactly as declared in the source code. Like the sizeof operator, decltype's operand is not evaluated.

Motivation

With the introduction of templates into the C++ programming language, and the advent of generic programming techniques pioneered by the Standard Template Library, the need for a mechanism for obtaining the type of an expression, commonly referred to as typeof, was recognized. In generic programming, it is often difficult or impossible to express types that depend on template parameters, in particular the return type of function template instantiations.

Many vendors provide the typeof operator as a compiler extension. As early as 1997, before C++ was fully standardized, Brian Parker proposed a portable solution based on the sizeof operator. His work was expanded on by Bill Gibbons, who concluded that the technique had several limitations and was generally less powerful than an actual typeof mechanism. In an October 2000 article of *Dr. Dobb's Journal*, Andrei Alexandrescu remarked that "having a typeof would make much template code easier to write and understand." He also noted that "typeof and sizeof share the same backend, because sizeof has to compute the type anyway." Andrew Koenig and Barbara E. Moo also recognized the usefulness of a built-in typeof facility, with the caveat that "using it often invites subtle programming errors, and there are some problems that it cannot solve." They characterized the use of type conventions, like the typedefs provided by the Standard Template Library, as a more powerful and general technique. However, Steve Dewhurst argued that such conventions are "costly to design and promulgate", and that it would be "much easier to ... simply extract the type of the expression." In a 2011 article on C++0x, Koenig and Moo predicted that "decltype will be widely used to make everyday programs easier to write."

In 2002, Bjarne Stroustrup suggested extending the C++ language with mechanisms for querying the type of an expression, and initializing objects without specifying the type. Stroustrup observed that the reference-dropping semantics offered by the typeof operator provided by the GCC and EDG compilers could be problematic. Conversely, an operator returning a reference type based on the lvalue-ness of the expression was deemed too confusing. The initial proposal to the C++ standards committee outlined a combination of the two variants; the operator would return a reference type only if the declared type of the expression included a reference. To emphasize that the deduced type would reflect the "declared type" of the expression, the operator was proposed to be named decltype.

One of the cited main motivations for the decltype proposal was the ability to write perfect forwarding function templates. It is sometimes desirable to write a generic forwarding function that returns the same type as the wrapped function, regardless of the type it is instantiated with. Without decltype, it is not generally possible to accomplish this. An example, which also utilizes the *trailing-return-type*:

```
int& foo(int& i);

float foo(float& f);



template <class T> auto transparent_forwarder(T& t) -> decl-
type(foo(t)) {

   return foo(t);

}
```

decltype is essential here because it preserves the information about whether the wrapped function returns a reference type.

Semantics

Similarly to the sizeof operator, the operand of decltype is unevaluated. Informally, the type returned by decltype(e) is deduced as follows:

1. If the expression e refers to a variable in local or namespace scope, a static member variable or a function parameter, then the result is that variable's or parameter's *declared type*

2. Otherwise, if e is an lvalue, decltype(e) is T&, where T is the type of e; if e is an xvalue, the result is T&&; otherwise, e is a prvalue and the result is T.

These semantics were designed to fulfill the needs of generic library writers, while at the same time being intuitive for novice programmers, because the return type of decltype always matches the type of the object or function exactly as declared in the source code. More formally, Rule 1 applies to unparenthesized *id-expressions* and class member access expressions. Example:

```
const int&& foo();

const int bar();

int i;

struct A { double x; };

const A* a = new A();

decltype(foo()) x1; // type is const int&&

decltype(bar()) x2; // type is int

decltype(i) x3; // type is int
```

```
decltype(a->x) x4; // type is double

decltype((a->x)) x5; // type is const double&
```

The reason for the difference between the latter two invocations of decltype is that the parenthesized expression (a->x) is neither an *id-expression* nor a member access expression, and therefore does not denote a named object. Because the expression is an lvalue, its deduced type is "reference to the type of the expression", or const double&.

In December 2008, a concern was raised to the committee by Jaakko Järvi over the inability to use decltype to form a *qualified-id*, which is inconsistent with the intent that decltype(e) should be treated "as if it were a *typedef-name*". While commenting on the formal Committee Draft for C++0x, the Japanese ISO member body noted that "a scope operator(::) cannot be applied to decltype, but it should be. It would be useful in the case to obtain member type(nested-type) from an instance as follows":

```
vector<int> v;

decltype(v)::value_type i = 0; // int i = 0;
```

This, and similar issues pertaining to the wording inhibiting the use of decltype in the declaration of a derived class and in a destructor call, were addressed by David Vandevoorde, and voted into the working paper in March 2010.

Availability

decltype is included in the C++ Language Standard since C++11. It is provided by a number of compilers as an extension. Microsoft's Visual C++ 2010 and later compilers provide a decltype type specifier that closely mimics the semantics as described in the standards committee proposal. It can be used with both managed and native code. The documentation states that it is "useful primarily to developers who write template libraries." decltype was added to the mainline of the GCC C++ compiler in version 4.3, released on March 5, 2008. decltype is also present in Codegear's C++ Builder 2009, the Intel C++ Compiler, and Clang.

References

- Stanley B. Lippman, Josee Lajoie (1999). C++ Primer (third ed.). Massachusetts: Addison-Wesley. pp. 1109–1112. ISBN 0-201-82470-1.

- Bjarne Stroustrup (1997 3rd Printing). The C++ programming language. Addison-Wesley. pp. 637–640. ISBN 0-201-88954-4.

- Vandevoorde, Daveed; Josuttis, Nicolai (2002). C++ Templates: The Complete Guide. Addison Wesley. ISBN 0-201-73484-2.

- Gregor, Douglas; Järvi, Jaakko; Siek, Jeremy; Stroustrup, Bjarne (2003-04-28). "Decltype and auto" (PDF). ISO/IEC JTC1/SC22/WG21 – The C++ Standards Committee. Retrieved 2015-08-28.

- Koenig, Andrew; Barbara E. Moo (2011-07-19). "4 Useful New Features in C++0x". Dr. Dobb's Journal. Retrieved 2012-01-12.

- Miller, William M. (2010-03-29). "C++ Standard Core Language Defect Reports, Revision 69". ISO/IEC JTC1/SC22/WG21 – The C++ Standards Committee. Retrieved 2010-04-10.

- Vandevoorde, Daveed (2010-02-03). "Core issues 743 and 950: Additional decltype(...) uses" (PDF). ISO/IEC JTC1/SC22/WG21 – The C++ Standards Committee. Retrieved 2010-04-10.

Methods and Tools of C++

Subroutine is a sequence of programming which is assigned to perform precise tasks, packaged as a unit. Exception safety on the other hand is a set of guidelines that can be used by clients when handling safety in any programming language, specifically C++. This chapter strategically encompasses and incorporates the major methods and tools of C++, providing a complete understanding.

C++ Classes

A class in C++ is a user defined type or data structure declared with keyword *class* that has data and functions (also called methods) as its members whose access is governed by the three access specifiers *private*, *protected* or *public* (by default access to members of a class is *private*). A class in C++ differs from a structure (declared with keyword *struct*) as by default, members are *private* in a class while they are *public* in a structure. The private members are not accessible outside the class; they can be accessed only through methods of the class. The public members form an interface to the class and are accessible outside the class. Instances of these data types are known as objects and can contain member variables, constants, member functions, and overloaded operators defined by the programmer.

Differences between Struct and Classes in C++

In C++, a *structure* is a class defined with the struct keyword. Its members and base classes are public by default. A class defined with the class keyword has private members and base classes by default. This is the only difference between structs and classes in C++.

Aggregate classes

An aggregate class is a class with no user-declared constructors, no private or protected non-static data members, no base classes, and no virtual functions. Such a class can be initialized with a brace-enclosed comma-separated list of initializer-clauses. The following code has the same semantics in both C and C++.

```
struct C

{
```

```
    int a;

    double b;

};


struct D

{

    int a;

    double b;

    C c;

};


// initialize an object of type C with an initializer-list

C c = {1, 2.0};


// D has a sub-aggregate of type C. In such cases initializ-
er-clauses can be nested

D d = {10, 20.0, {1, 2.0}};
```

POD-Structs

A POD-struct (Plain Old Data Structure) is an aggregate class that has no non-static data members of type non-POD-struct, non-POD-union (or array of such types) or reference, and has no user-defined assignment operator and no user-defined destructor. A POD-struct could be said to be the C++ equivalent of a C struct. In most cases, a POD-struct will have the same memory layout as a corresponding struct declared in C. For this reason, POD-structs are sometimes colloquially referred to as "C-style structs".

Properties Shared Between Structs in C and Pod-structs in C++

- Data members are allocated so that later members have higher addresses within an object, except where separated by an access-specifier.

- Two POD-struct types are layout-compatible if they have the same number of nonstatic data members, and corresponding nonstatic data members (in order) have layout-compatible types.

- A POD-struct may contain unnamed padding.

- A pointer to a POD-struct object, suitably converted using a reinterpret cast, points to its initial member and vice versa, implying that there is no padding at the beginning of a POD-struct.

- A POD-struct may be used with the offsetof macro.

Declaration and Usage

C++ classes have their own members. These members include variables (including other structures and classes), functions (specific identifiers or overloaded operators) known as methods, constructors and destructors. Members are declared to be either publicly or privately accessible using the public: and private: access specifiers respectively. Any member encountered after a specifier will have the associated access until another specifier is encountered. There is also inheritance between classes which can make use of the protected: specifier.

Global and Local Class

A class defined outside all methods is a global class because its objects can be created from anywhere in the program. If it is defined within a function body then it's a local class because objects of such a class are local to the function scope.

Basic Declaration and Member Variables

Classes are declared with the class or struct keyword. Declaration of members are placed within this declaration.

```
struct person              class person

{                          {

    string name;             public:

    int age;                   string
                           name;

                               int age;

};                         };
```

The above definitions are functionally equivalent. Either code will define objects of type person as having two public data members, name and age. The semicolons after the closing braces are mandatory.

After one of these declarations (but not both), person can be used as follows to create newly defined variables of the person datatype:

```cpp
#include <iostream>
#include <string>
using namespace std;

class person
{
  public:
    string name;
    int age;
};

int main()
{
  person a, b;
  a.name = "Calvin";
  b.name = "Hobbes";
  a.age = 30;
  b.age = 20;
  cout << a.name << ": " << a.age << endl;
  cout << b.name << ": " << b.age << endl;
  return 0;
}
```

Executing the above code will output

```
Calvin: 30
Hobbes: 20
```

Member Functions

An important feature of the C++ class and structure are member functions. Each data-type can have its own built-in functions (referred to as methods) that have access to all (public and private) members of the datatype. In the body of these non-static member functions, the keyword this can be used to refer to the object for which the function is called. This is commonly implemented by passing the address of the object as an implicit first argument to the function. Take the above person type as an example again:

```
class person

{

   std::string name;

   int age;

public:

   person()  :  age(5)  {  }

   void print() const;

};


void person::print() const

{

   cout << name << ":" << age << endl;

   /* "name" and "age" are the member variables.

      The "this" keyword is an expression whose value is the ad-
dress

      of the object for which the member was invoked. Its type
is

      const person*, because the function is declared const.

   */

}
```

In the above example the print() function is declared in the body of the class and defined by qualifying it with the name of the class followed by ::. Both name and age are private (default for class) and print() is declared as public which is necessary if it is to be used from outside the class.

With the member function print(), printing can be simplified into:

```
a.print();

b.print();
```

where a and b above are called senders, and each of them will refer to their own member variables when the print() function is executed.

It is common practice to separate the class or structure declaration (called its interface) and the definition (called its implementation) into separate units. The interface, needed by the user, is kept in a header and the implementation is kept separately in either source or compiled form.

Inheritance

The layout of non-POD classes in memory is not specified by the C++ standard. For example, many popular C++ compilers implement single inheritance by concatenation of the parent class fields with the child class fields, but this is not required by the standard. This choice of layout makes referring to a derived class via a pointer to the parent class type a trivial operation.

For example, consider

```
class P
{
    int x;
};
class C : public P
{
    int y;
};
```

An instance of P with a P* p pointing to it might look like this in memory:

```
+----+
|P::x|
+----+

↑

p
```

An instance of C with a P* p pointing to it might look like this:

```
+----+----+
|P::x|C::y|
```

```
+----+----+
```

↑

p

Therefore, any code that manipulates the fields of a P object can manipulate the P fields inside the C object without having to consider anything about the definition of C's fields. A properly written C++ program shouldn't make any assumptions about the layout of inherited fields, in any case. Using the static_cast or dynamic_cast type conversion operators will ensure that pointers are properly converted from one type to another.

Multiple inheritance is not as simple. If a class D inherits P and C, then the fields of both parents need to be stored in some order, but (at most) only one of the parent classes can be located at the front of the derived class. Whenever the compiler needs to convert a pointer from the D type to either P or C, the compiler will provide an automatic conversion from the address of the derived class to the address of the base class fields (typically, this is a simple offset calculation).

Overloaded Operators

In C++, operators, such as + - * /, can be overloaded to suit the needs of programmers. These operators are called overloadable operators.

By convention, overloaded operators should behave nearly the same as they do in built-in datatypes (int, float, etc.), but this is not required. One can declare a structure called integer in which the variable *really* stores an integer, but by calling integer * integer the sum, instead of the product, of the integers might be returned:

```
struct integer
{
    int i;
    integer(int j = 0) : i(j) {}
    integer operator*(const integer &k) const
    {
        return integer (i + k.i);
    }
};
```

The code above made use of a constructor to "construct" the return value. For clearer presentation (although this could decrease efficiency of the program if the compiler cannot optimize the statement into the equivalent one above), the above code can be rewritten as:

```
integer operator*(const integer &k) const

{

    integer m;

    m.i = i + k.i;

    return m;

}
```

Programmers can also put a prototype of the operator in the struct declaration and define the function of the operator in the global scope:

```
struct integer

{

    int i;


    integer(int j = 0) : i(j) {}


    integer operator* (const integer &k) const;

};



integer integer::operator* (const integer &k) const

{

    return integer(i * k.i);

}
```

i above represents the sender's own member variable, while k.i represents the member variable from the argument variable k.

The const keyword appears twice in the above code. The first occurrence, the argument const integer &k, indicated that the argument variable will not be changed by the function. The second incidence at the end of the declaration promises the compiler that the sender would not be changed by the function run.

In const integer &k, the ampersand (&) means "pass by reference". When the function is called, a pointer to the variable will be passed to the function, rather than the value of the variable.

The same overloading properties above apply also to classes.

Note that arity, associativity and precedence of operators cannot be changed.

Binary Overloadable Operators

Binary operators (operators with two arguments) are overloaded by declaring a function with an "identifier" *operator (something)* which calls one single argument. The variable on the left of the operator is the sender while that on the right is the argument.

```
integer i = 1;

/* we can initialize a structure variable this way as

    if calling a constructor with only the first

    argument specified. */

integer j = 3;

/* variable names are independent of the names of the

    member variables of the structure. */

integer k = i * j;

cout << k.i << endl;

'3' would be printed.
```

The following is a list of binary overloadable operators:

Operator	General usage
+ - * / %	Arithmetic calculation
^ & | << >>	Bitwise calculation
< > == != <= >=	Logical comparison
&&	Logical conjunction
||	Logical disjunction
+= -= *= /= %= ^= &= |= <<= >>=	Compound assignment
,	(no general usage)

The '=' (assignment) operator between two variables of the same structure type is overloaded by default to copy the entire content of the variables from one to another. It can be overwritten with something else, if necessary.

Operators must be overloaded one by one, in other words, no overloading is associated with one another. For example, < is not necessarily the opposite of >.

Unary Overloadable Operators

While some operators, as specified above, takes two terms, sender on the left and the argument on the right, some operators have only one argument - the sender, and they are said to be "unary". Examples are the negative sign (when nothing is put on the left of it) and the "logical NOT" (exclamation mark, !).

Sender of unary operators may be on the left or on the right of the operator. The following is a list of unary overloadable operators:

Operator	General usage	Position of sender
+ -	Positive / negative sign	right
* &	Dereference	right
! ~	Logical / bitwise NOT	right
++ --	Pre-increment / decrement	right
++ --	Post-increment / decrement	left

The syntax of an overloading of a unary operator, where the sender is on the right, is as follows:

```
return_type operator@ ()
```

When the sender is on the left, the declaration is:

```
return_type operator@ (int)
```

@ above stands for the operator to be overloaded. Replace return_type with the datatype of the return value (int, bool, structures etc.)

The int parameter essentially means nothing but a convention to show that the sender is on the left of the operator.

const arguments can be added to the end of the declaration if applicable.

Overloading Brackets

The square bracket [] and the round bracket () can be overloaded in C++ structures. The square bracket must contain exactly one argument, while the round bracket can contain any specific number of arguments, or no arguments.

The following declaration overloads the square bracket.

```
return_type operator[] (argument)
```

The content inside the bracket is specified in the argument part.

Round bracket is overloaded a similar way.

```
return_type operator() (arg1, arg2, ...)
```

Contents of the bracket in the operator call are specified in the second bracket.

In addition to the operators specified above, the arrow operator (->), the starred arrow (->*), the new keyword and the delete keyword can also be overloaded. These memory-or-pointer-related operators must process memory-allocating functions after overloading. Like the assignment (=) operator, they are also overloaded by default if no specific declaration is made.

Constructors

Sometimes programmers may want their variables to take a default or specific value upon declaration. This can be done by declaring constructors.

```
person::person(string N, int A)

{

    name = N;

    age = A;

}
```

Member variables can be initialized in an initializer list, with utilization of a colon, as in the example below. This differs from the above in that it initializes (using the constructor), rather than using the assignment operator. This is more efficient for class types, since it just needs to be constructed directly; whereas with assignment, they must be first initialized using the default constructor, and then assigned a different value. Also some types (like references and const types) cannot be assigned to and therefore must be initialized in the initializer list.

```
person(std::string N, int A) : name(N), age(A) {}
```

Note that the curly braces cannot be omitted, even if empty.

Default values can be given to the last arguments to help initializing default values.

```
person(std::string N = "", int A = 0) : name(N), age(A) {}
```

When no arguments are given to the constructor in the example above, it is equivalent to calling the following constructor with no arguments (a default constructor):

```
person() : name(""), age(0) {}
```

The declaration of a constructor looks like a function with the same name as the data-type. In fact, a call to a constructor can take the form of a function call. In that case a person type variable would be the return value:

```
int main()

{

    person r = person("Wales", 40);

    r.print();

}
```

The above code creates a temporary person object, and then assigns it to r using the copy constructor. A better way of creating the object (without unnecessary copying) is:

```
int main()

{

    person r ("Wales", 40);

    r.print ();

}
```

Specific program actions, which may or may not relate to the variable, can be added as part of the constructor.

```
person()

{

    std::cout << "Hello!" << endl;

}
```

With the above constructor, a "Hello!" will be printed in case a person variable with no specific value is initialized.

Default Constructor

Default constructors are called when constructors are not defined for the classes.

```
class A { int b;};

//Object created using parentheses
```

```
A *a = new A(); //Calls default constructor, and b will be ini-
tialized with '0'

//Object created using no parentheses

A *a = new A; // allocate memory, then call default construc-
tor, and b will have value '0'

//Object creation without new

A a;   //Just allocate memory, and b will have unknown garbage
value
```

However, if a *user defined constructor* was defined for the class, both of the above declarations will call this user defined constructor, whose defined code will be executed, but no default values will be assigned to the variable b.

Destructors

A destructor is the reverse of a constructor. It is called when an instance of a class is destroyed, e.g. when an object of a class created in a block (set of curly braces "{}") is deleted after the closing brace, then the destructor is called automatically. It will be called upon emptying of the memory location storing the variable. Destructors can be used to release resources, such as heap-allocated memory and opened files when an instance of that class is destroyed.

The syntax for declaring a destructor is similar to that of a constructor. There is no return value and the name of the method is the same as the name of the class with a tilde (~) in front.

```
~person()

{

    cout << "I'm deleting " << name << " with age " << age <<
endl;

}
```

Similarities between Constructors and Destructors

- Both have same name as the class in which they are declared.

- If not declared by user both are available in a class by default but they now can only allocate and deallocate memory from the objects of a class when an object is declared or deleted.

Class Templates

In C++, class declarations can be generated from class templates. Such class templates represent a family of classes. An actual class declaration is obtained by *instantiating* the template with one or more template arguments. A template instantiated with a particular set of arguments is called a template specialization.

Properties

The syntax of C++ tries to make every aspect of a structure look like that of the basic datatypes. Therefore, overloaded operators allow structures to be manipulated just like integers and floating-point numbers, arrays of structures can be declared with the square-bracket syntax (some_structure variable_name[size]), and pointers to structures can be dereferenced in the same way as pointers to built-in datatypes.

Memory Consumption

The memory consumption of a structure is at least the sum of the memory sizes of constituent variables. Take the twonums structure below as an example.

```
struct twonums

{

    int a;

    int b;

};
```

The structure consists of two integers. In many current C++ compilers, integers are 32-bit integers by default, so each of the member variables consume four bytes of memory. The entire structure, therefore, consumes at least (or exactly) eight bytes of memory, as follows.

```
+----+----+

| a  | b  |

+----+----+
```

However, the compiler may add padding between the variables or at the end of the structure to ensure proper data alignment for a given computer architecture, often padding variables to be 32-bit aligned. For example, the structure

```
struct bytes_and_such

{

    char c;

    char C;
```

```
    short int s;

    int i;

    double d;

};
```

could look like

```
+-+-+--+--+--+--+--------+
|c|C|XX|s |  i  |   d    |
+-+-+--+--+--+--+--------+
```

in memory, where XX are two unused bytes.

As structures may make use of pointers and arrays to declare and initialize its member variables, memory consumption of structures is not necessarily constant. Another example of non-constant memory size is template structures.

Bit Fields

Bit fields are used to define the class members that can occupy less storage than an integral type. This field is applicable only for integral types (int, char, short, long, etc.) and excludes float or double.

```
struct A

{
        unsigned a:2; // Possible values 0..3, occupies first 2
bits of int
        unsigned b:3; // Possible values 0..7, occupies next 3
bits of int
        unsigned :0;  // Moves to end of next integral type
        unsigned c:2;
        unsigned :4;  // Pads 4 bits in between c & d
        unsigned d:1;
        unsigned e:3;
};
```

- Memory structure

        4 byte int   4 byte int

```
[1] [2] [3] [4] [5] [6] [7] [8]
    [1]                          [2]                          [3]
[4]
    [a] [a] [b] [b] [b] [ ] [ ] [ ]  [ ] [ ] [ ] [ ] [ ] [ ] [ ] [ ]  [ ] [
] [ ] [ ] [ ] [ ] [ ] [ ]  [ ] [ ] [ ] [ ] [ ] [ ] [ ]

    [5]                          [6]                          [7]
[8]
    [c] [c] [ ] [ ] [ ] [ ] [ ] [d] [e]  [e] [e] [ ] [ ] [ ] [ ] [ ] [ ]  [ ] [
] [ ] [ ] [ ] [ ] [ ]  [ ] [ ] [ ] [ ] [ ] [ ] [ ]
```

Bit fields are not allowed in a union. It is applicable only for the classes defined using the keyword struct or class.

Pass by Reference

Many programmers prefer to use the ampersand (&) to declare the arguments of a function involving structures. This is because by using the dereferencing ampersand only one word (typically 4 bytes on a 32 bit machine, 8 bytes on a 64 bit machine) is required to be passed into the function, namely the memory location to the variable. Otherwise, if pass-by-value is used, the argument needs to be copied every time the function is called, which is costly with large structures.

Since pass-by-reference exposes the original structure to be modified by the function, the const keyword should be used to guarantee that the function does not modify the parameter, when this is not intended.

The This Keyword

To facilitate structures' ability to reference themselves, C++ implements the this keyword for all member functions. The this keyword acts as a pointer to the current object. Its type is that of a pointer to the current object.

The this keyword is especially important for member functions with the structure itself as the return value:

```
complex& operator+=(const complex & c)

{

    realPart += c.realPart;

    imagPart += c.imagPart;
```

```
    return *this;

}
```

As stated above, this is a pointer, so the use of the asterisk (*) is necessary to convert it into a reference to be returned.

Subroutine

In computer programming, a subroutine is a sequence of program instructions that perform a specific task, packaged as a unit. This unit can then be used in programs wherever that particular task should be performed. Subprograms may be defined within programs, or separately in libraries that can be used by multiple programs. In different programming languages, a subroutine may be called a procedure, a function, a routine, a method, or a subprogram. The generic term callable unit is sometimes used.

The name *subprogram* suggests a subroutine behaves in much the same way as a computer program that is used as one step in a larger program or another subprogram. A subroutine is often coded so that it can be started (called) several times and from several places during one execution of the program, including from other subroutines, and then branch back (*return*) to the next instruction after the *call*, once the subroutine's task is done. Maurice Wilkes, David Wheeler, and Stanley Gill are credited with the invention of this concept, which they termed a *closed subroutine*, contrasted with an *open subroutine* or macro.

Subroutines are a powerful programming tool, and the syntax of many programming languages includes support for writing and using them. Judicious use of subroutines (for example, through the structured programming approach) will often substantially reduce the cost of developing and maintaining a large program, while increasing its quality and reliability. Subroutines, often collected into libraries, are an important mechanism for sharing and trading software. The discipline of object-oriented programming is based on objects and methods (which are subroutines attached to these objects or object classes).

In the compiling method called threaded code, the executable program is basically a sequence of subroutine calls.

Main Concepts

The content of a subroutine is its body, which is the piece of program code that is executed when the subroutine is called or invoked.

A subroutine may be written so that it expects to obtain one or more data values from the calling program (its parameters or formal parameters). The calling program pro-

vides actual values for these parameters, called arguments. Different programming
languages may use different conventions for passing arguments:

Convention	Description	Common use
Call by value	Argument is evaluated and copy of value is passed to subroutine	Default in most Algol-like languages after Algol 60, such as Pascal, Delphi, Simula, CPL, PL/M, Modula, Oberon, Ada, and many others. C, C++, Java (References to objects and arrays are also passed by value)
Call by reference	Reference to argument, typically its address is passed	Selectable in most Algol-like languages after Algol 60, such as Algol 68, Pascal, Delphi, Simula, CPL, PL/M, Modula, Oberon, Ada, and many others. C++, Fortran, PL/I
Call by result	Parameter value is copied back to argument on return from the subroutine	Ada OUT parameters
Call by value-result	Parameter value is copied back on entry to the subroutine and again on return	Algol
Call by name	Like a macro – replace the parameters with the unevaluated argument expressions	Algol, Scala
Call by constant value	Like call by value except that the parameter is treated as a constant	PL/I NONASSIGNABLE parameters, Ada IN parameters

The subroutine may return a computed value to its caller (its return value), or provide
various result values or output parameters. Indeed, a common use of subroutines is to
implement mathematical functions, in which the purpose of the subroutine is purely to
compute one or more results whose values are entirely determined by the parameters
passed to the subroutine. (Examples might include computing the logarithm of a number or the determinant of a matrix.)

A subroutine call may also have side effects such as modifying data structures in a computer memory, reading from or writing to a peripheral device, creating a file, halting the
program or the machine, or even delaying the program's execution for a specified time.
A subprogram with side effects may return different results each time it is called, even
if it is called with the same arguments. An example is a random number function, available in many languages, that returns a different pseudo-random number each time it is
called. The widespread use of subroutines with side effects is a characteristic of imperative programming languages.

A subroutine can be coded so that it may call itself recursively, at one or more places,
to perform its task. This method allows direct implementation of functions defined by
mathematical induction and recursive divide and conquer algorithms.

A subroutine whose purpose is to compute one boolean-valued function (that is, to answer a yes/no question) is sometimes called a predicate. In logic programming languages, often all subroutines are called predicates, since they primarily determine success or failure. For example, any type of function is a subroutine but not main().

Language Support

High-level programming languages usually include specific constructs to:

- delimit the part of the program (body) that makes up the subroutine
- assign an identifier (name) to the subroutine
- specify the names and data types of its parameters and return values
- provide a private naming scope for its temporary variables
- identify variables outside the subroutine that are accessible within it
- call the subroutine
- provide values to its parameters
- specify the return values from within its body
- return to the calling program
- dispose of the values returned by a call
- handle any exceptional conditions encountered during the call
- package subroutines into a module, library, object, class, etc.

Some programming languages, such as Pascal, Fortran, Ada and many dialects of BASIC, distinguish between functions or function subprograms, which provide an explicit return value to the calling program, and subroutines or procedures, which do not. In those languages, function calls are normally embedded in expressions (e.g., a sqrt function may be called as y = z + sqrt(x)). Procedure calls either behave syntactically as statements (e.g., a print procedure may be called as if x > 0 then print(x) or are explicitly invoked by a statement such as CALL or GOSUB (e.g. call print(x)). Other languages, such as C and Lisp, do not distinguish between functions and subroutines.

In strictly functional programming languages such as Haskell, subprograms can have no side effects, which means that various internal states of the program will not change. Functions will always return the same result if repeatedly called with the same arguments. Such languages typically only support functions, since subroutines that do not return a value have no use unless they can cause a side effect.

In programming languages such as C, C++, and C#, subroutines may also simply be called functions, not to be confused with mathematical functions or functional programming, which are different concepts.

A language's compiler will usually translate procedure calls and returns into machine instructions according to a well-defined calling convention, so that subroutines can be compiled separately from the programs that call them. The instruction sequences corresponding to call and return statements are called the procedure's prologue and epilogue.

Advantages

The advantages of breaking a program into subroutines include:

- Decomposing a complex programming task into simpler steps: this is one of the two main tools of structured programming, along with data structures

- Reducing duplicate code within a program

- Enabling reuse of code across multiple programs

- Dividing a large programming task among various programmers, or various stages of a project

- Hiding implementation details from users of the subroutine

- Improving traceability (i.e. most languages offer ways to obtain the call trace which includes the names of the involved subroutines and perhaps even more information such as file names and line numbers); by not decomposing the code into subroutines, debugging would be impaired severely

Disadvantages

Invoking a subroutine (versus using in-line code) imposes some computational overhead in the call mechanism.

The subroutine typically requires standard housekeeping code – both at entry to, and exit from, the function (function prologue and epilogue – usually saving general purpose registers and return address as a minimum).

History

The idea of a subroutine was worked out after computing machines had already existed for some time. The arithmetic and conditional jump instructions were planned ahead of time and have changed relatively little; but the special instructions used for procedure calls have changed greatly over the years. The earliest computers and microprocessors, such as the Small-Scale Experimental Machine and the RCA 1802, did not have a single subroutine call instruction. Subroutines could be implemented, but they required programmers to use the call sequence—a series of instructions—at each call site. Some very early computers and microprocessors, such as the IBM 1620, the Intel 8008, and the PIC microcontrollers, have a single-instruction subroutine call that uses dedicated hardware stack to store return addresses—such hardware supports only a few levels of subroutine nesting, but can support recursive subroutines. Machines before the mid 1960s—such as the UNIVAC I, the PDP-1, and the IBM 1130—typically use a calling convention which saved the instruction counter in the first memory location of the called subroutine. This allows arbitrarily deep levels of subroutine nesting, but does not support recursive subroutines. The PDP-11 (1970) is one of the first computers with a stack-pushing subroutine call instruction; this feature supports both arbitrarily deep subroutine nesting and also supports recursive subroutines.

Language Support

In the very early assemblers, subroutine support was limited. Subroutines were not explicitly separated from each other or from the main program, and indeed the source code of a subroutine could be interspersed with that of other subprograms. Some assemblers would offer predefined macros to generate the call and return sequences. By the 1960s, assemblers usually had much more sophisticated support for both inline and separately assembled subroutines that could be linked together.

Subroutine Libraries

Even with this cumbersome approach, subroutines proved very useful. For one thing they allowed use of the same code in many different programs. Moreover, memory was a very scarce resource on early computers, and subroutines allowed significant savings in the size of programs.

Many early computers loaded the program instructions into memory from a punched paper tape. Each subroutine could then be provided by a separate piece of tape, loaded or spliced before or after the main program (or "mainline"); and the same subroutine tape could then be used by many different programs. A similar approach applied in computers which used punched cards for their main input. The name *subroutine library* originally meant a library, in the literal sense, which kept indexed collections of tapes or card-decks for collective use.

Return by Indirect Jump

To remove the need for self-modifying code, computer designers eventually provided an *indirect jump* instruction, whose operand, instead of being the return address itself, was the location of a variable or processor register containing the return address.

On those computers, instead of modifying the subroutine's return jump, the calling program would store the return address in a variable so that when the subroutine completed, it would execute an indirect jump that would direct execution to the location given by the predefined variable.

Jump to Subroutine

Another advance was the *jump to subroutine* instruction, which combined the saving of the return address with the calling jump, thereby minimizing overhead significantly.

In the IBM System/360, for example, the branch instructions BAL or BALR, designed for procedure calling, would save the return address in a processor register specified in the instruction. To return, the subroutine had only to execute an indirect branch instruction (BR) through that register. If the subroutine needed that register for some other purpose (such as calling another subroutine), it would save the register's contents to a private memory location or a register stack.

In systems such as the HP 2100, the JSB instruction would perform a similar task, except that the return address was stored in the memory location that was the target of the branch. Execution of the procedure would actually begin at the next memory location. In the HP 2100 assembly language, one would write, for example

```
      . . .

      JSB MYSUB      (Calls subroutine MYSUB.)

 BB   . . .          (Will return here after MYSUB is done.)
```

to call a subroutine called MYSUB from the main program. The subroutine would be coded as

```
 MYSUB NOP           (Storage for MYSUB's return address.)

 AA    . . .         (Start of MYSUB's body.)

       . . .

       JMP MYSUB,I   (Returns to the calling program.)
```

The JSB instruction placed the address of the NEXT instruction (namely, BB) into the location specified as its operand (namely, MYSUB), and then branched to the NEXT location after that (namely, AA = MYSUB + 1). The subroutine could then return to the main program by executing the indirect jump JMP MYSUB,I which branched to the location stored at location MYSUB.

Compilers for Fortran and other languages could easily make use of these instructions when available. This approach supported multiple levels of calls; however, since the return address, parameters, and return values of a subroutine were assigned fixed memory locations, it did not allow for recursive calls.

Incidentally, a similar method was used by Lotus 1-2-3, in the early 1980s, to discover the recalculation dependencies in a spreadsheet. Namely, a location was reserved in each cell to store the *return* address. Since circular references are not allowed for natural recalculation order, this allows a tree walk without reserving space for a stack in memory, which was very limited on small computers such as the IBM PC.

Call Stack

Most modern implementations use a call stack, a special case of the stack data structure, to implement subroutine calls and returns. Each procedure call creates a new entry, called a *stack frame*, at the top of the stack; when the procedure returns, its stack frame is deleted from the stack, and its space may be used for other procedure calls. Each stack frame contains the *private data* of the corresponding call, which typically includes the procedure's parameters and internal variables, and the return address.

The call sequence can be implemented by a sequence of ordinary instructions (an approach still used in reduced instruction set computing (RISC) and very long instruction word (VLIW) architectures), but many traditional machines designed since the late 1960s have included special instructions for that purpose.

The call stack is usually implemented as a contiguous area of memory. It is an arbitrary design choice whether the bottom of the stack is the lowest or highest address within this area, so that the stack may grow forwards or backwards in memory; however, many architectures chose the latter.

Some designs, notably some Forth implementations, used two separate stacks, one mainly for control information (like return addresses and loop counters) and the other for data. The former was, or worked like, a call stack and was only indirectly accessible to the programmer through other language constructs while the latter was more directly accessible.

When stack-based procedure calls were first introduced, an important motivation was to save precious memory. With this scheme, the compiler does not have to reserve separate space in memory for the private data (parameters, return address, and local variables) of each procedure. At any moment, the stack contains only the private data of the calls that are currently *active* (namely, which have been called but haven't returned yet). Because of the ways in which programs were usually assembled from libraries, it was (and still is) not uncommon to find programs that include thousands of subroutines, of which only a handful are active at any given moment. For such programs, the call stack mechanism could save significant amounts of memory. Indeed, the call stack mechanism can be viewed as the earliest and simplest method for automatic memory management.

However, another advantage of the call stack method is that it allows recursive subroutine calls, since each nested call to the same procedure gets a separate instance of its private data.

Delayed Stacking

One disadvantage of the call stack mechanism is the increased cost of a procedure call and its matching return. The extra cost includes incrementing and decrementing the stack pointer (and, in some architectures, checking for stack overflow), and accessing the local variables and parameters by frame-relative addresses, instead of absolute addresses. The cost may be realized in increased execution time, or increased processor complexity, or both.

This overhead is most obvious and objectionable in *leaf procedures* or *leaf functions*, which return without making any procedure calls themselves. To reduce that overhead, many modern compilers try to delay the use of a call stack until it is really needed. For example, the call of a procedure *P* may store the return address and parameters of the called procedure in certain processor registers, and transfer control to the procedure's body by a simple jump. If procedure *P* returns without making any other call, the call stack is not used at all. If *P* needs to call another procedure *Q*, it will then use the call stack to save the contents of any registers (such as the return address) that will be needed after *Q* returns.

C and C++ Examples

In the C and C++ programming languages, subprograms are termed *functions* (or *member functions* when associated with a class). These languages use the special keyword void to indicate that a function takes no parameters (especially in C) or does not return any value. Note that C/C++ functions can have side-effects, including modifying any variables whose addresses are passed as parameters (i.e., *passed by reference*). Examples:

```
void function1(void) { /* some code */ }
```

The function does not return a value and has to be called as a stand-alone function, e.g., function1();

```
int function2(void)

{

    return 5;

}
```

This function returns a result (the number 5), and the call can be part of an expression, e.g., x + function2()

```
char function3(int number)

{

    char selection[] = {'S','M','T','W','T','F','S'};
```

```
        return selection[number];

}
```

This function converts a number between 0 and 6 into the initial letter of the corresponding day of the week, namely 0 to 'S', 1 to 'M', ..., 6 to 'S'. The result of calling it might be assigned to a variable, e.g., num_day = function3(number);.

```
void function4(int *pointer_to_var)

{

        (*pointer_to_var)++;

}
```

This function does not return a value but modifies the variable whose address is passed as the parameter; it would be called with "function4(&variable_to_increment);".

Visual Basic 6 Examples

In the Visual Basic 6 language, subprograms are termed *functions* or *subs* (or *methods* when associated with a class). Visual Basic 6 uses various terms called *types* to define what is being passed as a parameter. By default, an unspecified variable is registered as a variant type and can be passed as *ByRef* (default) or *ByVal*. Also, when a function or sub is declared, it is given a public, private, or friend designation, which determines whether it can be accessed outside the module or project that it was declared in.

- By value [ByVal] – a way of passing the value of an argument to a procedure instead of passing the address. This allows the procedure to access a copy of the variable. As a result, the variable's actual value can't be changed by the procedure to which it is passed.

- By reference [ByRef] – a way of passing the address of an argument to a procedure instead of passing the value. This allows the procedure to access the actual variable. As a result, the variable's actual value can be changed by the procedure to which it is passed. Unless otherwise specified, arguments are passed by reference.

- Public (optional) – indicates that the function procedure is accessible to all other procedures in all modules. If used in a module that contains an Option Private, the procedure is not available outside the project.

- Private (optional) – indicates that the function procedure is accessible only to other procedures in the module where it is declared.

- Friend (optional) – used only in a class module. Indicates that the Function procedure is visible throughout the project, but not visible to a controller of an instance of an object.

```
Private Function Function1()

    ` Some Code Here

End Function
```

The function does not return a value and has to be called as a stand-alone function, e.g., Function1

```
Private Function Function2() as Integer

    Function2 = 5

End Function
```

This function returns a result (the number 5), and the call can be part of an expression, e.g., x + Function2()

```
Private Function Function3(ByVal intValue as Integer) as String

    Dim strArray(6) as String

    strArray = Array("M", "T", "W", "T", "F", "S", "S")

    Function3 = strArray(intValue)

End Function
```

This function converts a number between 0 and 6 into the initial letter of the corresponding day of the week, namely 0 to 'M', 1 to 'T', ..., 6 to 'S'. The result of calling it might be assigned to a variable, e.g., num_day = Function3(number).

```
Private Function Function4(ByRef intValue as Integer)

    intValue = intValue + 1

End Function
```

This function does not return a value but modifies the variable whose address is passed as the parameter; it would be called with "Function4(variable_to_increment)".

PL/I Example

In PL/I a called procedure may be passed a *descriptor* providing information about the argument, such as string lengths and array bounds. This allows the procedure to be more general and eliminates the need for the programmer to pass such information. By default PL/I passes arguments by reference. A (trivial) subroutine to change the sign of each element of a two-dimensional array might look like:

```
change_sign: procedure(array);

  declare array(*,*) float;

  array = -array;

  end change_sign;
```

This could be called with various arrays as follows:

```
/* first array bounds from -5 to +10 and 3 to 9 */

declare array1 (-5:10, 3:9)float;

/* second array bounds from 1 to 16 and 1 to 16 */

declare array2 (16,16) float;

call change_sign(array1);

call change_sign(array2);
```

Local Variables, Recursion and Reentrancy

A subprogram may find it useful to make use of a certain amount of *scratch* space; that is, memory used during the execution of that subprogram to hold intermediate results. Variables stored in this scratch space are termed *local variables*, and the scratch space is termed an *activation record*. An activation record typically has a return address that tells it where to pass control back to when the subprogram finishes.

A subprogram may have any number and nature of call sites. If recursion is supported, a subprogram may even call itself, causing its execution to suspend while another *nested* execution of the same subprogram occurs. Recursion is a useful means to simplify some complex algorithms, and breaking down complex problems. Recursive languages generally provide a new copy of local variables on each call. If the programmer desires the value of local variables to stay the same between calls, they can be declared *static* in some languages, or global values or common areas can be used. Here is an example of recursive subroutine in C/C++ to find Fibonacci numbers:

```
int fib(int n)

{

        if(n<=1) return n;

        return fib(n-1)+fib(n-2);

}
```

Early languages like Fortran did not initially support recursion because variables were statically allocated, as well as the location for the return address. Most computers before the late 1960s such as the PDP-8 did not have support for hardware stack registers.

Modern languages after ALGOL such as PL/1 and C almost invariably use a stack, usually supported by most modern computer instruction sets to provide a fresh activation record for every execution of a subprogram. That way, the nested execution is free to modify its local variables without concern for the effect on other suspended executions in progress. As nested calls accumulate, a call stack structure is formed, consisting of one activation record for each suspended subprogram. In fact, this stack structure is virtually ubiquitous, and so activation records are commonly termed *stack frames*.

Some languages such as Pascal and Ada also support nested subroutines, which are subroutines callable only within the scope of an outer (parent) subroutine. Inner subroutines have access to the local variables of the outer subroutine that called them. This is accomplished by storing extra context information within the activation record, also termed a *display*.

If a subprogram can function properly even when called while another execution is already in progress, that subprogram is said to be *reentrant*. A recursive subprogram must be reentrant. Reentrant subprograms are also useful in multi-threaded situations, since multiple threads can call the same subprogram without fear of interfering with each other. In the IBM CICS transaction processing system, *quasi-reentrant* was a slightly less restrictive, but similar, requirement for application programs that were shared by many threads.

In a multi-threaded environment, there is generally more than one stack. An environment that fully supports coroutines or lazy evaluation may use data structures other than stacks to store their activation records.

Overloading

In strongly typed languages, it is sometimes desirable to have a number of functions with the same name, but operating on different types of data, or with different parameter profiles. For example, a square root function might be defined to operate on reals, complex values or matrices. The algorithm to be used in each case is different, and the return result may be different. By writing three separate functions with the same name, the programmer has the convenience of not having to remember different names for each type of data. Further if a subtype can be defined for the reals, to separate positive and negative reals, two functions can be written for the reals, one to return a real when the parameter is positive, and another to return a complex value when the parameter is negative.

In object-oriented programming, when a series of functions with the same name can accept different parameter profiles or parameters of different types, each of the functions is said to be overloaded.

Here is an example of subroutine overloading in C++:

```cpp
#include <iostream>


double area (double h, double w) {

    return h * w;

}


double area (double r) {

    return r * r * 3.14;

}


int main () {

    double rectangle_area = area(3, 4);

    double circle_area = area(5);


    std::cout << "Area of a rectangle is " << rectangle_area << std::endl;

    std::cout << "Area of a circle is " << circle_area << std::endl;


    return 0;

}
```

In this code there are two functions of same name but they have different parameters.

As another example, a subroutine might construct an object that will accept directions, and trace its path to these points on screen. There are a plethora of parameters that could be passed in to the constructor (colour of the trace, starting x and y co-ordinates, trace speed). If the programmer wanted the constructor to be able to accept only the color parameter, then he could call another constructor that accepts only color, which in turn calls the constructor with all the parameters passing in a set of *default values* for all the other parameters (X and Y would generally be centered on screen or placed at the origin, and the speed would be set to another value of the coder's choosing).

Closures

A *closure* is a subprogram together with the values of some of its variables captured from the environment in which it was created. Closures were a notable feature of the Lisp programming language, introduced by John McCarthy. Depending on the implementation, closures can serve as a mechanism for side-effects.

Conventions

A wide number of conventions for the coding of subroutines have been developed. Pertaining to their naming, many developers have adopted the approach that the name of a subroutine should be a verb when it does a certain task, an adjective when it makes some inquiry, and a noun when it is used to substitute variables.

Some programmers suggest that a subroutine should perform only one task, and if a subroutine does perform more than one task, it should be split up into more subroutines. They argue that subroutines are key components in code maintenance, and their roles in the program must remain distinct.

Proponents of modular programming (modularizing code) advocate that each subroutine should have minimal dependency on other pieces of code. For example, the use of global variables is generally deemed unwise by advocates for this perspective, because it adds tight coupling between the subroutine and these global variables. If such coupling is not necessary, their advice is to refactor subroutines to accept passed parameters instead. However, increasing the number of parameters passed to subroutines can affect code readability.

Return Codes

Besides its *main* or *normal* effect, a subroutine may need to inform the calling program about *exceptional* conditions that may have occurred during its execution. In some languages and programming standards, this is often done through a *return code*, an integer value placed by the subroutine in some standard location, which encodes the normal and exceptional conditions.

In the IBM System/360, where a return code was expected from the subroutine, the return value was often designed to be a multiple of 4—so that it could be used as a direct branch table index into a branch table often located immediately after the call instruction to avoid extra conditional tests, further improving efficiency. In the System/360 assembly language, one would write, for example:

```
          BAL   14,SUBRTN01      go to subroutine, storing return
address in R14

          B     TABLE(15)        use returned value in reg 15 to
index the branch table,

*                                 branching to the appropriate
branch instr.

TABLE     B     OK               return code =00   GOOD
}

          B     BAD              return code =04   Invalid input
} Branch table

          B     ERROR            return code =08   Unexpected
condition }
```

Optimization of Subroutine Calls

There is a significant runtime overhead in a calling a subroutine, including passing the arguments, branching to the subprogram, and branching back to the caller. The overhead often includes saving and restoring certain processor registers, allocating and reclaiming call frame storage, etc.. In some languages, each subroutine call also implies automatic testing of the subroutine's return code, or the handling of exceptions that it may raise. In object-oriented languages, a significant source of overhead is the intensively used dynamic dispatch for method calls.

There are some seemingly obvious optimizations of procedure calls that cannot be applied if the procedures may have side effects. For example, in the expression $(f(x)-1)/(f(x)+1)$, the function f must be called twice, because the two calls may return different results. Moreover, the value of x must be fetched again before the second call, since the first call may have changed it. Determining whether a subprogram may have a side effect is very difficult (indeed, undecidable). So, while those optimizations are safe in purely functional programming languages, compilers of typical imperative programming usually have to assume the worst.

Inlining

A method used to eliminate this overhead is *inline expansion* or *inlining* of the subprogram's body at each call site (versus branching to the subroutine and back). Not only does this avoid the call overhead, but it also allows the compiler to optimize the procedure's *body* more effectively by taking into account the context and arguments at that call. The inserted body can be optimized by the compiler. Inlining however, will usually increase the code size, unless the program contains only one call to the subroutine, or the subroutine body is less code than the call overhead.

Exception Safety

Exception safety guarantees, originally formalized by David Abrahams, are a set of contractual guidelines that class library implementers and clients can use when reasoning about exception handling safety in any programming language that uses exceptions, particularly C++.

There are several levels of exception safety (in decreasing order of safety):

1. No-throw guarantee, also known as failure transparency: Operations are guaranteed to succeed and satisfy all requirements even in exceptional situations. If an exception occurs, it will be handled internally and not observed by clients.

2. Strong exception safety, also known as commit or rollback semantics: Operations can fail, but failed operations are guaranteed to have no side effects, so all data retain their original values.

3. Basic exception safety, also known as a no-leak guarantee: Partial execution of failed operations can cause side effects, but all invariants are preserved and there are no resource leaks (including memory leaks). Any stored data will contain valid values, even if they differ from what they were before the exception.

4. No exception safety: No guarantees are made.

Usually, at least basic exception safety is required to write robust code in such languages. Higher levels of safety can sometimes be difficult to achieve, and might incur an overhead due to extra copying. A key mechanism for exception safety is a finally clause, or similar exception handling syntax, which ensure that certain code is *always* run when a block is exited, including by exceptions. Several languages have constructs that simplify this, notably using the dispose pattern, named as using, with, or try-with-resources.

Example

Consider a smart vector type, such as C++'s std::vector or Java's ArrayList. When an item x is added to a vector v, the vector must actually add x to the internal list of objects and update a count field that says how many objects are in v. It may also need to allocate new memory if the existing capacity isn't sufficient.

Exception safety alternatives:

No-throw guarantee

> Very difficult or impossible to implement, since memory allocation may fail and throw an exception. Handling allocation failure would then be problematic, since repeated attempts are also likely to fail.

Strong exception safety

> Can be implemented fairly easily by doing any allocation first and then copying into a temporary buffer that is eventually swapped if no errors are encountered. In this case, insertion of x into v will either succeed, or v will remain unchanged.

Basic exception safety

> Implemented by ensuring that the size field is guaranteed to be updated if x is successfully inserted. Also, all allocations need to be handled in a way that prevents any chance of a resource leak, regardless of failure.

No exception safety

> Implementation in which an insertion failure might lead to corrupted content in v, an incorrect size value, or a resource leak.

Rule of Three (C++ Programming)

The *rule of three* and *rule of five* are rules of thumb in C++ for the building of exception-safe code and for formalizing rules on resource management. It accomplishes this by prescribing how the default members of a class should be used to accomplish this task in a systematic manner.

Rule of Three

The *rule of three* (also known as the Law of The Big Three or The Big Three) is a rule of thumb in C++ (prior to C++11) that claims that if a class defines one (or more) of the following it should probably explicitly define all three:

- destructor
- copy constructor
- copy assignment operator

These three functions are special member functions. If one of these functions is used without first being declared by the programmer it will be implicitly implemented by the compiler with the following default semantics:

- *Destructor* – Call the destructors of all the object's class-type members

- *Copy constructor* – Construct all the object's members from the corresponding members of the copy constructor's argument, calling the copy constructors of the object's class-type members, and doing a plain assignment of all non-class type (e.g., *int* or pointer) data members

- *Copy assignment operator* – Assign all the object's members from the corresponding members of the assignment operator's argument, calling the copy assignment operators of the object's class-type members, and doing a plain assignment of all non-class type (e.g. *int* or pointer) data members.

The Rule of Three claims that if one of these had to be defined by the programmer, it means that the compiler-generated version does not fit the needs of the class in one case and it will probably not fit in the other cases either. The term "Rule of three" was coined by Marshall Cline in 1991.

An amendment to this rule is that if the class is designed in such a way that Resource Acquisition Is Initialization (RAII) is used for all its (nontrivial) members, the destructor may be left undefined (also known as The Law of The Big Two). A ready-to-go example of this approach is the use of smart pointers instead of plain ones.

Because implicitly-generated constructors and assignment operators simply copy all class data members ("shallow copy"), one should define explicit copy constructors and copy assignment operators for classes that encapsulate complex data structures or have external references such as pointers, if you need to copy the objects pointed to by the class members. If the default behavior ("shallow copy") is actually the intended one, then an explicit definition, although redundant, will be a "self-documenting code" indicating that it was an intention rather than an oversight.

Rule of Five

With the advent of C++11 the rule of three can be broadened to *the rule of five* as C++11 implements *move semantics*, allowing destination objects to *grab* (or *steal*) data from temporary objects. The following example also shows the new moving members: move constructor and move assignment operator. Consequently, for *the rule of five* we have the following *special members*:

- destructor

- copy constructor

- move constructor

- copy assignment operator

- move assignment operator

Situations exist where classes may need destructors, but cannot sensibly implement copy and move constructors and copy and move assignment operators. This happens, for example, when the base class does not support these latter *Big Four* members, but the derived class's constructor allocates memory for its own use. In C++11, this can be simplified by explicitly specifying the five members as default.

Example in C++

```cpp
#include <cstring>

#include <iostream>


class Foo

{

public:

    /** Default constructor */

    Foo() :

        data (new char)

    {

        std::strcpy(data, "Hello, World!");

    }


    /** Copy constructor */

    Foo (const Foo& other) :

        data (new char[std::strlen (other.data) + 1])

    {

        std::strcpy(data, other.data);

    }


    /** Move constructor */

    Foo (Foo&& other) noexcept : /* noexcept needed to enable
optimizations in containers */

        data(other.data)

    {
```

```
        other.data = nullptr;

    }


    /** Destructor */

    ~Foo() noexcept /* explicitly specified destructors should
be annotated noexcept as best-practice */

    {

        delete[] data;

    }


    /** Copy assignment operator */

    Foo& operator= (const Foo& other)

    {

        Foo tmp(other);          // re-use copy-constructor

        *this = std::move(tmp); // re-use move-assignment

        return *this;

    }


    /** Move assignment operator */

    Foo& operator= (Foo&& other) noexcept

    {

        delete[] data;

        data = other.data;

        other.data = nullptr;

        return *this;

    }
```

```cpp
private:

    friend std::ostream& operator<< (std::ostream& os, const
Foo& foo)

    {

        os << foo.data;

        return os;

    }


    char* data;

};


int main()

{

    const Foo foo;

    std::cout << foo << std::endl;


    return 0;

}
```

Trait (Computer Programming)

In computer programming, a *trait* is a concept used in object-oriented programming, which represents a set of methods that can be used to extend the functionality of a class.

Characteristics

Traits both provide a set of methods that implement behaviour to a class, and require that the class implement a set of methods that parameterize the provided behaviour.

For inter-object communication (and sharing between objects), traits are somewhat between an object-oriented protocol (interface) and a mixin. An interface may define one or more behaviors via method signatures, while a trait defines behaviors via full method definitions: i.e., it includes the body of the methods. In contrast, mixins include full method definitions and may also carry state through member variable, while traits usually don't.

Hence an object defined as a trait is created as the composition of methods, which can be used by other classes without requiring multiple inheritance. In case of a naming collision, when more than one trait to be used by a class has a method with the same name, the programmer must explicitly disambiguate which one of those methods will be used in the class; thus manually solving the *diamond problem* of multiple inheritance. This is different from other composition methods in object-oriented programming, where conflicting names are automatically resolved by scoping rules.

Whereas mixins can be composed only using the inheritance operation, traits offer a much wider selection of operations, including:

- *symmetric sum*: an operation that merges two disjoint traits to create a new trait

- *override* (or *asymmetric sum*): an operation that forms a new trait by adding methods to an existing trait, possibly overriding some of its methods

- *alias*: an operation that creates a new trait by adding a new name for an existing method

- *exclusion*: an operation that forms a new trait by removing a method from an existing trait. (Combining this with the alias operation yields a *shallow rename* operation).

Traits are composed in the following ways:

- Trait composition is commutative; the ordering of adding traits does not matter. For example, given trait $S = A + B$, then trait $T = B + A$ is the same as S.

- Conflicting methods are excluded from the composition.

- Nested traits are equivalent to flattened traits; the composition hierarchy does not affect the traits behaviour. For example given trait $S = A + X$, where $X = B + C$, then trait $T = A + B + C$ is the same as S.

Supported Languages

Traits come originally from the programming language Self and are supported by the following programming languages:

- AmbientTalk: Combines the properties of Self traits (object-based multiple inheritance) and Smalltalk's Squeak traits (requiring explicit composition of traits by the programmer). It builds on the research on *stateful* and *freezable* traits to enable state within traits, which was not allowed in the first definitions.

- C++: Used in Standard Template Library and the C++ standard library to support generic container classes and in the Boost TypeTraits library.

- Curl: Abstract classes as mixins permit method implementations and thus constitute traits by another name.

- D: Since version 2.003, the __traits language extension and std.traits module helper templates provide compile-time traits. Together with other language features (notably templates and mixins), they allow flexible automatic generation of methods based on interfaces and types. D also allows explicit aliasing of member methods and variables, including forwarding to multiple member classes.

- Fortress

- Groovy: Since version 2.3

- Java: Since version 8, Java has support for *default methods*, which have some properties of traits.

- JavaScript: Traits can be implemented via functions and delegations or through libraries that provide traits.

- Kotlin: Traits have been called *interfaces* since M12.

- Lasso

- Perl: Called *roles*, they are implemented in Perl 5 libraries such as Moose, Role::Tiny and Role::Basic. Roles are part of the language in Perl 6.

- PHP: Since version 5.4, PHP allows users to specify templates that provide the ability to "inherit" from more than one (trait-)class, as a pseudo multiple inheritance.

- Python: Via a third-party library, or via higher-order mixin classes

- Racket: Supports traits as a library and uses macros, structures, and first-class classes to implement them.

- Ruby: *Module mixins* can be used to implement traits.

- Rust

- Scala trait is builtin supported with the key word *trait*.

- Smalltalk: Traits are implemented in two dialects of Smalltalk, Squeak and Pharo.

- Swift: Traits can be implemented with *protocol extensions.*

Examples

PHP

This example uses a trait to enhance other classes:

```php
// The template

trait TSingleton

{

    private static $_instance = null;


    public static function getInstance()

    {

        if (null === self::$_instance)

        {

            self::$_instance = new self();

        }


        return self::$_instance;

    }

}


class FrontController

{

    use TSingleton;

}
```

```
// Can also be used in already extended classes
class WebSite extends SomeClass
{
    use TSingleton;
}
```

This allows simulating aspects of multiple inheritance:

```
trait TBounding
{
    public $x, $y, $width, $height;
}


trait TMoveable
{
    public function moveTo($x, $y)
    {
        // ...
    }
}


trait TResizeable
{
    public function resize($newWidth, $newHeight)
    {
        // ...
    }
```

```
}


class Rectangle

{

    use TBounding, TMoveable, TResizeable;


    public function fillColor($color)

    {

        // ...

    }

}
```

Charm++

Charm++ is a parallel object-oriented programming language based on C++ and developed in the Parallel Programming Laboratory at the University of Illinois. Charm++ is designed with the goal of enhancing programmer productivity by providing a high-level abstraction of a parallel program while at the same time delivering good performance on a wide variety of underlying hardware platforms. Programs written in Charm++ are decomposed into a number of cooperating message-driven objects called *chares*. When a programmer invokes a method on an object, the Charm++ runtime system sends a message to the invoked object, which may reside on the local processor or on a remote processor in a parallel computation. This message triggers the execution of code within the chare to handle the message asynchronously.

Chares may be organized into indexed collections called *chare arrays* and messages may be sent to individual chares within a chare array or to the entire chare array simultaneously.

The chares in a program are mapped to physical processors by an adaptive runtime system. The mapping of chares to processors is transparent to the programmer, and this transparency permits the runtime system to dynamically change the assignment of chares to processors during program execution to support capabilities such as measurement-based load balancing, fault tolerance, automatic checkpointing, and the ability to shrink and expand the set of processors used by a parallel program.

The molecular dynamics simulation packages NAMD and OpenAtom are implemented using Charm++.

Adaptive MPI (AMPI) is an implementation of the Message Passing Interface standard on top of the Charm++ runtime system and provides the capabilities of Charm++ in a more traditional MPI programming model. AMPI encapsulates each MPI process within a user-level migratable thread that is bound within a Charm++ object. By embedding each thread with a chare, AMPI programs can automatically take advantage of the features of the Charm++ runtime system with little or no changes to the underlying MPI program.

History

Charm++ was developed at the Parallel Programming Laboratory, University of Illinois, by Wennie Shu and Kevin Nomura working with Laxmikant Kale. The second prototype was called Chare Kernel(2.0) was written by Manish Gupta. Charm(3.0) had significant design changes and was developed by a team consisting of Attila Gürsoy, Balkrishna Ramkumar, Amitabh B. Sinha, and Laxmikant Kale. A new translator was written by Nimish Shah. Sanjeev Krishnan made the Charm++ implementation. Charm(4.0) included Charm++. It was released in fall 1993. Charm(4.5) was developed by Attila Gürsoy, Sanjeev Krishnan, Milind Bhandarkar, Joshua Yelon, Narain Jagathesan, and Laxmikant Kale. The same team also developed Charm(4.8) that included Converse, a parallel runtime system that allows interoperability among modules that were written using different paradigms within a single application. After that, the Charm++ runtime system was re-targeted at Converse. Syntactic extensions in Charm++ were dropped, and a simple interface translator was developed (by Sanjeev Krishnan and Jay DeSouza), which became the Charm++ language. The version is 5.8 Revision 1 includes

1. completely rewritten runtime system and the interface translator (done by Milind Bhandarkar).

2. several new features such as Chare Arrays (developed by Robert Brunner and Orion Lawlor), and

3. various libraries (written by Terry Wilmarth, Gengbin Zheng, Laxmikant Kale, Zehra Sura, Milind Bhandarkar, Robert Brunner, and Krishnan Varadarajan.)

After that, a coordination language "Structured Dagger" has been implemented on top of Charm++ by Milind Bhandarkar that was included in this version. Several features have also been added to Converse. Dynamic seed-based load balancing has been implemented (Terry Wilmarth and Joshua Yelon), a client-server interface for Converse programs, and debugging support has been added (Parthasarathy Ramachandran, Jeff Wright, and Milind Bhandarkar). Converse has been ported to platforms including ASCI Red (Joshua Yelon), Cray T3E (Robert Brunner), and SGI Origin2000 (Milind Bhandarkar). There exists also a test suite for Charm++ developed by Michael Lang,

Jackie Wang, and Fang Hu. Projections, the performance visualization and analysis tool, was redesigned and rewritten using Java by Michael Denardo. Orion Lawlor, Gengbin Zheng, and Milind Bhandarkar are responsible for changes to the system since the last release.

Example

Here is some Charm++ code for demonstration purposes:

Header file (hello.h)

```
#ifndef __HELLO_H__
#define __HELLO_H__


class Hello : public CBase_Hello {

  public:

    /// Constructors ///
    Hello();
    Hello(CkMigrateMessage *msg);

    /// Entry Methods ///
    void sayHi(int from);
};


#endif //__HELLO_H__
```

Interface file (hello.ci)

```
module hello {

  array [1D] Hello {
```

```
      entry Hello();

      entry void sayHi(int);

   };


};
```

Source file (hello.C)

```
#include "hello.decl.h"


#include "hello.h"

#include "main.decl.h"


extern /* readonly */ CProxy_Main mainProxy;

extern /* readonly */ int numElements;


Hello::Hello() {

  // Nothing to do when the Hello chare object is created.

  // This is where member variables would be initialized

  // just like in a C++ class constructor.

}


// Constructor needed for chare object migration (ignore for
now)

// NOTE: This constructor does not need to appear in the ".ci"
file

Hello::Hello(CkMigrateMessage *msg) { }


void Hello ::sayHi(int from) {
```

```
// Have this chare object say hello to the user.
CkPrintf("\"Hello\" from Hello chare # %d on "
         "processor %d (told by %d).\n",
         thisIndex, CkMyPe(), from);


// Tell the next chare object in this array of chare objects
// to also say hello. If this is the last chare object in
// the array of chare objects, then tell the main chare
// object to exit the program.
if (thisIndex < (numElements - 1))
  thisProxy[thisIndex + 1].sayHi(thisIndex);
else
  mainProxy.done();
}


#include "hello.def.h"
```

References

- Donald E. Knuth. The Art of Computer Programming, Volume I: Fundamental Algorithms. Addison-Wesley. ISBN 0-201-89683-4.

- O.-J. Dahl; E. W. Dijkstra; C. A. R. Hoare (1972). Structured Programming. Academic Press. ISBN 0-12-200550-3.

- Abrahams, D. (2000). Exception-Safety in Generic Components. Generic Programming. LNCS. 1766. Springer. pp. 69–79. doi:10.1007/3-540-39953-4_6. ISBN 978-3-540-41090-4.

- Stroustrup, Bjarne (2000). The C++ Programming Language (3 ed.). Addison-Wesley. pp. 283–4. ISBN 978-0-201-70073-2.

- Bjarne Stroustrup. "Appendix E: Standard-Library Exception Safety in "The C++ Programming Language" (3rd Edition).Addison-Wesley, ISBN 0-201-88954-4".

- Myers, Nathan C. (June 1995). "Traits: a new and useful template technique". C++ Report. Retrieved January 23, 2016.

- Steele, Guy; Maessen, Jan-Willem (June 11, 2006). "Fortress Programming Language Tutorial"

(PDF). Sun Microsystems. Retrieved January 23, 2016.

- Forslund, Emil (February 3, 2016). "Definition of the Trait Pattern in Java". Age of Java. Retrieved February 3, 2016.

- Neward, Ted (April 29, 2008). "The busy Java developer's guide to Scala: Of traits and behaviors". IBM developerWorks. IBM. Retrieved January 23, 2016.

- U.S. Election Assistance Commission (2007). "Definitions of Words with Special Meanings". Voluntary Voting System Guidelines. Retrieved 2013-01-14.

- Dainith, John. ""open subroutine." A Dictionary of Computing. 2004..". Encyclopedia.com. Retrieved January 14, 2013.

- Marr, Stefan (January 9, 2011). "Request for Comments: Horizontal Reuse for PHP". PHP.net wiki. The PHP Group. Retrieved January 31, 2011.

Various C++ Compilers

Generic programming has softwares such as Ada, Delphi, Eiffel, Java and C# whereas metaprogramming writes programs with the skill to treat programs as their data. Which means if a data is being analyzed it can simultaneously be modified also. C++ programming is best understood in confluence with the major topics listed in following chapter.

C++Builder

C++Builder is a rapid application development (RAD) environment, originally developed by Borland and as of 2009 owned by Embarcadero Technologies, for writing programs in the C++ programming language targeting Windows NT (IA-32 and x64), OS X, iOS and Android. C++Builder combines the Visual Component Library and IDE written in Delphi with a C++ compiler. Most components developed in Delphi can be used in C++Builder with no or little modification, although the reverse is not true.

C++Builder includes tools that allow drag-and-drop visual development, making programming easier by incorporating a WYSIWYG graphical user interface builder.

Technology

C++Builder uses the same IDE as Delphi, and shares many core libraries. Notable shared Delphi (Object Pascal code) and C++ Builder routines include the FastMM4 memory manager, which was developed as a community effort within the FastCode project, the entire UI framework known as the VCL, which is written in Object Pascal, as well as base system routines, many of which have been optimised for both Delphi and C++Builder through the FastCode project.

C++Builder projects can include Delphi code. The Delphi compiler emits C++ headers, allowing C++ code to link to Delphi classes and methods as though they were written in C++. The reverse (C++ code being used by Delphi) is not possible.

History

Borland C++Builder

C++Builder originally targeted only the Microsoft Windows platform. Later versions incorporated Borland CLX, a cross-platform development visual component library based on Qt, that supports Windows and Linux, however CLX is now abandoned. A cross-platform version for Linux and OS X is reportedly planned.

Traditionally, the release cycle was such that Delphi got major enhancements first, with C++Builder following, though recent versions have been released at the same time as their Delphi equivalents.

1.0

Original Borland C++Builder editions include Client/Server Suite, Professional, Standard.

Borland C++Builder 4

New features include:

- Integrated Inprise Corporation's VisiBroker 3.3 with event and naming services

- New multi-standard flexible C++ compiler

- Support for the latest ANSI/ISO C++ language specifications, including a host of compiler enhancements including Dynamic Compilation and Adaptive Compiler Technology (ACT), which radically speed compiler build processes; full ANSI/ISO template implementation; full ANSI/ISO STL (standard template library) support; and a high-performance 32-bit ANSI C++ native code compiler.

- Fully customizable AppBrowser IDE

- Latest support for Windows 98, 95, and NT including multiple monitors, common controls, docking forms and toolbars, and more.

- New Code and Parameter completion, and the new ClassExplorer live structured class view and member creation wizards.

- Exclusive C++ debugging tools, including remote debugging for distributed development (COM and CORBA); multi-process and cross-process debugging with debug inspectors, dynamic watch windows, and debug tooltips.

- Internet tools, including ActiveForms for building Web browser C++ applications and WebBroker for building CGI, WinCGI, ISAPI, and NSAPI C++ applications and over 25 Internet protocol components for instantly adding HTTP, FTP, SMTP, POP, NNTP, HTML, and TCP/IP support to any C++ application.

- Multi-Tier Database Development Services (MIDAS) Development Kit, including MIDAS 2.

- Support for industry standards, including Oracle Corporation's Oracle8i database server; Microsoft Corporation's Microsoft Foundation Classes (MFC), Microsoft Active Template Library (ATL), Microsoft SQL Server 7 and MTS (Microsoft Transaction Server); and Inprise Corporation's Object Windows Library (OWL) and Visual Component Library (VCL).

- EZ-COM, which simplifies C++ COM client development and One-Step ActiveX Control creation with new Data Binding support.

Borland C++Builder 5

It was launched in 2000.

Borland C++Builder 6

Launched in 2001.

Borland C++BuilderX

In Sep 15, 2003, Borland Software Corporation announced the release of *Borland C++BuilderX* (CBX), which was also included as part of the latest Borland Enterprise Studio for Mobile. CBX was written using the same framework as JBuilder and bore little resemblance to either C++Builder or Delphi. This product was aimed at developing large programs for enterprises, but did not sell well.

In Sep 22, 2003, Borland Software Corporation and PalmSource, Inc. announced Borland has licensed the PalmSource software development kits (SDKs) and will support Palm OS development in the Borland C++BuilderX Integrated Development Environment (IDE) and latest Borland Application Lifecycle Management (ALM) solutions for C++.

At the end of 2004 Borland announced that it would continue to develop the earlier C++Builder and bundle it with the Delphi development suite, abandoning C++BuilderX.

C++ Builder 2006

In Oct 10, 2005, Borland Software Corporation announced the release of Borland C++Builder (previously codenamed "DeXter").

About a year after the announcement Borland released *Borland Developer Studio 2006* which includes *Borland C++Builder 2006* that provides improved configuration management and bug fixes. *Borland Developer Studio 2006* is a single package containing Delphi, C++Builder, and C#Builder.

In 2006 Borland's Developer Tools Group, developers of C++Builder, was transferred to a wholly owned subsidiary, CodeGear.

CodeGear Borland C++Builder

In 2007 CodeGear released *C++Builder 2007*, providing full API support for Microsoft Vista, increased ANSI C++ conformance, up to 500% faster in-IDE build performance, support for MSBuild, DBX4 database architecture, and "VCL for the Web" which supports Ajax. The API support for Microsoft Vista includes themed applications and seamless VCL support for Aero and Vista Desktop. *CodeGear RAD Studio 2007* incorporates *C++Builder 2007* and *Delphi*. Also in 2007 Borland revived the "Turbo" brand and released two "Turbo" editions of C++Builder: Turbo C++ Professional, and Turbo C++ Explorer (no longer available from CodeGear), based on *Borland C++Builder 2006*.

In 2008 CodeGear was purchased by Embarcadero Technologies, who continued development.

Embarcadero C++Builder

C++Builder 2009 was released in August 2008, with the most notable improvements being full Unicode support throughout VCL and RTL, early adoption of the C++0x standard, full ITE (Integrated Translation Environment) support, native Ribbon components and the inclusion of the Boost library. *C++Builder 2010* then followed in August 2009, adding in particular the touch and gesture support newly introduced to the VCL and a C++ specific class explorer. C++Builder XE was released in August 2010.

Embarcadero moved to a different versioning scheme in 2010. Rather than using numbers, they use XE. "C++ Builder XE" was released in August 2010, "C++Builder XE2" was released in August 2011, "C++ Builder XE3" was released in August 2012. No notable major changes were included in those three years except for bug fixes and the inclusion of 'FireMonkey' for creating cross-platform GUIs.

In April 2013, "C++ Builder XE4" was released, which included a 64-bit Windows compiler based on Clang 3.1. The 32-bit compiler is still based on Embarcadero's older technology.

XE5 (19)

Changes to C++Builder XE5 include:

- Time Picker control for Windows and OS X

- Built-in search filtering for TListView on Windows and OS X

- FM Platform performance optimizations

- Professional edition includes expanded FireDAC support for local databases, including Microsoft Access database, SQLite database, InterBase ToGo / IB-

Lite, InterBase on localhost, MySQL Embedded, MySQL Server on localhost, Advantage Database local engine, PostgreSQL on localhost, Firebird Embedded, and Firebird on localhost

- FireDAC integrated into the C++Builder install for Professional, Enterprise, Ultimate and Architect editions

- REST Client support for simplified invocation of REST services

- Authorization support including Basic Authentication, Plan Authentication, OAuth1, OAuth2

- TRestClient, TRestRequest, and TRestResponse components

- REST Debugger tool for testing REST calls and their parameters

C++Builder XE5 Starter Edition includes:

- Develop 32-bit Windows application using the C++Builder VCL and FireMonkey application platform

- IDE and visual development environment

- Hundreds of included components

- License for use until user's individual revenue from C++Builder applications or company revenue reaches $1,000 US or development team expands to more than five developers

Available editions include Architect, Ultimate, Enterprise, Professional, Starter.

RAD Studio XE5 also includes C++Builder XE5.

XE6 to 8

- Include changes for stability of the IDE, updated FMX and VCL libraries

10 Seattle

Released in late August 2015 Seattle updates the C++ compiler suite to CLANG 3.3 with the following exceptions:

- OS X compiler is still proprietary Borland

- iOS 64 bit compiler is Clang 3.5

- Changes to the IDE and compiler can be found here: www.embarcadero.com/products/cbuilder/whats-new

10.1 Berlin

Released in late April 2016.

- FireUI App Previews - Lets you preview your FireMonkey application on iOS, Android, OS X and Windows as you are designing the app.

- Address Book for iOS and Android - Supports the TAddressBook component which lets your applications access the device's Address Book.

OS X Support

C++Builder XE2 was released in August 2011, introducing OS X support to the compiler for the first time. This allows the creation of cross-platform executables from a single source using the included FireMonkey libraries, however the IDE is only compatible with Microsoft Windows.

C++Builder XE3 was released in August 2012 containing further OS X support and an upgraded version of FireMonkey.

C++Builder XE4 was released in April 2013 containing further OS X support and Fire-Monkey version 3.

Version History

The following is a rough outline of product release information.

Year	Version	Released by	Target platforms
4 Feb. 1997	1	Borland International, Inc.	Windows
8 Feb. 1998	3	Borland International, Inc.	Windows
26 Jan. 1999	4	Inprise Corporation	Windows
30 Jan. 2000	5	Inprise Corporation, Borland Software Corporation	Windows
1 Feb. 2002	6	Borland Software Corporation	Windows
28 Aug. 2003	X	Borland Software Corporation	Windows, Linux, Solaris
23 Nov. 2005	2006 (10)	Borland Software Corporation, CodeGear	Windows
5 June 2007	2007 (11)	CodeGear	Windows
25 Aug. 2008	2009 (12)	Embarcadero Technologies	Windows
24 Aug. 2009	2010 (14)	Embarcadero Technologies	Windows
30 Aug. 2010	XE (15)	Embarcadero Technologies	Windows
31 Aug. 2011	XE2 (16)	Embarcadero Technologies	Windows, OS X

4 Sept. 2012	XE3 (17)	Embarcadero Technologies	Windows, OS X
22 April 2013	XE4 (18)	Embarcadero Technologies	Windows, OS X
11 Sept. 2013	XE5 (19)	Embarcadero Technologies	Windows, OS X, iOS
15 April 2014	XE6 (20)	Embarcadero Technologies	Windows, OS X, iOS, Android
2 Sept. 2014	XE7 (21)	Embarcadero Technologies	Windows, OS X, iOS, Android
7 April 2015	XE8 (22)	Embarcadero Technologies	Windows, OS X, iOS, Android
31 Aug. 2015	10 Seattle (23)	Embarcadero Technologies	Windows, OS X, iOS, Android
20 April 2016	10.1 Berlin (24)	Embarcadero Technologies	Windows, OS X, iOS, Android

Editions

C++ Builder is available in four editions with increasing features and price:

- Starter - only compiles 32-bit Windows applications and has a limited commercial-use license.

- Professional - adds 64-bit Windows applications, cross-platform compilation for macOS, iOS and Android, library source code, code formatting, local database connectivity and a full commercial license.

- Enterprise - adds client/server database connectivity, Enterprise Mobility Services, and DataSnap multi-tier SDK.

- Architect - adds data modeling tools.

IBM XL C/C++ Compilers

XL C/C++ is the name of IBM's proprietary optimizing C/C++ compiler for IBM-supported environments.

The IBM XL compilers are built from modularized components consisting of front ends (for different programming languages), a platform agnostic high level optimizer, and platform-specific low-level optimizers/code generators to target specific hardware and operating systems. The XL C/C++ compilers target POWER, BlueGene/Q, and z Systems hardware architectures.

A common high level optimizer across the POWER and z/OS XL C/C++ compilers optimizes the source program using platform-agnostic optimizations such as inter-procedural analysis, profile-directed feedback, and loop and vector optimizations.

A low-level optimizer on each platform performs function-level optimizations, and generates optimized code for a specific operating system and hardware platform.

The particular optimizations performed for any given compilation depend upon the optimization level chosen under option control (O2 to O5) along with any other optimization-related options, such as those for interprocedural analysis or loop optimizations.

A 60-day installable evaluation version is available for download for the XL C/C++ for AIX, XL C/C++ for Linux on Power, and XL C/C++ for Linux on z compilers. z/OS XL C/C++ is available for a 15-day zero install trial via the IBM Integrated Solution for z Systems Development.

In June 2016, IBM introduced XL C/C++ for Linux Community Edition which is free of charge. It can be downloaded from this link.

The XL compilers on AIX have delivered leadership scores in the SPEC CPU2000 and CPU2006 benchmarks, in combination with specific IBM POWER system processor announcements, for example CPU2006 Floating Point score of 71.5 in May 2010 and SPEC CPU2000 Floating Point score of 4051 in August 2006.

Current (2016) versions of the XL C/C++ compilers support a subset of the C++03 standard on AIX; while XL C/C++ for Linux (Power) v13.1.3 supports C++11.

The XL C/C++ compiler for Linux on Power little endian edition, released in December 2014, is based on the open source Clang front end (part of the Clang/LLVM open source project) and therefore provides a higher level of language and GCC compatibility than IBM C/C++ compilers on other platforms, although that support is a subset of what Clang/LLVM itself supports.

Products

The XL C/C++ compiler family consists of the following products, with most recent version and release dates where known:

- XL C/C++ for z/VM (Version 1.3, December 2011)
- z/OS XL C/C++ (Version 2.2, September 2015)
- XL C/C++ for Linux on z Systems (Version 1.1, January 2015)
- XL C/C++ for AIX (Version 13.1, June 2014)
- XL C for AIX (Version 13.1, June 2014)
- XL C/C++ for Linux on Power (Version 13.1.1, December 2014)
- XL C/C++ for Blue Gene/Q (Version 12.1, June 2012)

- XL C/C++ Advanced Edition for Blue Gene (Version 9.0, September 2007, withdrawn August 2009)

Turbo C++

Turbo C++ is a discontinued C++ compiler and integrated development environment and computer language originally from Borland. Most recently it was distributed by Embarcadero Technologies, which acquired all of Borland's compiler tools with the purchase of its CodeGear division in 2008. The original Turbo C++ product line was put on hold after 1994 and was revived in 2006 as an introductory-level IDE, essentially a stripped-down version of their flagship C++Builder. Turbo C++ 2006 was released on September 5, 2006 and was available in 'Explorer' and 'Professional' editions. The Explorer edition was free to download and distribute while the Professional edition was a commercial product. In October 2009 Embarcadero Technologies discontinued support of its 2006 C++ editions. As such, the Explorer edition is no longer available for download and the Professional edition is no longer available for purchase from Embarcadero Technologies. Turbo C++ is succeeded by C++Builder.

History

The first release of Turbo C++ was made available during the MS-DOS era on personal computers. Version 1.0, running on MS-DOS, was released in May 1990. An OS/2 version was produced as well. Version 1.01 was released on February 28, 1991, running on MS-DOS. The latter was able to generate both COM and EXE programs and was shipped with Borland's Turbo Assembler compiler for Intel x86 processors. The initial version of the Turbo C++ compiler was based on a front end developed by TauMetric (TauMetric was later acquired by Sun Microsystems and their front end was incorporated in Sun C++ 4.0, which shipped in 1994).This compiler supported the AT&T 2.0 release of C++.

Turbo C++ 3.0 was released in 1991 (shipping on November 20), and came in amidst expectations of the coming release of Turbo C++ for Microsoft Windows. Initially released as an MS-DOS compiler, 3.0 supported C++ templates, Borland's inline assembler, and generation of MS-DOS mode executables for both 8086 real mode and 286 protected mode (as well as the Intel 80186.) 3.0 implemented AT&T C++ 2.1, the most recent at the time. The separate Turbo Assembler product was no longer included, but the inline-assembler could stand in as a reduced functionality version.

Soon after the release of Windows 3.0, Borland updated Turbo C++ to support Windows application development. The Turbo C++ 3.0 for Windows product was quickly followed by Turbo C++ 3.1 (and then Turbo C++ 4.5). It's possible that the jump from version 1.x to version 3.x was in part an attempt to link Turbo C++ release numbers with Microsoft Windows versions; however, it seems more likely that this jump was simply to synchronize Turbo C and Turbo C++, since Turbo C 2.0 (1989) and Turbo C++ 1.0 (1990) had come out roughly at the same time, and the next generation 3.0 was a merger of both the C and C++ compiler.

Starting with version 3.0, Borland segmented their C++ compiler into two distinct product-lines: "Turbo C++" and "Borland C++". Turbo C++ was marketed toward the hobbyist and entry-level compiler market, while Borland C++ targeted the professional application development market. Borland C++ included additional tools, compiler code-optimization, and documentation to address the needs of commercial developers. Turbo C++ 3.0 could be upgraded with separate add-ons, such as Turbo Assembler and Turbo Vision 1.0.

Version 4.0 was released in November 1993 and was notable (among other things) for its robust support of templates. In particular, Borland C++ 4 was instrumental in the development of the Standard Template Library, expression templates, and the first advanced applications of template metaprogramming. With the success of the Pascal-evolved product Delphi, Borland ceased work on their Borland C++ suite and concentrated on C++Builder for Windows. C++Builder shared Delphi's front-end application framework, but retained the Borland C++ back-end compiler. Active development on Borland C++/Turbo C++ was suspended until 2006.

Legacy Software

- Turbo C++ v1.01 and Turbo C v2.01 can be downloaded, free of charge, from Borland's Antique Software website.

- Turbo C 3.0 (DOS) was included in the Turbo C Suite 1.0, which is no longer sold by Borland.

Norcroft C Compiler

 The Norcroft C compiler (also referred to as the Norcroft compiler suite) in computing is a portable set of C/C++ programming tools written by Codemist, available for a wide range of processor architectures.

Norcroft C was developed by Codemist, established in November 1987 by a group of academics from the University of Cambridge and University of Bath; Arthur Norman, Alan Mycroft and John Fitch. Development took place from at least 1985; the company was dissolved in May 2016. The name *Norcroft* is derived from the original authors' surnames.

Supported Architectures

Acorn C/C++

Acorn C/C++ was released for the RISC OS operating system, developed in collaboration with Acorn Computers.

INMOS Transputer C Compiler

This compiler for the INMOS Transputer was developed in collaboration with Perihelion Software.

Cambridge Consultants XAP

This compiler for Cambridge Consultants' XAP processor is another Norcroft compiler.

Watcom C/C++

Watcom C/C++ (currently Open Watcom C/C++) is a compiler for C, C++ and Fortran. It was developed by Watcom International Corporation.

History

Though no longer sold commercially by Sybase, the Watcom C/C++ compiler and the Watcom Fortran compiler have been made available free of charge – for non commercial usage, as the *Open Watcom* package.

The Open Watcom C/C++ version 1.4 release on December 2005 introduced Linux x86 as an experimental target, supported from NT or OS/2 host platforms. There is code for an abandoned QNX version, but libraries necessary for it to be compiled could not be released as open source.

Stable version 1.9 was released in June 2010.

A forked version 2.0 beta was released that supports 64-bit hosts (Window and Linux), built-in text editor, 2-phase build system, and the DOS version supports long filenames (LFN).

Release History

The *Open Watcom* has a comprehensive history.

Date	Product	Notes
1984	Waterloo C for S/370	

1985		Work on current code generator codebase started
1988	Watcom C 6.0	• DOS host and target only • Included a debugger and full set of runtime libraries • Generated better code than other compilers at the time • Watcom C Version 6.5 contained Graphics Library similar to Microsoft Graphics Library
1989	Watcom C 7.0	
1989	Watcom C 7.0/386	• First 32-bit version, DOS host and target only • Supported Phar Lap DOS extender • Did not come with a linker or debugger
1990	Watcom C 8.0	
1990	Watcom C 8.0/386	• Added linker, librarian, debugger, and profiler
1991	Watcom C 8.5	
1991	Watcom C 8.5/386	• Shipped with DOS/4GW • Windows 3.0 supported (Win386 extender) • Unicode support • OS/2 hosted executables added
1992	Watcom C 9.0	
1992	Watcom C 9.0/386	• OS/2 2.0 host and target support • 486 optimizations • Based pointer support
	Watcom C 9.01/386	• Windows 3.1 support
1993	Watcom C/ C++ 9.5	
1993	Watcom C/ C++ 9.5/386	• C++ compiler added • Pentium optimizations • Windows NT host and target support

Year	Version	Features
1994	Watcom C/C++ 10.0	• MFC included • Precompiled header support • 16-bit and 32-bit tools merged into single package • Redesigned debugger • C++ class browser added • Windows resource editors added • Graphical IDE for Windows and OS/2
1995	Watcom C/C++ 10.5	• Native C++ exception handling on OS/2 and Win32 • Windows 95 and NT 3.5 support • TCP/IP remote debugging
1996	Watcom C/C++ 10.6	• Structured exception handling in C • Improved compatibility with Microsoft compilers
1997	Watcom C/C++ 11.0	• *Namespace*, RTTI, and new style cast support in C++ compiler • 64-bit integer support • Multi-byte character support in libraries • Incremental linking support • COFF and ELF object file support in linker and librarian • Microsoft clone tools added • DLL based tools for better IDE integration
1998	Watcom C/C++ 11.0B	
1999		Sybase issues end-of-life notice for Watcom C/C++ 11.0
2000		Sybase announces open sourcing of Watcom tools
2001-09-27	Watcom C/C++ 11.0c Beta	
2002-12-21	Watcom C/C++ 11.0c	
2003-01-28	Open Watcom 1.0	
2003-08-12	Open Watcom 1.1	
2004-01-07	Open Watcom 1.2	
2004-08-03	Open Watcom 1.3	

Date	Version	Notes
2005-12-14	Open Watcom 1.4	
2006-04-26	Open Watcom 1.5	
2006-12-15	Open Watcom 1.6	
2007-08-18	Open Watcom 1.7	
2007-10-23	Open Watcom 1.7a	
2009-02-21	Open Watcom 1.8	
2010-06-02	Open Watcom 1.9	**Current Official Version**
2015-04-02	Open Watcom 2.0 Beta	GitHub V2 Fork. Open Watcom ported to 64-bit hosts (Window and Linux), Resource compiler and Resource editor support WIN64 executables, built-in text editor, 2-phase build system, DOS version of tools support long filenames (LFN), numerous fixes.

License

The Open Source Initiative has approved the license as open source, but Debian, Fedora and the Free Software Foundation have rejected it because "It requires you to publish the source code publicly whenever you "Deploy" the covered software, and "Deploy" is defined to include many kinds of private use."

Design

The compiler can be operated from, and generate executable code for, the DOS (MS-DOS, FreeDOS), OS/2, Windows, Linux operating systems. It also supports NLM targets for Novell NetWare. There is ongoing work to extend the targeting to Linux and modern BSD (e.g., FreeBSD) operating systems, running on x86, PowerPC, and other processors.

The code is portable and, like many other open source compiler projects such as GCC or LCC the compiler backend (code generator) is retargetable.

Uses

In the mid-1990s some of the most technically ambitious MS-DOS computer games such as *Doom, Descent, Duke Nukem 3D*, and *Rise of the Triad* were built using Watcom C/C++, some such as ROTT using the DOS/4GW protected mode extender with the Watcom compiler.

C++: The Programming Language

It was used to port the game Retro City Rampage to MS-DOS in 2015.

Variants

There is an unofficial fork of Open Watcom V2 on GitHub. A variant of the 16bit DOS CRT library startup was created with WASM.

Compatibility

Open Watcom's syntax supports many conventions introduced by other compilers, such as Microsoft's and Borland's, including differing conventions regarding (for instance) the number of leading underscores on the "asm" tag. Code written specifically for another compiler rather than standard-compliant C or C++ will often compile with the Watcom compiler.

The compiler supports C89/C90 standards by default.

Open Watcom supports partial compatibility with the C99 standard. It implements the most commonly used parts of the standard. However, they are enabled only through the undocumented command-line switch "-za99". Three C99 features have been bundled as C90 Extension since pre-v1.0: C++ style comments (//), flexible array members, trailing comma allowed in enum declaration.

The compiler currently doesn't support any new major C11 features, though the C library does include "Safe C" functions. It is specified in ISO/IEC TR 24731-1 and known as "Bounds-checking interfaces (Annex K)" in C11. Some function name examples are strcpy_s(), memcpy_s(), printf_s(). This library was released along with Open Watcom 1.5 in April 2006.

Visual C++

Microsoft Visual C++ (often abbreviated as MSVC or VC++) is an integrated development environment (IDE) product from Microsoft for the C, C++, and C++/CLI programming languages. MSVC is proprietary software; it was originally a standalone product but later became a part of Visual Studio and made available in both trialware and freeware forms. It features tools for developing and debugging C++ code, especially code written for Windows API, DirectX and .NET Framework.

Many applications require redistributable Visual C++ packages to function correctly. These packages are often installed independently of applications, allowing multiple applications to make use of the package while only having to install it once. These Visual C++ redistributable and runtime packages are mostly installed for standard libraries that many applications use.

History

The predecessor to Visual C++ was called *Microsoft C/C++*. There was also a *Microsoft QuickC* 2.5 and a *Microsoft QuickC for Windows* 1.0. The Visual C++ compiler is still known as *Microsoft C/C++* and as of the release of Visual C++ 2015 Update 2, is on version 19.00.23918.

16-bit Versions

- Microsoft C 1.0, based on Lattice C, was Microsoft's first C product in 1983. It was not K&R C.

- C 2.0 added large model support.

- C 3.0 was the first version developed inside Microsoft. This version intended compatibility with K&R and the later ANSI standard. It was being used inside Microsoft (for Windows and Xenix development) in early 1984. It shipped as a product in 1985.

- C 4.0 added optimizations and CodeView, a source level debugger.

- C 5.0 added loop optimizations and *Huge Model* (arrays bigger than 64k) support. Microsoft Fortran and the first 32 bit compiler for 80386 were also part of this project.

- C 5.1 released in 1988 allowed compiling programs for OS/2 1.x.

- C 6.0 released in 1989. It added global flow analysis, a source browser, and a new debugger, and included an optional C++ front end.

- C/C++ 7.0 was released in 1992. Added built-in support for C++ and MFC (Microsoft Foundation Class Library) 1.0.

- Visual C++ 1.0, which included MFC 2.0, was the first version of Visual C++, released in February 1993. It was Cfront 2.1 compliant and available in two editions:

  o Standard – replaced QuickC for Windows.

  o Professional – replaced C/C++ 7.0. Included the ability to build both DOS and Windows applications, an optimizing compiler, a source profiler, and the Windows 3.1 SDK. The Phar Lap 286 DOS Extender Lite was also included.

- Visual C++ 1.5 was released in December 1993, included MFC 2.5, and added OLE 2.0 and ODBC support to MFC. It was the first version of Visual C++ that came only on CD-ROM.

o   Visual C++ 1.51 and 1.52 were available as part of a subscription service.

o   Visual C++ 1.52b is similar to 1.52, but does not include the Control Development Kit.

o   Visual C++ 1.52c was a patched version of 1.5. It is the last, and arguably most popular, development platform for Microsoft Windows 3.x. It is available through Microsoft Developer Network.

Strictly 32-bit Versions

- Visual C++ 1.0 (original name: Visual C++ 32-bit Edition) was the first version for 32-bit development. Although released when 16-bit 1.5 was available, it did not include support for OLE2 and ODBC. It was also available in a bundle called Visual C++ 16/32-bit Suite, which included Visual C++ 1.5.

- Visual C++ 2.0, which included MFC 3.0, was the first version to be 32-bit only. In many ways, this version was ahead of its time, since Windows 95, then codenamed "Chicago", was not yet released, and Windows NT had only a small market share. As a result, this release was almost a "lost generation". Microsoft included and updated Visual C++ 1.5 as part of the 2.x releases up to 2.1, which included Visual C++ 1.52, and both 16-bit and 32-bit version of the Control Development Kit (CDK) were included. Visual C++ 2.x also supported Win32s development. It is available through Microsoft Developer Network. There was a Visual C++ 2.0 RISC Edition for MIPS and Alpha processors, as well as a cross-platform edition for the Macintosh (68000 instruction set).

    o   Visual C++ 2.1 and 2.2 were updates for 2.0 available through subscription.

- Visual C++ 4.0, released on 1995-12-11 introduced the Developer Studio IDE. Its then-novel tiled layout of non-overlapping panels — navigation panel, combination editor/source level debugger panel, and console output panel— continues through the Visual Studio product line (as of 2013). Visual C++ 4.0 included MFC 4.0, was designed for Windows 95 and Windows NT. To allow support of legacy (Windows 3.x/DOS) projects, 4.0 came bundled with the Visual C++ 1.52 installation CD. Updates available through subscription included Visual C++ 4.1, which came with the Microsoft Game SDK (later released separately as the DirectX SDK), and Visual C++ 4.2. Version number 3.0 was skipped to achieve version number parity between Visual C++ 4.0 and MFC 4.0.

- Visual C++ 4.2 did not support Windows 3.x (Win32s) development. This was the final version with a cross-platform edition for the Macintosh available and it differed from the 2.x version in that it also allowed compilation for the PowerPC instruction set.

- Visual C++ 5.0, which included MFC 4.21 and was released 1997-04-28, was a major upgrade from 4.2. Available in four editions: Learning, Professional, Enterprise, and RISC.

- Visual C++ 6.0 (commonly known as VC6), which included MFC 6.0, was released in 1998. The release was somewhat controversial since it did not include an expected update to MFC. Visual C++ 6.0 is still quite popular and often used to maintain legacy projects. There are, however, issues with this version under Windows XP, especially under the debugging mode (for example, the values of static variables do not display). The debugging issues can be solved with a patch called the "Visual C++ 6.0 Processor Pack". Version number: 12.00.8804

- Visual C++ .NET 2002 (also known as Visual C++ 7.0), which included MFC 7.0, was released in 2002 with support for link time code generation and debugging runtime checks, .NET 1.0, and Visual C# and Managed C++. The new user interface used many of the hot keys and conventions of Visual Basic, which accounted for some of its unpopularity among C++ developers. Version number: 13.00.9466

- Visual C++ .NET 2003 (also known as Visual C++ 7.1), which included MFC 7.1, was released in 2003 along with .NET 1.1 and was a major upgrade to Visual C++ .NET 2002. It was considered a patch to Visual C++ .NET 2002. Accordingly, the English language upgrade version of Visual Studio .NET 2003 shipped for minimal cost to owners of the English-language version of Visual Studio .NET 2002. This was the last version to support Windows 95 and NT 4.0 as a target. Version number: 13.10.3077

- eMbedded Visual C++ in various versions was used to develop for some versions of the Windows CE operating system. Initially it replaced a development environment consisting of tools added onto Visual C++ 6.0. eMbedded Visual C++ was replaced as a separate development environment by Microsoft Visual Studio 2005.

32-bit and 64-Bit Versions

- Visual C++ 2005 (also known as Visual C++ 8.0), which included MFC 8.0, was released in November 2005. This version supports .NET 2.0 and includes a new version of C++ targeted to the .NET framework (C++/CLI) with the purpose of replacing the previous version (Managed C++). Managed C++ for CLI is still available via compiler options, though. It also introduced OpenMP. With Visual C++ 2005, Microsoft also introduced Team Foundation Server. Visual C++ 8.0 has problems compiling MFC AppWizard projects that were created using Visual Studio 6.0, so maintenance of legacy projects can be continued with the original IDE if rewriting is not feasible.

Visual C++ 2005 is the last version able to target Windows 98 and Windows Me. SP1 version (14.00.50727.762) is also available in Microsoft Windows SDK Update for Windows Vista.

- Visual C++ 2008 (also known as Visual C++ 9.0) was released in November 2007. This version supports .NET 3.5. Managed C++ for CLI is still available via compiler options. By default, all applications compiled against the Visual C++ 2008 Runtimes (static and dynamic linking) will only work under Windows 2000 and later. A feature pack released for VC9, later included in SP1, added support for C++ TR1 library extensions. SP1 version (15.00.30729.01) is also available in Microsoft Windows SDK for Windows 7.

- Visual C++ 2010 (also known as Visual C++ 10.0) was released on April 12, 2010. It uses a SQL Server Compact database to store information about the source code, including IntelliSense information, for better IntelliSense and code-completion support. However, Visual C++ 2010 does not support Intellisense for C++/CLI. This version adds a C++ parallel computing library called the Parallel Patterns Library, partial support for C++11, significantly improved IntelliSense based on the Edison Design Group front end, and performance improvements to both the compiler and generated code. This version is built on .NET 4.0, but supports compiling to machine code. The partial C++11 support mainly consists of six compiler features: lambdas, rvalue references, auto, decltype, static_assert, and nullptr. C++11 also supports library features (e.g., moving the TR1 components from std::tr1 namespace directly to std namespace). Variadic templates were also considered, but delayed until some future version due to having a lower priority, which stemmed from the fact that — unlike other costly-to-implement features (lambda, rvalue references) — variadic templates would benefit only a minority of library writers rather than the majority of compiler end users. By default, all applications compiled against Visual C++ 2010 Runtimes only work on Windows XP SP2 and later. The RTM version (16.00.30319) is also available in Windows SDK for Windows 7 and .NET Framework 4 (WinSDK v7.1). SP1 version (16.00.40219) is available as part of Visual Studio 2010 Service Pack 1 or through the Microsoft Visual C++ 2010 Service Pack 1 Compiler Update for the Windows SDK 7.1.

- Visual C++ 2012 (also known as Visual C++ 11.0) was released on August 15, 2012. It features improved C++11 support, and support for Windows Runtime development.

- Visual C++ 2013 (also known as Visual C++ 12.0) was released on October 17, 2013. It features further C++11 and C99 support, and introduces a REST SDK.

- Visual C++ 2015 (also known as Visual C++ 14.0) was released on July 20, 2015. It features improved C++11/14/17 support.

Compatibility

ABI

The Visual C++ compiler ABI have historically changed between major compiler releases. This is especially the case for STL containers, where container sizes have varied a lot between compiler releases. Microsoft therefore recommends against using C++ interfaces at module boundaries when one wants to enable client code compiled using a different compiler version. Instead of C++, Microsoft recommends using C or COM interfaces, which are designed to have a stable ABI between compiler releases.

C Runtime Libraries

Visual C++ ships with different versions of C runtime libraries. This means users can compile their code with any of the available libraries. However, this can cause some problems when using different components (DLLs, EXEs) in the same program. A typical example is a program using different libraries. The user should use the same C Run-Time for all the program's components unless the implications are understood. Microsoft recommends using the multithreaded, dynamic link library (/MD or /MDd compiler option) to avoid possible problems.

C99

Although the product originated as an IDE for the C programming language, for many years the compiler's support for that language conformed only to the original edition of the C standard, dating from 1989. The later revisions of the standard, C99 and C11, were not supported at all until Visual C++ 2012, which added support for various C99 features in its C mode (including designated initializers, compound literals, and the _Bool type). Visual C++ 2013 significantly improved the C99 support, though it is still not complete. Visual C++ 2015 further improves the C99 support, with full support of the C99 Standard Library, except for features that require C99 language features not yet supported by the compiler.

Common MSVC Version

The predefined macro _MSC_VER indicates the major and minor version numbers of the Visual C++ compiler. The macro's value is an integer literal in which the last two digits indicate the minor version number and the preceding digits indicate the major version number.

Here are values of _MSC_VER for various versions of the Visual C++ compiler:

```
MSVC++ 5.0   _MSC_VER == 1100

MSVC++ 6.0   _MSC_VER == 1200
```

```
MSVC++ 7.0   _MSC_VER == 1300

MSVC++ 7.1   _MSC_VER == 1310 (Visual Studio 2003)

MSVC++ 8.0   _MSC_VER == 1400 (Visual Studio 2005)

MSVC++ 9.0   _MSC_VER == 1500 (Visual Studio 2008)

MSVC++ 10.0 _MSC_VER == 1600 (Visual Studio 2010)

MSVC++ 11.0 _MSC_VER == 1700 (Visual Studio 2012)

MSVC++ 12.0 _MSC_VER == 1800 (Visual Studio 2013)

MSVC++ 14.0 _MSC_VER == 1900 (Visual Studio 2015)
```

These version numbers refer to the major version number of Visual Studio, which can be seen inside the Visual Studio "About" box. It does not refer to the year in the name. A thorough list is available.

Controversy

Without any announcement from Microsoft, Visual Studio 2015 Update 2 started generating telemetry calls in compiled binaries. After some users contacted Microsoft about this problem, Microsoft said they would remove these telemetry calls when compiling with the future Visual Studio 2015 Update 3. The function in question was removed from the Visual C++ CRT static libraries in Visual Studio 2015 Update 3.

References

- Toth, Viktor (1996). "1". Visual C++ 4.0 unleashed. Indianapolis: SAMS Publishing. ISBN 9780672308741. Retrieved 26 July 2013.

- "What's New for Visual C++ in Visual Studio 2012". Microsoft Developer Network. Microsoft. Retrieved September 20, 2015.

- Free Software Foundation. "Various Licenses and Comments about Them". GNU Operating System. Retrieved Dec 23, 2014.

Diverse Aspects of C++ Programming Language

Generic programming is a style of computer programming where the algorithms written in generic programming are written in terms of types to-be-specified-later. The other diverse aspects of C++ are metaprogramming, compatibility of C and C++, criticism of C++ and Sieve C++ Parallel programming system. This topic will provide an integrated understanding of C++ programming language.

Generic Programming

In the simplest definition, generic programming is a style of computer programming in which algorithms are written in terms of types *to-be-specified-later* that are then *instantiated* when needed for specific types provided as parameters. This approach, pioneered by ML in 1973, permits writing common functions or types that differ only in the set of types on which they operate when used, thus reducing duplication. Such software entities are known as *generics* in Ada, Delphi, Eiffel, Java, C#, F#, Objective-C, Swift, and Visual Basic .NET; *parametric polymorphism* in ML, Scala, Haskell (the Haskell community also uses the term "generic" for a related but somewhat different concept) and Julia; *templates* in C++ and D; and *parameterized types* in the influential 1994 book *Design Patterns*. The authors of *Design Patterns* note that this technique, especially when combined with delegation, is very powerful but also quote the following

Dynamic, highly parameterized software is harder to understand than more static software.

— Gang of Four, Design Patterns (Chapter 1)

The term generic programming was originally coined by David Musser and Alexander Stepanov in a more specific sense than the above, to describe a programming paradigm whereby fundamental requirements on types are abstracted from across concrete examples of algorithms and data structures and formalised as concepts, with generic functions implemented in terms of these concepts, typically using language genericity mechanisms as described above.

Stepanov–Musser and Other Generic Programming Paradigms

Generic programming is defined in Musser & Stepanov (1989) as follows,

Generic programming centers around the idea of abstracting from concrete, efficient algorithms to obtain generic algorithms that can be combined with different data representations to produce a wide variety of useful software.

—Musser, David R.; Stepanov, Alexander A., Generic Programming

Generic programming paradigm is an approach to software decomposition whereby fundamental requirements on types are abstracted from across concrete examples of algorithms and data structures and formalised as concepts, analogously to the abstraction of algebraic theories in abstract algebra. Early examples of this programming approach were implemented in Scheme and Ada, although the best known example is the Standard Template Library (STL), which developed a theory of iterators that is used to decouple sequence data structures and the algorithms operating on them.

For example, given N sequence data structures, e.g. singly linked list, vector etc., and M algorithms to operate on them, e.g. find, sort etc., a direct approach would implement each algorithm specifically for each data structure, giving $N \times M$ combinations to implement. However, in the generic programming approach, each data structure returns a model of an iterator concept (a simple value type which can be dereferenced to retrieve the current value, or changed to point to another value in the sequence) and each algorithm is instead written generically with arguments of such iterators, e.g. a pair of iterators pointing to the beginning and end of the subsequence to process. Thus, only $N + M$ data structure-algorithm combinations need be implemented. Several iterator concepts are specified in the STL, each a refinement of more restrictive concepts e.g. forward iterators only provide movement to the next value in a sequence (e.g. suitable for a singly linked list or a stream of input data), whereas a random-access iterator also provides direct constant-time access to any element of the sequence (e.g. suitable for a vector). An important point is that a data structure will return a model of the most general concept that can be implemented efficiently—computational complexity requirements are explicitly part of the concept definition. This limits which data structures a given algorithm can be applied to and such complexity requirements are a major determinant of data structure choice. Generic programming similarly has been applied in other domains, e.g. graph algorithms.

Note that although this approach often utilizes language features of compile-time genericity/templates, it is in fact independent of particular language-technical details. Generic programming pioneer Alexander Stepanov wrote,

Generic programming is about abstracting and classifying algorithms and data structures. It gets its inspiration from Knuth and not from type theory. Its goal is the incremental construction of systematic catalogs of useful, efficient and abstract algorithms and data structures. Such an undertaking is still a dream.

—Alexander Stepanov, Short History of STL

I believe that iterator theories are as central to Computer Science as theories of rings or Banach spaces are central to Mathematics.

—Alexander Stepanov, An Interview with A. Stepanov

Bjarne Stroustrup noted,

Following Stepanov, we can define generic programming without mentioning language features: Lift algorithms and data structures from concrete examples to their most general and abstract form.

—Bjarne Stroustrup, Evolving a language in
and for the real world: C++ 1991-2006

Other programming paradigms that have been described as generic programming include *Datatype generic programming* as described in "Generic Programming — an Introduction". The *Scrap your boilerplate* approach is a lightweight generic programming approach for Haskell.

In this article we distinguish the high-level programming paradigms of *generic programming*, above, from the lower-level programming language *genericity mechanisms* used to implement them. For further discussion and comparison of generic programming paradigms.

Programming Language Support for Genericity

Genericity facilities have existed in high-level languages since at least the 1970s in languages such as ML, CLU and Ada, and were subsequently adopted by many object-based and object-oriented languages, including BETA, C++, D, Eiffel, Java, and DEC's now defunct Trellis-Owl language.

Genericity is implemented and supported differently in various programming languages; the term "generic" has also been used differently in various programming contexts. For example, in Forth the compiler can execute code while compiling and one can create new *compiler keywords* and new implementations for those words on the fly. It has few *words* that expose the compiler behaviour and therefore naturally offers *genericity* capacities which, however, are not referred to as such in most Forth texts. Similarly, dynamically typed languages, especially interpreted ones, usually offer *genericity* by default as both passing values to functions and value assignment are type-indifferent and such behavior is often utilized for abstraction or code terseness, however this is not typically labeled *genericity* as it's a direct consequence of dynamic typing system employed by the language. The term has been used in functional programming, specifically in Haskell-like languages, which use a structural type system where types are always parametric and the actual code on those types is generic. These usages still serve a similar purpose of code-saving and the rendering of an abstraction.

Arrays and structs can be viewed as predefined generic types. Every usage of an array or struct type instantiates a new concrete type, or reuses a previous instantiated type. Array element types and struct element types are parameterized types, which are used to instantiate the corresponding generic type. All this is usually built-in in the compiler and the syntax differs from other generic constructs. Some extensible programming languages try to unify built-in and user defined generic types.

A broad survey of genericity mechanisms in programming languages follows. For a specific survey comparing suitability of mechanisms for generic programming.

In Object-oriented Languages

When creating container classes in statically typed languages, it is inconvenient to write specific implementations for each datatype contained, especially if the code for each datatype is virtually identical. For example, in C++, this duplication of code can be circumvented by defining a class template:

```
template<typename T>

class List

{

    /* class contents */

};



List<Animal> list_of_animals;

List<Car> list_of_cars;
```

Above, T is a placeholder for whatever type is specified when the list is created. These "containers-of-type-T", commonly called templates, allow a class to be reused with different datatypes as long as certain contracts such as subtypes and signature are kept. This genericity mechanism should not be confused with *inclusion polymorphism*, which is the algorithmic usage of exchangeable sub-classes: for instance, a list of objects of type Moving_Object containing objects of type Animal and Car. Templates can also be used for type-independent functions as in the Swap example below:

```
template<typename T>

void Swap(T & a, T & b) //"&" passes parameters by reference

{

    T temp = b;
```

```
    b = a;

    a = temp;

}
```

```
string hello = "world!", world = "Hello, ";

Swap( world, hello );

cout << hello << world << endl; //Output is "Hello, world!"
```

The C++ template construct used above is widely cited as the genericity construct that popularized the notion among programmers and language designers and supports many generic programming idioms. The D programming language also offers fully generic-capable templates based on the C++ precedent but with a simplified syntax. The Java programming language has provided genericity facilities syntactically based on C++'s since the introduction of J2SE 5.0.

C# 2.0, Chrome 1.5 and Visual Basic .NET 2005 have constructs that take advantage of the support for generics present in the Microsoft .NET Framework since version 2.0.

Generics in Ada

Ada has had generics since it was first designed in 1977–1980. The standard library uses generics to provide many services. Ada 2005 adds a comprehensive generic container library to the standard library, which was inspired by C++'s standard template library.

A *generic unit* is a package or a subprogram that takes one or more *generic formal parameters*.

A *generic formal parameter* is a value, a variable, a constant, a type, a subprogram, or even an instance of another, designated, generic unit. For generic formal types, the syntax distinguishes between discrete, floating-point, fixed-point, access (pointer) types, etc. Some formal parameters can have default values.

To *instantiate* a generic unit, the programmer passes *actual* parameters for each formal. The generic instance then behaves just like any other unit. It is possible to instantiate generic units at run-time, for example inside a loop.

Example

The specification of a generic package:

```
generic
```

```
   Max_Size : Natural; -- a generic formal value

   type Element_Type is private; -- a generic formal type; ac-
cepts any nonlimited type

package Stacks is

   type Size_Type is range 0 .. Max_Size;

   type Stack is limited private;

   procedure Create (S : out Stack;

                       Initial_Size : in Size_Type := Max_Size);

   procedure Push (Into : in out Stack; Element : in Element_
Type);

   procedure Pop (From : in out Stack; Element : out Element_
Type);

   Overflow : exception;

   Underflow : exception;

private

   subtype Index_Type is Size_Type range 1 .. Max_Size;

   type Vector is array (Index_Type range <>) of Element_Type;

   type Stack (Allocated_Size : Size_Type := 0) is record

      Top : Index_Type;

      Storage : Vector (1 .. Allocated_Size);

   end record;

end Stacks;
```

Instantiating the generic package:

```
type Bookmark_Type is new Natural;

-- records a location in the text document we are editing


package Bookmark_Stacks is new Stacks (Max_Size => 20,

                                        Element_Type => Book-
```

```
mark_Type);
```

-- Allows the user to jump between recorded locations in a document

Using an instance of a generic package:

```
type Document_Type is record

    Contents : Ada.Strings.Unbounded.Unbounded_String;

    Bookmarks : Bookmark_Stacks.Stack;

end record;


procedure Edit (Document_Name : in String) is

  Document : Document_Type;

begin

  -- Initialise the stack of bookmarks:

  Bookmark_Stacks.Create (S => Document.Bookmarks, Initial_Size
=> 10);

  -- Now, open the file Document_Name and read it in...

end Edit;
```

Advantages and Limitations

The language syntax allows precise specification of constraints on generic formal parameters. For example, it is possible to specify that a generic formal type will only accept a modular type as the actual. It is also possible to express constraints *between* generic formal parameters; for example:

```
generic

    type Index_Type is (<>); -- must be a discrete type

    type Element_Type is private; -- can be any nonlimited type

    type Array_Type is array (Index_Type range <>) of Element_
Type;
```

In this example, Array_Type is constrained by both Index_Type and Element_Type. When instantiating the unit, the programmer must pass an actual array type that satisfies these constraints.

The disadvantage of this fine-grained control is a complicated syntax, but, because all generic formal parameters are completely defined in the specification, the compiler can instantiate generics without looking at the body of the generic.

Unlike C++, Ada does not allow specialised generic instances, and requires that all generics be instantiated explicitly. These rules have several consequences:

- the compiler can implement *shared generics*: the object code for a generic unit can be shared between all instances (unless the programmer requests inlining of subprograms, of course). As further consequences:

  - there is no possibility of code bloat (code bloat is common in C++ and requires special care, as explained below).

  - it is possible to instantiate generics at run-time, as well as at compile time, since no new object code is required for a new instance.

  - actual objects corresponding to a generic formal object are always considered to be nonstatic inside the generic.

- all instances of a generic being exactly the same, it is easier to review and understand programs written by others; there are no "special cases" to take into account.

- all instantiations being explicit, there are no hidden instantiations that might make it difficult to understand the program.

- Ada does not permit "template metaprogramming", because it does not allow specialisations.

Templates in C++

C++ uses templates to enable generic programming techniques. The C++ Standard Library includes the Standard Template Library or STL that provides a framework of templates for common data structures and algorithms. Templates in C++ may also be used for template metaprogramming, which is a way of pre-evaluating some of the code at compile-time rather than run-time. Using template specialization, C++ Templates are considered Turing complete.

Technical Overview

There are two kinds of templates: function templates and class templates. A *function template* is a pattern for creating ordinary functions based upon the parameterizing types supplied when instantiated. For example, the C++ Standard Template Library contains the function template max(x, y) which creates functions that return either *x* or *y,* whichever is larger. max() could be defined like this:

```
template <typename T>

T max(T x, T y)

{

    return x < y ? y : x;

}
```

Specializations of this function template, instantiations with specific types, can be called just like an ordinary function:

```
cout << max(3, 7);    // outputs 7
```

The compiler examines the arguments used to call max and determines that this is a call to max(int, int). It then instantiates a version of the function where the parameterizing type T is int, making the equivalent of the following function:

```
int max(int x, int y)

{

    return x < y ? y : x;

}
```

This works whether the arguments x and y are integers, strings, or any other type for which the expression x < y is sensible, or more specifically, for any type for which operator< is defined. Common inheritance is not needed for the set of types that can be used, and so it is very similar to duck typing. A program defining a custom data type can use operator overloading to define the meaning of < for that type, thus allowing its use with the max() function template. While this may seem a minor benefit in this isolated example, in the context of a comprehensive library like the STL it allows the programmer to get extensive functionality for a new data type, just by defining a few operators for it. Merely defining < allows a type to be used with the standard sort(), stable_sort(), and binary_search() algorithms or to be put inside data structures such as sets, heaps, and associative arrays.

C++ templates are completely type safe at compile time. As a demonstration, the standard type complex does not define the < operator, because there is no strict order on complex numbers. Therefore, max(x, y) will fail with a compile error if x and y are complex values. Likewise, other templates that rely on < cannot be applied to complex data unless a comparison (in the form of a functor or function) is provided. E.g.: A complex cannot be used as key for a map unless a comparison is provided. Unfortunately, compilers historically generate somewhat esoteric, long, and unhelpful error messages for this sort of error. Ensuring that a certain object adheres to a method protocol can alleviate this issue. Languages which use compare instead of < can also use complex values as keys.

The second kind of template, a *class template*, extends the same concept to classes. A class template specialization is a class. Class templates are often used to make generic containers. For example, the STL has a linked list container. To make a linked list of integers, one writes list<int>. A list of strings is denoted list<string>. A list has a set of standard functions associated with it, which work for any compatible parameterizing types.

Template Specialization

A powerful feature of C++'s templates is *template specialization*. This allows alternative implementations to be provided based on certain characteristics of the parameterized type that is being instantiated. Template specialization has two purposes: to allow certain forms of optimization, and to reduce code bloat.

For example, consider a sort() template function. One of the primary activities that such a function does is to swap or exchange the values in two of the container's positions. If the values are large (in terms of the number of bytes it takes to store each of them), then it is often quicker to first build a separate list of pointers to the objects, sort those pointers, and then build the final sorted sequence. If the values are quite small however it is usually fastest to just swap the values in-place as needed. Furthermore, if the parameterized type is already of some pointer-type, then there is no need to build a separate pointer array. Template specialization allows the template creator to write different implementations and to specify the characteristics that the parameterized type(s) must have for each implementation to be used.

Unlike function templates, class templates can be partially specialized. That means that an alternate version of the class template code can be provided when some of the template parameters are known, while leaving other template parameters generic. This can be used, for example, to create a default implementation (the *primary specialization*) that assumes that copying a parameterizing type is expensive and then create partial specializations for types that are cheap to copy, thus increasing overall efficiency. Clients of such a class template just use specializations of it without needing to know whether the compiler used the primary specialization or some partial specialization in each case. Class templates can also be *fully specialized*, which means that an alternate implementation can be provided when all of the parameterizing types are known.

Advantages and Disadvantages

Some uses of templates, such as the max() function, were previously filled by function-like preprocessor macros (a legacy of the C programming language). For example, here is a possible max() macro:

```
#define max(a,b) ((a) < (b) ? (b) : (a))
```

Macros are expanded by preprocessor, before compilation proper; templates are expanded at compile time. Macros are always expanded inline; templates can also be expanded as inline functions when the compiler deems it appropriate. Thus both function-like macros and function templates have no run-time overhead.

However, templates are generally considered an improvement over macros for these purposes. Templates are type-safe. Templates avoid some of the common errors found in code that makes heavy use of function-like macros, such as evaluating parameters with side effects twice. Perhaps most importantly, templates were designed to be applicable to much larger problems than macros.

There are three primary drawbacks to the use of templates: compiler support, poor error messages, and code bloat. Many compilers historically have poor support for templates, thus the use of templates can make code somewhat less portable. Support may also be poor when a C++ compiler is being used with a linker which is not C++-aware, or when attempting to use templates across shared library boundaries. Most modern compilers however now have fairly robust and standard template support, and the new C++ standard, C++11, further addresses these issues.

Almost all compilers produce confusing, long, or sometimes unhelpful error messages when errors are detected in code that uses templates. This can make templates difficult to develop.

Finally, the use of templates requires the compiler to generate a separate *instance* of the templated class or function for every permutation of type parameters used with it. (This is necessary because types in C++ are not all the same size, and the sizes of data fields are important to how classes work.) So the indiscriminate use of templates can lead to code bloat, resulting in excessively large executables. However, judicious use of template specialization and derivation can dramatically reduce such code bloat in some cases:

So, can derivation be used to reduce the problem of code replicated because templates are used? This would involve deriving a template from an ordinary class. This technique proved successful in curbing code bloat in real use. People who do not use a technique like this have found that replicated code can cost megabytes of code space even in moderate size programs.

> — *Bjarne Stroustrup, The Design and Evolution of C++, 1994*

In simple cases templates can be transformed into generics (not causing code bloat) by creating a class getting a parameter derived from a type in compile time and wrapping a template around this class. It is a nice approach for creating generic heap-based containers.

The extra instantiations generated by templates can also cause debuggers to have difficulty working gracefully with templates. For example, setting a debug breakpoint within a template from a source file may either miss setting the breakpoint in the actual instantiation desired or may set a breakpoint in every place the template is instantiated.

Also, because the compiler needs to perform macro-like expansions of templates and generate different instances of them at compile time, the implementation source code for the templated class or function must be available (e.g. included in a header) to the code using it. Templated classes or functions, including much of the Standard Template Library (STL), if not included in header files, cannot be compiled. (This is in contrast to non-templated code, which may be compiled to binary, providing only a declarations header file for code using it.) This may be a disadvantage by exposing the implementing code, which removes some abstractions, and could restrict its use in closed-source projects.

Templates in D

The D programming language supports templates based in design on C++. Most C++ template idioms will carry over to D without alteration, but D adds some additional functionality:

- Template parameters in D are not restricted to just types and primitive values, but also allow arbitrary compile-time values (such as strings and struct literals), and aliases to arbitrary identifiers, including other templates or template instantiations.

- Template constraints and the static if statement provide an alternative to C++'s substitution failure is not an error (SFINAE) mechanism, similar to C++ concepts.

- The is(...) expression allows speculative instantiation to verify an object's traits at compile time.

- The auto keyword and the typeof expression allow type inference for variable declarations and function return values, which in turn allows "Voldemort types" (types which do not have a global name).

Templates in D use a different syntax as in C++: whereas in C++ template parameters are wrapped in angular brackets (Template<param1, param2>), D uses an exclamation sign and parentheses: Template!(param1, param2). This avoids the C++ parsing difficulties due to ambiguity with comparison operators. If there is only one parameter, the parentheses can be omitted.

Conventionally, D combines the above features to provide compile-time polymorphism using trait-based generic programming. For example, an input range is defined as any type which satisfies the checks performed by isInputRange, which is defined as follows:

```
template isInputRange(R)

{

    enum bool isInputRange = is(typeof(
```

```
    (inout int = 0)

    {

        R r = R.init;       // can define a range object

        if (r.empty) {}     // can test for empty

        r.popFront();       // can invoke popFront()

        auto h = r.front;   // can get the front of the range

    }));

}
```

A function which accepts only input ranges can then use the above template in a template constraint:

```
auto fun(Range)(Range range)

    if (isInputRange!Range)

{

    // ...

}
```

Code Generation

In addition to template metaprogramming, D also provides several features to enable compile-time code generation:

- The import expression allows reading a file from disk and using its contents as a string expression.

- Compile-time reflection allows enumerating and inspecting declarations and their members during compilation.

- User-defined attributes allow users to attach arbitrary identifiers to declarations, which can then be enumerated using compile-time reflection.

- Compile-Time Function Execution (CTFE) allows a subset of D (restricted to safe operations) to be interpreted during compilation.

- String mixins allow evaluating and compiling the contents of a string expression as D code which becomes part of the program.

Combining the above allows generating code based on existing declarations. For example, D serialization frameworks can enumerate a type's members and generate specialized functions for each serialized type to perform serialization and deserialization. User-defined attributes could further indicate serialization rules.

The import expression and compile-time function execution also allow efficiently implementing domain-specific languages. For example, given a function which takes a string containing an HTML template and returns equivalent D source code, it is possible to use it in the following way:

```
// Import the contents of example.htt as a string manifest con-
stant.
enum htmlTemplate = import("example.htt");
```

```
// Transpile the HTML template to D code.
enum htmlDCode = htmlTemplateToD(htmlTemplate);
```

```
// Paste the contents of htmlDCode as D code.
mixin(htmlDCode);
```

Genericity in Eiffel

Generic classes have been a part of Eiffel since the original method and language design. The foundation publications of Eiffel, use the term *genericity* to describe the creation and use of generic classes.

Basic/Unconstrained Genericity

Generic classes are declared with their class name and a list of one or more *formal generic parameters*. In the following code, class LIST has one formal generic parameter G

```
class

    LIST [G]

            . . .

feature    -- Access

    item: G

            -- The item currently pointed to by cursor

        . . .
```

```
feature    -- Element change

   put (new_item: G)

            -- Add `new_item' at the end of the list

            ...
```

The formal generic parameters are placeholders for arbitrary class names which will be supplied when a declaration of the generic class is made, as shown in the two *generic derivations* below, where ACCOUNT and DEPOSIT are other class names. ACCOUNT and DEPOSIT are considered *actual generic parameters* as they provide real class names to substitute for G in actual use.

```
    list_of_accounts: LIST [ACCOUNT]

              -- Account list



     list_of_deposits: LIST [DEPOSIT]

              -- Deposit list
```

Within the Eiffel type system, although class LIST [G] is considered a class, it is not considered a type. However, a generic derivation of LIST [G] such as LIST [ACCOUNT] is considered a type.

Constrained Genericity

For the list class shown above, an actual generic parameter substituting for G can be any other available class. To constrain the set of classes from which valid actual generic parameters can be chosen, a *generic constraint* can be specified. In the declaration of class SORTED_LIST below, the generic constraint dictates that any valid actual generic parameter will be a class which inherits from class COMPARABLE. The generic constraint ensures that elements of a SORTED_LIST can in fact be sorted.

```
class

    SORTED_LIST [G -> COMPARABLE]
```

Generics in Java

Support for the *generics*, or "containers-of-type-T" was added to the Java programming language in 2004 as part of J2SE 5.0. In Java, generics are only checked at compile time for type correctness. The generic type information is then removed via a process called type erasure, to maintain compatibility with old JVM implementations, making it unavailable at runtime. For example, a List<String> is converted to the raw type List. The compiler inserts type casts to convert the elements to the String type when they are retrieved from the list, reducing performance compared to other implementations such as C++ templates.

Genericity in .NET [C#, VB.NET]

Generics were added as part of .NET Framework 2.0 in November 2005, based on a research prototype from Microsoft Research started in 1999. Although similar to generics in Java, .NET generics do not apply type erasure, but implement generics as a first class mechanism in the runtime using reification. This design choice provides additional functionality, such as allowing reflection with preservation of generic types, as well as alleviating some of the limitations of erasure (such as being unable to create generic arrays). This also means that there is no performance hit from runtime casts and normally expensive boxing conversions. When primitive and value types are used as generic arguments, they get specialized implementations, allowing for efficient generic collections and methods. As in C++ and Java, nested generic types such as Dictionary<string, List<int>> are valid types, however are advised against for member signatures in code analysis design rules.

.NET allows six varieties of generic type constraints using the where keyword including restricting generic types to be value types, to be classes, to have constructors, and to implement interfaces. Below is an example with an interface constraint:

```
using System;


class Sample
{
    static void Main()
    {
        int[] array = { 0, 1, 2, 3 };
        MakeAtLeast<int>(array, 2); // Change array to { 2, 2,
2, 3 }
        foreach (int i in array)
            Console.WriteLine(i); // Print results.
        Console.ReadKey(true);

    }
```

```
      static void MakeAtLeast<T>(T[] list, T lowest) where T :
IComparable<T>

      {

          for (int i = 0; i < list.Length; i++)

              if (list[i].CompareTo(lowest) < 0)

                  list[i] = lowest;

      }

}
```

The MakeAtLeast() method allows operation on arrays, with elements of generic type T. The method's type constraint indicates that the method is applicable to any type T that implements the generic IComparable<T> interface. This ensures a compile time error if the method is called if the type does not support comparison. The interface provides the generic method CompareTo(T).

The above method could also be written without generic types, simply using the non-generic Array type. However, since arrays are contravariant, the casting would not be type safe, and compiler may miss errors that would otherwise be caught while making use of the generic types. In addition, the method would need to access the array items as objects instead, and would require casting to compare two elements. (For value types like types such as int this requires a boxing conversion, although this can be worked around using the Comparer<T> class, as is done in the standard collection classes.)

A notable behavior of static members in a generic .NET class is static member instantiation per run-time type.

```
    //A generic class

    public class GenTest<T>

    {

        //A static variable - will be created for each type on
refraction

        static CountedInstances OnePerType = new CountedInstanc-
es();


        //a data member

        private T mT;
```

```
        //simple constructor

        public GenTest(T pT)

        {

            mT = pT;

        }

    }


    //a class

    public class CountedInstances

    {

        //Static variable - this will be incremented once per
instance

        public static int Counter;


        //simple constructor

        public CountedInstances()

        {

            //increase counter by one during object instantiation

            CountedInstances.Counter++;

        }

    }


//main code entry point

//at the end of execution, CountedInstances.Counter = 2

GenTest<int> g1 = new GenTest<int>(1);

GenTest<int> g11 = new GenTest<int>(11);

GenTest<int> g111 = new GenTest<int>(111);
```

```
GenTest<double> g2 = new GenTest<double>(1.0);
```

Genericity in Delphi

Delphi's Object Pascal dialect acquired generics in the Delphi 2007 release, initially only with the (now discontinued) .NET compiler before being added to the native code one in the Delphi 2009 release. The semantics and capabilities of Delphi generics are largely modelled on those had by generics in .NET 2.0, though the implementation is by necessity quite different. Here's a more or less direct translation of the first C# example shown above:

```
program Sample;


{$APPTYPE CONSOLE}


uses
  Generics.Defaults; //for IComparer<>


type
  TUtils = class
    class procedure MakeAtLeast<T>(Arr: TArray<T>; const Lowest:
T;
      Comparer: IComparer<T>); overload;
    class procedure MakeAtLeast<T>(Arr: TArray<T>; const Lowest:
T); overload;
  end;


class procedure TUtils.MakeAtLeast<T>(Arr: TArray<T>; const Low-
est: T;
  Comparer: IComparer<T>);
var
  I: Integer;
begin
  if Comparer = nil then Comparer := TComparer<T>.Default;
```

```
  for I := Low(Arr) to High(Arr) do

    if Comparer.Compare(Arr[I], Lowest) < 0 then

      Arr[I] := Lowest;
end;


class procedure TUtils.MakeAtLeast<T>(Arr: TArray<T>; const Low-
est: T);
begin

  MakeAtLeast<T>(Arr, Lowest, nil);

end;


var

  Ints: TArray<Integer>;

  Value: Integer;
begin

  Ints := TArray<Integer>.Create(0, 1, 2, 3);

  TUtils.MakeAtLeast<Integer>(Ints, 2);

  for Value in Ints do

    WriteLn(Value);

  ReadLn;
end.
```

As with C#, methods as well as whole types can have one or more type parameters. In
the example, TArray is a generic type (defined by the language) and MakeAtLeast a
generic method. The available constraints are very similar to the available constraints
in C#: any value type, any class, a specific class or interface, and a class with a parame-
terless constructor. Multiple constraints act as an additive union.

Genericity in Free Pascal

Free Pascal implemented generics before Delphi, and with different syntax and semantics. However, work is now underway to implement Delphi generics alongside native
FPC ones. This allows Free Pascal programmers to use generics in whatever style they

prefer.

Delphi and Free Pascal example:

```
// Delphi style
unit A;

{$ifdef fpc}
  {$mode delphi}
{$endif}

interface

type
  TGenericClass<T> = class
    function Foo(const AValue: T): T;
  end;

implementation

function TGenericClass<T>.Foo(const AValue: T): T;
begin
  Result := AValue + AValue;
end;

end.

// Free Pascal's ObjFPC style
```

```
unit B;

{$ifdef fpc}
  {$mode objfpc}
{$endif}

interface

type
  generic TGenericClass<T> = class
    function Foo(const AValue: T): T;
  end;

implementation

function TGenericClass.Foo(const AValue: T): T;
begin
  Result := AValue + AValue;
end;

end.

// example usage, Delphi style
program TestGenDelphi;

{$ifdef fpc}
  {$mode delphi}
```

```
{$endif}

uses
  A,B;

var
  GC1: A.TGenericClass<Integer>;
  GC2: B.TGenericClass<String>;
begin
  GC1 := A.TGenericClass<Integer>.Create;
  GC2 := B.TGenericClass<String>.Create;
  WriteLn(GC1.Foo(100)); // 200
  WriteLn(GC2.Foo('hello')); // hellohello
  GC1.Free;
  GC2.Free;
end.

// example usage, ObjFPC style
program TestGenDelphi;

{$ifdef fpc}
  {$mode objfpc}
{$endif}

uses
  A,B;
```

```
// required in ObjFPC

type

  TAGenericClassInt = specialize A.TGenericClass<Integer>;

  TBGenericClassString = specialize B.TGenericClass<String>;

var

  GC1: TAGenericClassInt;

  GC2: TBGenericClassString;

begin

  GC1 := TAGenericClassInt.Create;

  GC2 := TBGenericClassString.Create;

  WriteLn(GC1.Foo(100)); // 200

  WriteLn(GC2.Foo('hello')); // hellohello

  GC1.Free;

  GC2.Free;

end.
```

Functional Languages

Genericity in Haskell

The type class mechanism of Haskell supports generic programming. Six of the predefined type classes in Haskell (including Eq, the types that can be compared for equality, and Show, the types whose values can be rendered as strings) have the special property of supporting *derived instances*. This means that a programmer defining a new type can state that this type is to be an instance of one of these special type classes, without providing implementations of the class methods as is usually necessary when declaring class instances. All the necessary methods will be "derived" – that is, constructed automatically – based on the structure of the type. For instance, the following declaration of a type of binary trees states that it is to be an instance of the classes Eq and Show:

```
data BinTree a = Leaf a | Node (BinTree a) a (BinTree a)

     deriving
```

This results in an equality function (==) and a string representation function being automatically defined for any type of the form BinTree T provided that T itself supports those operations.

The support for derived instances of Eq and Show makes their methods == and show generic in a qualitatively different way from parametrically polymorphic functions: these "functions" (more accurately, type-indexed families of functions) can be applied to values of various types, and although they behave differently for every argument type, little work is needed to add support for a new type. Ralf Hinze (2004) has shown that a similar effect can be achieved for user-defined type classes by certain programming techniques. Other researchers have proposed approaches to this and other kinds of genericity in the context of Haskell and extensions to Haskell (discussed below).

PolyP

PolyP was the first generic programming language extension to Haskell. In PolyP, generic functions are called *polytypic*. The language introduces a special construct in which such polytypic functions can be defined via structural induction over the structure of the pattern functor of a regular datatype. Regular datatypes in PolyP are a subset of Haskell datatypes. A regular datatype t must be of kind $* \rightarrow *$, and if a is the formal type argument in the definition, then all recursive calls to t must have the form $t\ a$. These restrictions rule out higher-kinded datatypes as well as nested datatypes, where the recursive calls are of a different form. The flatten function in PolyP is here provided as an example:

```
flatten :: Regular d => d a -> [a]

  flatten = cata fl


  polytypic fl :: f a [a] -> [a]

    case f of

      g+h -> either fl fl

      g*h -> \(x,y) -> fl x ++ fl y

      () -> \x -> []

      Par -> \x -> [x]

      Rec -> \x -> x

      d@g -> concat . flatten . pmap fl

      Con t -> \x -> []


    cata :: Regular d => (FunctorOf d a b -> b) -> d a -> b
```

Generic Haskell

Generic Haskell is another extension to Haskell, developed at Utrecht University in the Netherlands. The extensions it provides are:

- *Type-indexed values* are defined as a value indexed over the various Haskell type constructors (unit, primitive types, sums, products, and user-defined type constructors). In addition, we can also specify the behaviour of a type-indexed values for a specific constructor using *constructor cases*, and reuse one generic definition in another using *default cases*.

The resulting type-indexed value can be specialised to any type.

- *Kind-indexed types* are types indexed over kinds, defined by giving a case for both $*$ and $k \rightarrow k'$. Instances are obtained by applying the kind-indexed type to a kind.

- Generic definitions can be used by applying them to a type or kind. This is called *generic application*. The result is a type or value, depending on which sort of generic definition is applied.

- *Generic abstraction* enables generic definitions be defined by abstracting a type parameter (of a given kind).

- *Type-indexed types* are types which are indexed over the type constructors. These can be used to give types to more involved generic values. The resulting type-indexed types can be specialised to any type.

As an example, the equality function in Generic Haskell:

```
type Eq {[ * ]} t1 t2 = t1 -> t2 -> Bool

type Eq {[ k -> l ]} t1 t2 = forall u1 u2. Eq {[ k ]} u1 u2
-> Eq {[ l ]} (t1 u1) (t2 u2)


eq {| t :: k |} :: Eq {[ k ]} t t

eq {| Unit |} _ _ = True

eq {| :+: |} eqA eqB (Inl a1) (Inl a2) = eqA a1 a2

eq {| :+: |} eqA eqB (Inr b1) (Inr b2) = eqB b1 b2

eq {| :+: |} eqA eqB _ _ = False

eq {| :*: |} eqA eqB (a1 :*: b1) (a2 :*: b2) = eqA a1 a2 &&
eqB b1 b2

eq {| Int |} = (==)
```

```
eq {| Char |} = (==)
eq {| Bool |} = (==)
```

Clean

Clean offers generic programming based PolyP and the generic Haskell as supported by the GHC>=6.0. It parametrizes by kind as those but offers overloading.

Other Languages

The ML family of programming languages support generic programming through parametric polymorphism and generic modules called *functors*. Both Standard ML and OCaml provide functors, which are similar to class templates and to Ada's generic packages. Scheme syntactic abstractions also have a connection to genericity – these are in fact a superset of templating à la C++.

A Verilog module may take one or more parameters, to which their actual values are assigned upon the instantiation of the module. One example is a generic register array where the array width is given via a parameter. Such the array, combined with a generic wire vector, can make a generic buffer or memory module with an arbitrary bit width out of a single module implementation.

VHDL, being derived from Ada, also have generic ability.

Metaprogramming

Metaprogramming is the art of writing of computer programs with the ability to treat programs as their data. It means that a program could be designed to read, generate, analyse or transform other programs, and even modify itself while running. In some cases, this allows programmers to minimize the number of lines of code to express a solution (hence reducing development time), or it gives programs greater flexibility to efficiently handle new situations without recompilation. One of the types of metaprogramming only involves writing their program is generic programming.

Metaprogramming is used to move the computations from the run-time to compile-time,enable self-adapting code and generate code using compile time computations.

The language in which the metaprogram is written is called the metalanguage. The language of the programs that are manipulated is called the *object language*. The ability of a programming language to be its own metalanguage is called *reflection* or *reflexivity*.

Reflection is a valuable language feature to facilitate metaprogramming. Having the programming language itself as a first-class data type (as in Lisp, Prolog, SNOBOL, or Rebol) is also very useful; this is known as *homoiconicity*. Generic programming invokes a metaprogramming facility within a language, in those languages supporting it.

Metaprogramming usually works in one of three ways. The first way is to expose the internals of the run-time engine to the programming code through application programming interfaces (APIs) like Microsoft IL Emiter. The second approach is dynamic execution of expressions that contain programming commands, often composed from strings, but can also be from other methods using arguments or context, like Javascript. Thus, "programs can write programs." Although both approaches can be used in the same language, most languages tend to lean toward one or the other.

The third way is to step outside the language entirely. General purpose program transformation systems such as compilers, which accept language descriptions and can carry out arbitrary transformations on those languages, are direct implementations of general metaprogramming. This allows metaprogramming to be applied to virtually any target language without regard to whether that target language has any metaprogramming abilities of its own.

Approaches

In Statically Typed Functional Languages

- Usage of dependent types allows proving that generated code is never invalid.

Template Metaprogramming

- C "X Macros"
- C++ Templates

Staged Meta-Programming

- MetaML
- MetaOCaml

Macro Systems

- Scheme hygienic macros
- MacroML
- Template Haskell

IBM/360 Assembler

The IBM/360 and derivatives had powerful assembler macro facilities that were often used to generate complete programs or sections of programs (for different operating systems for instance). Macros provided with CICS transaction processing system had assembler macros that generated COBOL statements as a pre-processing step.

'Metaclass'

- Python
- SmallTalk-80
- Ruby
- Objective C

Examples

A simple example of a metaprogram is this POSIX Shell script, which is an example of generative programming:

```
#!/bin/sh

# metaprogram

echo '#!/bin/sh' >program

for I in $(seq 992)

do

        echo "echo $I" >> program

done

chmod +x program
```

This script (or program) generates a new 993-line program that prints out the numbers 1–992. This is only an illustration of how to use code to write more code; it is not the most efficient way to print out a list of numbers. Nonetheless, a programmer can write and execute this metaprogram in less than a minute, and will have generated exactly 1000 lines of code in that amount of time.

A quine is a special kind of metaprogram that produces its own source code as its output.

Not all metaprogramming involves generative programming. If programs are modifiable at runtime or if incremental compilation is available (such as in C#, Forth, Frink, Groovy, JavaScript, Lisp, Lua, Perl, PHP, Python, REBOL, Ruby, Smalltalk, and Tcl), then techniques can be used to perform metaprogramming without actually generating source code.

Lisp is probably the quintessential language with metaprogramming facilities, both because of its historical precedence and because of the simplicity and power of its metaprogramming. In Lisp metaprogramming, the unquote operator (typically a comma) introduces code that is evaluated at program definition time rather than at run time; Self-evaluating forms and quoting in Lisp. The metaprogramming language is thus identical to the host programming language, and existing Lisp routines can be directly reused for metaprogramming, if desired.

This approach has been implemented in other languages by incorporating an interpreter in the program, which works directly with the program's data. There are implementations of this kind for some common high-level languages, such as RemObjects' Pascal Script for Object Pascal.

One style of metaprogramming is to employ domain-specific languages (DSLs). A fairly common example of using DSLs involves generative metaprogramming: lex and yacc, two tools used to generate lexical analyzers and parsers, let the user describe the language using regular expressions and context-free grammars, and embed the complex algorithms required to efficiently parse the language.

Challenges of Metaprogramming

We have seen that metaprogramming can help us to give more flexibility and configurability at runtime. However the wrong use of the metaprogramming can result in unwarranted and unexpected errors. Some of the common problems which can occur due to wrong use of metaprogramming are inability of the compiler to identify missing configuration parameters, invalid or incorrect data can result in unknown exception or different results

Implementations

- ASF+SDF Meta Environment

- DMS Software Reengineering Toolkit

- Joose (JavaScript)

- JetBrains MPS

- Moose (Perl)

- Nemerle

- Rascal Metaprogramming Language

- Stratego/XT

- Template Haskell

Compatibility of C and C++

The C and C++ programming languages are closely related. C++ grew out of C, as it was designed to be source-and-link compatible with C. Due to this, development tools for the two languages (such as IDEs and compilers) are often integrated into a single product, with the programmer able to specify C or C++ as their source language. However, most non-trivial C programs will not compile as C++ code without modification — C is not a subset of C++.

Likewise, C++ introduces many features that are not available in C and in practice almost all code written in C++ is not conforming C code. This article, however, focuses on differences that cause conforming C code to be ill-formed C++ code, or to be conforming/well-formed in both languages, but to behave differently in C and C++.

Bjarne Stroustrup, the creator of C++, has suggested that the incompatibilities between C and C++ should be reduced as much as possible in order to maximize inter-operability between the two languages. Others have argued that since C and C++ are two different languages, compatibility between them is useful but not vital; according to this camp, efforts to reduce incompatibility should not hinder attempts to improve each language in isolation. The official rationale for the 1999 C standard (C99) "endorse[d] the principle of maintaining the largest common subset" between C and C++ "while maintaining a distinction between them and allowing them to evolve separately", and stated that the authors were "content to let C++ be the big and ambitious language."

Several additions of C99 are or were not supported in C++ or conflicted with C++ features, such as variadic macros, compound literals, designated initializers, variable-length arrays, and native complex number types. The long long int datatype and restrict type qualifier defined in C99 were not included in the C++03 standard, but most mainstream compilers such as the GNU Compiler Collection, Microsoft Visual C++, and Intel C++ Compiler provided similar functionality as an extension. The long long datatype along with variadic macros are present in the subsequent C++ standard, C++11. On the other hand, C99 has reduced some other incompatibilities by incorporating C++ features such as // comments and mixed declarations and code.

Constructs Valid in C but not in C++

- One commonly encountered difference is C being more weakly-typed regarding pointers. For example, C allows a void* pointer to be assigned to any pointer type without a cast, while C++ doesn't; this idiom appears often in C code using malloc memory allocation, or in the passing of context pointers to the pthreads API and other frameworks involving callbacks. For example, the following is valid in C but not C++:

```
void* ptr;

/* Implicit conversion from void* to int* */

int *i = ptr;
```

or similarly:

```
int *j = malloc(sizeof(int) * 5);       /* Implicit conversion from
void* to int* */
```

In order to make the code compile as both C and C++, one must use an explicit cast, as follows (with some potentially unpleasant side effects in both languages):

```
void* ptr;

int *i = (int *)ptr;

int *j = (int *)malloc(sizeof(int) * 5);
```

- C++ adds numerous additional keywords to support its new features. This renders C code using those keywords for identifiers invalid in C++. For example:

```
struct template

{

    int new;

    struct template* class;

};
```

is valid C code, but is rejected by a C++ compiler, since the keywords "template", "new" and "class" are reserved.

- C++ compilers prohibit goto or switch from crossing an initialization, as in the following C99 code:

```
void fn(void)

{

    goto flack;

    int i = 1;

    flack:

        ;

}
```

- In C, struct, union, and enum types must be indicated as such whenever the type is referenced. In C++, all declarations of such types carry the typedef implicitly. As a result, C allows declaring type with the same name as a struct, union or enum.

```
enum BOOL {FALSE, TRUE};

typedef int BOOL;
```

- C allows for multiple tentative definition of a single global variable in a single translation unit.

```
int N;

int N = 10;
```

- Enumeration constants (enum values) are always of type int in C, whereas they are distinct types in C++ and may have a size different from that of int. C++11 allows the programmer to use custom integer types for the values of an enum.

- C++ changes some C standard library functions to add additional polymorphic functions with const type qualifiers, e.g. strchr returns char* in C, while C++ acts as if there were two polymorphic functions const char *strchr(const char *) and a char *strchr(char *).

- In both C and C++, one can define nested struct types, but the scope is interpreted differently (in C++, a nested struct is defined only within the scope/namespace of the outer struct).

- Non-prototype ("K&R"-style) function declarations are not allowed in C++, although they have also been deprecated in C since 1990. Similarly, implicit function declarations (using functions that have not been declared) are not allowed in C++, but have also been deprecated in C since 1999.

- C allows struct, union, and enum types to be declared in function prototypes, whereas C++ does not.

- In C, a function prototype without parameters, e.g. int foo();, implies that the parameters are unspecified. Therefore, it is legal to call such a function with one or more arguments, e.g. foo(42, "hello world"). In contrast, in C++ a function prototype without arguments means that the function takes no arguments, and calling such a function with arguments is ill-formed. In C, the correct way to declare a function that takes no arguments is by using 'void', as in int foo(void);, which is also valid in C++.

- C++ is more strict than C about pointer assignments that discard a const qualifier (e.g. assigning a const int* value to an int* variable): in C++ this is invalid and generates a compiler error (unless an explicit typecast is used), whereas in C this is allowed (although many compilers emit a warning).

- In C++ a const variable must be initialized; in C this is not necessary.

- Complex arithmetic using the float complex and double complex primitive data types was added in the C99 standard, via the _Complex keyword and complex convenience macro. In C++, complex arithmetic can be performed using the complex number class, but the two methods are not code-compatible.

- C99 and C11 added several additional features to C that have not been incorporated into standard C++, such as the restrict keyword, designated initializers, and flexible array members.

- Zero length arrays are valid in C99, but forbidden in ISO C++. The length of bytes field is zero. Such field must be the last field in the struct, struct cannot consist of only zero length array and struct can have only one zero length array.

```
struct X
{
    int n, m;
    char bytes[];
}
```

- Designated initializers for structs and arrays are valid only in C:

```
struct X a = {.n = 4, .m = 6};
char s = { = 'a', ='g'};
```

- Array parameter qualifiers in functions.

```
int foo(int a[const]);
int bar(char s[static 5]);
```

- Variable length arrays. This feature leads to possibly non-coplile time sizeof operator.

```
void foo(size_t x, int a[*]);   // VLA declaration
void foo(size_t x, int a[x])
{
    printf("%zu\n", sizeof a); // same as sizeof(int*)
    char s[x*2];
    printf("%zu\n", sizeof s); // will print x*2
}
```

Constructs that Behave Differently in C and C++

There are a few syntactical constructs that are valid in both C and C++, but produce different results in the two languages.

For example, character literals such as 'a' are of type int in C and of type char in C++, which means that sizeof 'a' will generally give different results in the two languages: in C++, it will be 1, while in C it will be sizeof(int). As another consequence of this type difference, in C, 'a' will always be a signed expression, regardless of whether or not char is a signed or unsigned type, whereas for C++ this is compiler implementation specific.

C++ implicitly treats any const global as file scope unless it is explicitly declared extern, unlike C in which extern is the default. Conversely, inline functions in C are of file scope whereas they have external linkage by default in C++.

Several of the other differences from the previous section can also be exploited to create code that compiles in both languages but behaves differently. For example, the following function will return different values in C and C++:

```
extern int T;


int size(void)

{

    struct T {  int i;  int j;  };


    return sizeof(T);

    /* C:    return sizeof(int)

     * C++: return sizeof(struct T)

     */

}
```

This is due to C requiring struct in front of structure tags (and so sizeof(T) refers to the variable), but C++ allowing it to be omitted (and so sizeof(T) refers to the implicit typedef). Beware that the outcome is different when the extern declaration is placed inside the function: then the presence of an identifier with same name in the function scope inhibits the implicit typedef to take effect for C++, and the outcome for C and C++ would be the same. Observe also that the ambiguity in the example above is due to the use of the parenthesis with the sizeof operator. Using sizeof T would expect T to be an expression and not a type, and thus the example would not compile with C++.

Both C99 and C++ have a boolean type bool with constants true and false, but they behave differently. In C++, bool is a built-in type and a reserved keyword. In C99, a new keyword, _Bool, is introduced as the new boolean type. In many aspects, it behaves much like an unsigned int, but conversions from other integer types or pointers always constrained to 0 and 1. Other than for other unsigned types, and as one would expect for a boolean type, such a conversion is 0 if and only if the expression in question evaluates to 0 and it is 1 in all other cases. The header stdbool.h provides macros bool, true and false that are defined as _Bool, 1 and 0, respectively.

Linking C and C++ Code

While C and C++ maintain a large degree of source compatibility, the object files their respective compilers produce can have important differences that manifest themselves when intermixing C and C++ code. Notably:

- C compilers do not name mangle symbols in the way that C++ compilers do.

- Depending on the compiler and architecture, it also may be the case that calling conventions differ between the two languages.

For these reasons, for C++ code to call a C function foo(), the C++ code must prototype foo() with extern "C". Likewise, for C code to call a C++ function bar(), the C++ code for bar() must be declared with extern "C".

A common practice for header files to maintain both C and C++ compatibility is to make its declaration be extern "C" for the scope of the header:

```
/* Header file foo.h */

#ifdef __cplusplus /* If this is a C++ compiler, use C linkage */

extern "C" {

#endif


/* These functions get C linkage */

void foo();


struct bar { /* ... */ };


#ifdef __cplusplus /* If this is a C++ compiler, end C linkage */
```

```
}

#endif
```

Differences between C and C++ linkage and calling conventions can also have subtle implications for code that uses function pointers. Some compilers will produce non-working code if a function pointer declared extern "C" points to a C++ function that is not declared extern "C".

For example, the following code:

```
1 void my_function();
2 extern "C" void foo(void (*fn_ptr)(void));
3
4 void bar()
5 {
6    foo(my_function);
7 }
```

Using Sun Microsystems' C++ compiler, this produces the following warning:

```
$ CC -c test.cc

"test.cc", line 6: Warning (Anachronism): Formal argument fn_
ptr of type

extern "C" void(*)() in call to foo(extern "C" void(*)()) is
being passed

void(*)().
```

This is because my_function() is not declared with C linkage and calling conventions, but is being passed to the C function foo().

Criticism of C++

C++ is a general-purpose programming language with imperative, object-oriented and generic programming features. Many criticisms have been leveled at the programming language from, among others, prominent software developers like Linus Torvalds, Richard Stallman, and Ken Thompson.

C++ is a multiparadigm programming language with backward compatibility with the programming language C. This article focuses not on C features like pointer arithmetic, operator precedence or preprocessor macros, but on pure C++ features that are often criticized.

Slow Compile Times

The natural interface between source files in C/C++ are header files. Each time a header file is modified, all source files that include the header file should recompile their code. Header files are slow because of them being textual and context dependent as a consequence of the preprocessor. C only has limited amounts of information in header files, the most important being struct declarations and function prototypes. C++ stores its classes in header files and they are not only exposing their public variables and public functions (like C with its structs and function prototypes) but also their private functions. This forces unnecessary recompiles of all source files that include the header file, each time when changing these private functions. This problem is magnified where the classes are written as templates, forcing all of their code into the slow header files, which is the case with the whole C++ standard library. Large C++ projects can therefore be extremely slow to compile.

One solution for this is to use the Pimpl idiom. By using pointers on the stack to the implementation object on the heap there is a higher chance all object sizes on the stack become equal. This of course comes with the cost of an unnecessary heap allocation for each object. Additionally precompiled headers can be used for header files that are fairly static.

One suggested solution is to use a module system.

Global Format State of <Iostream>

C++ <iostream> unlike C <stdio.h> relies on a global format state. This fits very poorly together with exceptions, when a function must interrupt the control flow, after an error, but before resetting the global format state. One fix for this is to use Resource Acquisition Is Initialization (RAII) which is implemented in Boost but is not a part of the C++ Standard Library.

The global state of <iostream> uses static constructors which causes overhead. Another source of bad performance is the use of std::endl instead of '\n' when doing output, because of it calling flush as a side effect. C++ <iostream> is by default synchronized with <stdio.h> which can cause performance problems. Shutting it off can improve performance but forces giving up thread safety.

Here follows an example where an exception interrupts the function before std::cout can be restored from hexadecimal to decimal. The error number in the catch statement will be written out in hexadecimal which probably isn't what one wants:

```
#include <iostream>
```

```
#include <vector>


int main() {

    try {

        std::cout << std::hex;

        std::cout << 0xFFFFFFFF << std::endl;

        std::vector<int> vector(0xFFFFFFFFFFFFFFFFL,0); // Ex-
ception

        std::cout << std::dec; // Never reached

    } catch(std::exception &e) {

        std::cout << "Error number: " << 10 << std::endl; // Not
in decimal

    }

    return(EXIT_SUCCESS);

}
```

It is acknowledged even by some members of the C++ standards body that the iostreams interface is an aging interface that needs to be replaced eventually. This design forces the library implementers to adopt solutions that impact performance greatly.

Heap Allocations in Containers

After the inclusion of the STL in C++, its templated containers were promoted while the traditional C arrays were strongly discouraged. One important feature of containers like std::string and std::vector is them having their memory on the heap instead of on the stack like C arrays. To stop them from allocating on the heap, one would be forced to write a custom allocator, which isn't standard. Heap allocation is slower than stack allocation which makes claims about the classical C++ containers being "just as fast" as C arrays somewhat untrue. They are just as fast to use, but not to construct. One way to solve this problem was to introduce stack allocated containers like boost::array or std::array.

As for strings there is the possibility to use SSO (short string optimization) where only strings exceeding a certain size are allocated on the heap. There is however no standard way in C++ for the user to decide this SSO limit and it remains hard coded and implementation specific.

Iterators

The philosophy of the Standard Template Library (STL) embedded in the C++ Standard Library is to use generic algorithms in the form of templates using iterators. Iterators are hard to implement efficiently which caused Alexander Stepanov to blame some compiler writers for their initial weak performance. The complex categories of iterators have also been criticized, and ranges have been proposed for the C++ standard library.

One big problem is that iterators often deal with heap allocated data in the C++ containers and becomes invalid if the data is independently moved by the containers. Functions that change the size of the container often invalidate all iterators pointing to it, creating dangerous cases of undefined behavior. Here is an example where the iterators in the for loop get invalidated because of the std::string container changing its size on the heap:

```cpp
#include <iostream>

#include <string>


int main() {

    std::string text = "One\nTwo\nThree\nFour\n";

    // Let's add an '!' where we find newlines

    for(auto i = text.begin(); i != text.end(); ++i) {

        if(*i == '\n') {

            // i =

            text.insert(i,'!')+1;

            // Without updating the iterator this program has

            // undefined behavior and will likely crash

        }

    }


    std::cout << text;

    return(EXIT_SUCCESS);

}
```

Uniform Initialization Syntax

The C++11 uniform initialization syntax and std::initializer_list share the same syntax which are triggered differently depending on the internal workings of the classes. If there is a std::initializer_list constructor then this is called. Otherwise the normal constructors are called with the uniform initialization syntax. This can be confusing for beginners and experts alike

```cpp
#include <iostream>

#include <vector>


int main() {

    int integer1{10}; // int

    int integer2(10); // int

    std::vector<int> vector1{10,0}; // std::initializer_list

    std::vector<int> vector2(10,0); // size_t,int


    std::cout << "Will print 10"

    << std::endl << integer1 << std::endl;

    std::cout << "Will print 10"

    << std::endl << integer2 << std::endl;


    std::cout << "Will print 10,0," << std::endl;

    for(auto &i : vector1) std::cout << i << ',';

    std::cout << std::endl;

    std::cout << "Will print 0,0,0,0,0,0,0,0,0,0," << std::endl;

    for(auto &i : vector2) std::cout << i << ',';


    return(EXIT_SUCCESS);

}
```

Exceptions

There have been concerns that the zero-overhead principle isn't compatible with exceptions. Most modern implementation has a zero performance overhead when exceptions are enabled but not used, but instead has an overhead in exception handling and in binary size due to the need for unroll tables. Many compilers support disabling exceptions from the language to save the binary overhead. Exceptions have also been criticized for being unsafe for state-handling, this safety issue has led to the invention of the RAII idiom, which has proven useful beyond making C++ exceptions safe.

Strings without Unicode

The C++ Standard Library offers no real support for Unicode. std::basic_string::length will only return the underlying array length which is acceptable when using ASCII or UTF-32 but not when using variable length encodings like UTF-8 or UTF-16. In these encodings the array length has little to do with the string length in code points. There is no support for advanced Unicode concepts like normalization, surrogate pairs, bidi or conversion between encodings.

This will print out the length of two strings with the equal amount of Unicode code points:

```
#include <iostream>

#include <string>

#include <cassert>


int main() {

    // This will print "22 18",

    // UTF-8 prefix just to be explicit

    std::string utf8  = u8"Vår gård på Öland!";

    std::string ascii = u8"Var gard pa Oland!";

    std::cout << utf8.length() << " " << ascii.length() << std::endl;

    assert(utf8.length() == ascii.length()); // Fail!

    return(EXIT_SUCCESS);

}
```

Verbose Assembly and Code Bloat

For a long time, there have been accusations about C++ generating code bloat.

Sieve C++ Parallel Programming System

The Sieve C++ Parallel Programming System is a C++ compiler and parallel runtime designed and released by Codeplay that aims to simplify the parallelization of code so that it may run efficiently on multi-processor or multi-core systems. It is an alternative to other well-known parallelisation methods such as OpenMP, the RapidMind Development Platform and Threading Building Blocks (TBB).

Introduction

Sieve is a C++ compiler that will take a section of serial code, which is annotated with sieve markers, and parallelize it automatically. The programmer wraps code they wish to parallelise inside a lexical scope, which is tagged as 'sieve'. Inside this scope, referred to commonly as a 'sieve block', certain rules apply :

- All side-effects within the sieve block are delayed until the end of the scope.

- Side-effects are defined to be any modifications to data declared outside the sieve block scope.

- Only functions annotated with sieve or immediate can be called.

Delaying side-effects removes many small dependencies which would usually impede automatic parallelization. Reads and writes can be safely reordered by the compiler as to allow better use of various data movement mechanisms, such as Direct Memory Access(DMA). In addition, alias analysis and dataflow analysis can be simplified . The compiler can then split up code within the sieve block much easier, to exploit parallelism.

Memory Configuration

This separation of scopes also means the Sieve System can be used in non-uniform memory architectures. Multi-core CPUs such as the Cell microprocessor used in the PlayStation 3 are of this type, in which the fast cores have local memories that must be utilized to exploit performance inherent in the system. It is also able to work on shared memory systems, like x86, meaning it can run on various architectures. Sieve blocks can also be nested for systems with a hierarchy of different memories and processing elements.

Parallelization and Scalability

The sieve compiler can split code within a sieve block into chunks either implicitly or explicitly though a 'splithere' statement. For instance, the following example shows parallelizing a loop:

```
sieve

{

    for (iterator i(0); i<length; ++i)

    {

        R[i] = A[i] * B[i]

        splithere;

    }

}
```

The compiler will implicitly add a splitpoint above the for loop construct body, as an entry point. Similarly one will be added after as an exit point.

In the Sieve System, only local variables to the sieve block scope may have dependencies. However, these dependencies must not cross splitpoints; they will generate compiler warnings. In order to parallelize this loop, a special 'Iterator' class may be used in place of a standard integer looping counter. It is safe for parallelization, and the programmer is free to create new Iterator classes at will . In addition to these Iterator classes, the programmer is free to implement classes called 'Accumulators' which are used to carry out reduction operations.

The way the Iterator classes are implemented opens up various means for scalability. The Sieve Parallel Runtime employs dynamic speculative execution when executing on a target platform. This can yield very good speedups, however running on a single core machine can incur overheads .

Determinism

Determinism is an unusual feature of the Sieve System. If executing a parallel Sieve program on a multi core machine yields a bug, the bug will not disappear when run on a single core to aid debugging. This has the advantage of eliminating race conditions, one of the most common bugs in concurrent programming. The removal of the need to consider concurrency control structures within a sieve block can speed up development time and results in safer code.

Supported Systems

The system is designed for hierarchical based systems with homogeneous or heterogeneous CPU cores which have local memories, connected via DMA engines or similar memory transfer models.

Sieve has been shown successfully operating on multi-core x86 systems, the Ageia PhysX Physics Processing Unit, and the IBM Cell microprocessor. ANSI C is generated if a compiler code generator is not available for a certain target platform. This allows for autoparallelization using existing C compilation toolkits .

References

- Lee, Kent D. (15 December 2008). Programming Languages: An Active Learning Approach. Springer Science & Business Media. pp. 9–10. ISBN 978-0-387-79422-8.

- Gamma, Erich; Helm, Richard; Johnson, Ralph; Vlissides, John (1994). Design Patterns. Addison-Wesley. ISBN 0-201-63361-2.

- Alexander Stepanov; Paul McJones (June 19, 2009). Elements of Programming. Addison-Wesley Professional. ISBN 978-0-321-63537-2.

- Verilog by Example, Section The Rest for Reference. Blaine C. Readler, Full Arc Press, 2011. ISBN 978-0-9834973-0-1.

- Lämmel, Ralf; Peyton Jones, Simon. "Scrap Your Boilerplate: A Practical Design Pattern for Generic Programming" (PDF). Microsoft. Retrieved 16 October 2016. CS1 maint: Multiple names: authors list (link)

- "Re: [RFC] Convert builin-mailinfo.c to use The Better String Library" (Mailing list). 6 September 2007. Retrieved 31 March 2015.

- for example, instance_eval in Ruby takes a string or an anonymous function. "Rdoc for Class: BasicObject (Ruby 1.9.3) - instance_eval". Retrieved 30 December 2011.

C++ Standard Library: An Integrated Study

C++ Standard Library is a collection of classes and functions. This collection is written in the core language. The topics discussed in this text are C++ string handling, functional (C++), sequence container (C++) and standard template library. The diverse aspects of C++ Standard Library have been carefully analyzed in this chapter.

C++ Standard Library

In the C++ programming language, the C++ Standard Library is a collection of classes and functions, which are written in the core language and part of the C++ ISO Standard itself. The C++ Standard Library provides several generic containers, functions to utilize and manipulate these containers, function objects, generic strings and streams (including interactive and file I/O), support for some language features, and functions for everyday tasks such as finding the square root of a number. The C++ Standard Library also incorporates 18 headers of the ISO C90 C standard library ending with ".h", but their use is deprecated. No other headers in the C++ Standard Library end in ".h". Features of the C++ Standard Library are declared within the std namespace.

The C++ Standard Library is based upon conventions introduced by the Standard Template Library (STL), and has been influenced by research in generic programming and developers of the STL such as Alexander Stepanov and Meng Lee. Although the C++ Standard Library and the STL share many features, neither is a strict superset of the other.

A noteworthy feature of the C++ Standard Library is that it not only specifies the syntax and semantics of generic algorithms, but also places requirements on their performance. These performance requirements often correspond to a well-known algorithm, which is expected but not required to be used. In most cases this requires linear time $O(n)$ or linearithmic time $O(n \log n)$, but in some cases higher bounds are allowed, such as quasilinear time $O(n \log^2 n)$ for stable sort (to allow in-place merge sort). Previously sorting was only required to take $O(n \log n)$ on average, allowing the use of quicksort, which is fast in practice but has poor worst-case performance, but introsort was introduced to allow both fast average performance and optimal worst-case complexity, and as of C++11, sorting is guaranteed to be at worst linearithmic. In other cases requirements remain laxer, such as selection, which is only required to be linear on average (as in quickselect), not requiring worst-case linear as in introselect.

The C++ Standard Library underwent ISO standardization as part of the C++ ISO Standardization effort, and is undergoing further work regarding standardization of expanded functionality.

Standard Headers

The following files contain the declarations of the C++ Standard Library.

Containers

<array>

> New in C++11 and TR1. Provides the container class template std::array, a container for a fixed sized array.

<bitset>

> Provides the specialized container class std::bitset, a bit array.

<deque>

> Provides the container class template std::deque, a double-ended queue.

<forward_list>

> New in C++11 and TR1. Provides the container class template std::forward_list, a singly linked list.

<list>

> Provides the container class template std::list, a doubly linked list.

<map>

> Provides the container class templates std::map and std::multimap, sorted associative array and multimap.

<queue>

> Provides the container adapter class std::queue, a single-ended queue, and std::priority_queue, a priority queue.

<set>

> Provides the container class templates std::set and std::multiset, sorted associative containers or sets.

\<stack\>

>   Provides the container adapter class std::stack, a stack.

\<unordered_map\>

>   New in C++11 and TR1. Provides the container class template std::unordered_ map and std::unordered_multimap, hash tables.

\<unordered_set\>

>   New in C++11 and TR1. Provides the container class template std::unordered_ set and std::unordered_multiset.

\<vector\>

>   Provides the container class template std::vector, a dynamic array.

General

\<algorithm\>

>   Provides definitions of many container algorithms.

\<chrono\>

>   Provides time elements, such as std::chrono::duration, std::chrono::time_ point, and clocks.

\<functional\>

>   Provides several function objects, designed for use with the standard algo- rithms.

\<iterator\>

>   Provides classes and templates for working with iterators.

\<memory\>

>   Provides facilities for memory management in C++, including the class tem- plate std::unique_ptr.

\<stdexcept\>

>   Contains standard exception classes such as std::logic_error and std::runtime_ error, both derived from std::exception.

\<tuple\>

New in C++11 and TR1. Provides a class template std::tuple, a tuple.

<utility>

Provides the template class std::pair, for working with object pairs (two-member tuples), and the namespace std::rel_ops, for easier operator overloading.

Localization

<locale>

Defines classes and declares functions that encapsulate and manipulate the information peculiar to a locale.

<codecvt>

Provides code conversion facets for various character encodings.

Strings

<string>

Provides the C++ standard string classes and templates.

<regex>

New in C++11. Provides utilities for pattern matching strings using regular expressions.

Streams and Input/Output

<fstream>

Provides facilities for file-based input and output.

<iomanip>

Provides facilities to manipulate output formatting, such as the base used when formatting integers and the precision of floating point values.

<ios>

Provides several types and functions basic to the operation of iostreams.

<iosfwd>

Provides forward declarations of several I/O-related class templates.

Provides C++ input and output fundamentals.

<istream>

Provides the template class std::istream and other supporting classes for input.

<ostream>

Provides the template class std::ostream and other supporting classes for output.

<sstream>

Provides the template class std::stringstream and other supporting classes for string manipulation.

<streambuf>

Provides reading and writing functionality to/from certain types of character sequences, such as external files or strings.

Language Support

<exception>

Provides several types and functions related to exception handling, including std::exception, the base class of all exceptions thrown by the Standard Library.

<limits>

Provides the template class std::numeric_limits, used for describing properties of fundamental numeric types.

<new>

Provides operators new and delete and other functions and types composing the fundamentals of C++ memory management.

<typeinfo>

Provides facilities for working with C++ run-time type information.

Thread Support Library

<thread>

New in C++11. Provide class and namespace for working with threads.

New in C++11. 30.4-1 This section provides mechanisms for mutual exclusion: mutexes, locks, and call once.

<condition_variable>

New in C++11. 30.5-1 Condition variables provide synchronization primitives used to block a thread until notified by some other thread that some condition is met or until a system time is reached.

<future>

New in C++11. 30.6.1-1 Describes components that a C++ program can use to retrieve in one thread the result (value or exception) from a function that has run in the same thread or another thread.

Numerics Library

Components that C++ programs may use to perform seminumerical operations.

<complex>

The header <complex> defines a class template, and numerous functions for representing and manipulating complex numbers.

<random>

Facility for generating (pseudo-)random numbers

<valarray>

Defines five class templates (valarray, slice_array, gslice_array, mask_array, and indirect_array), two classes (slice and gslice), and a series of related function templates for representing and manipulating arrays of values.

<numeric>

Generalized numeric operations.

C Standard Library

Each header from the C Standard Library is included in the C++ Standard Library under a different name, generated by removing the .h, and adding a 'c' at the start; for example, 'time.h' becomes 'ctime'. The only difference between these headers and the traditional C Standard Library headers is that where possible the functions should be placed into the std:: namespace. In ISO C, functions in the standard library are allowed to be implemented by macros, which is not allowed by ISO C++.

C++ String Handling

The C++ programming language has support for string handling, mostly implemented in its standard library. The language standard specifies several string types, some inherited from C, some newly designed to make use of the language's features, such as templates and the RAII resource management idiom.

Since the initial versions of C++ had only the "low-level" C string handling functionality and conventions, multiple incompatible designs for string handling classes have been designed over the years, and C++ programmers may need to handle multiple conventions in a single application.

History

The std::string type is the main string datatype in standard C++ since 1998, but it was not always part of C++, and still is not the only standard string type: from C, C++ inherited the convention of using null-terminated strings that are handled by a pointer to their first element, and a library of functions that manipulate such strings. In modern standard C++, a string literal such as "hello" still denotes a NUL-terminated array of characters and std::string has support for converting itself to such an array.

In a 1991 retrospective on the history of C++, its inventor Bjarne Stroustrup called the lack of a standard string type (and some other standard types) in C++ 1.0 the worst mistake he made in its development; "the absence of those led to everybody re-inventing the wheel and to an unnecessary diversity in the most fundamental classes". Over the years, C++ application, library and framework developers produced their own, incompatible string representations, such as the one in AT&T's Standard Components library (the first such implementation, 1983) or the CString type in Microsoft's MFC. While std::string standardized strings, legacy applications still commonly contain such custom string types and libraries may expect C-style strings, making it "virtually impossible" to avoid using multiple string types in C++ programs and requiring programmers to decide on the desired string representation ahead of starting a project.

Implementation Issues

The various vendors' string types have different implementation strategies and performance characteristics. In particular, some string types use a copy-on-write strategy, where an operation such as

```
string a = "hello!";

string b = a; // Copy constructor
```

does not actually copy the content of a to b; instead, both strings share their contents and a reference count on the content is incremented. The actual copying is postponed until a mutating operation, such as appending a character to either string, makes the strings' contents differ.

Though std::string no longer uses it, third-party string libraries may still implement copy-on-write strings; Qt's QString is an example.

Also, third-party string implementations may store 16-bit or 32-bit code points instead of bytes, in order to facilitate processing of Unicode text. However, it means that conversion to these types from std::string or from arrays of bytes is a slow and often a lossy operation, dependent on the "locale", and can throw exceptions.

Standard String Types

The std::string class is the standard representation for a text string since C++98. Compared to C-style strings (NUL-terminated arrays) and the associated standard functions, this class offers several the benefits of automated memory management and a reduced risk of out-of-bounds accesses. The class provides some typical string operations like comparison, concatenation, find and replace, and a function for obtaining substrings. An std::string can be constructed from a C-style string, and a C-style string can also be obtained from one.

The individual units making up the string are of type char, at least (and almost always) 8 bits each. In modern usage these are often not "characters", but parts of a multibyte character encoding such as UTF-8.

The copy-on-write strategy was deliberately allowed by the initial C++ Standard for std::string because it was deemed a useful optimization, and used by nearly all implementations. However, there were mistakes, for instance the operator[] returned a non-const reference, and must be treated as potentially-mutating, even *after* the operator has finished (the caller can legally store the reference and modify the byte after copying the string). This caused some implementations to abandon copy-on-write. Performance problems in multi-threaded applications, due to the locking needed to examine or change the reference count, were soon pointed out. The optimization was finally disallowed in C++11, with the result that even passing a std::string as an argument to a function, viz.

```
void print(std::string s)

{

    std::cout << s;

}
```

must be expected to perform a full copy of the string into newly allocated memory. The common idiom to avoid such copying is to pass by const reference:

```cpp
void print(std::string const &s)

{

    std::cout << s;

}
```

Example Usage

```cpp
#include <iostream>

#include <string>


int main()

{

    // Literals (double-quoted text) denote C strings, but std::string

    // instances can be initialized from such literals.

    std::string foo = "fighters";

    std::string bar = "stool";


    // The operator != compares string contents for inequality. This is different

    // from != on char pointers to C strings, where != would compare the memory

    // addresses of the strings rather than their contents.

    if (foo != bar) {

        std::cout << "The strings are different." << std::endl;

    }


    // Prints "stool fighters". The + operator denotes string concatenation.

    std::cout << (bar + " " + foo) << std::endl;
```

```
    return 0;

}
```

Related Classes

std::string is a typedef for a particular instantiation of the std::basic_string template class. Its definition is found in the <string> header:

```
typedef basic_string<char> string;
```

Thus string provides basic_string functionality for strings having elements of type char. There is a similar class std::wstring, which consists of wchar_t, and is most often used to store UTF-16 text on Windows and UTF-32 on most Unix-like platforms. The C++ standard, however, does not impose any interpretation as Unicode code points or code units on these types and does not even guarantee that a wchar_t holds more bits than a char. To resolve some of the incompatibilities resulting from wchar_t's properties, C++11 added two new classes: std::u16string and std::u32string (made up of the new types char16_t and char32_t), which are the given number of bits per code unit on all platforms. C++11 also added new string literals of 16-bit and 32-bit "characters" and syntax for putting Unicode code points into null-terminated (C-style) strings.

A basic_string is guaranteed to be specializable for any type with a char_traits struct to accompany it. As of C++11, only char, wchar_t, char16_t and char32_t specializations are required to be implemented in the standard library; any other types are implementation-defined. Each specialization is also a Standard Library container, and thus the Standard Library algorithms can be applied to the code units in strings.

Critiques

The design of std::string has held up as an example of monolithic design by Herb Sutter, who reckons that of the 103 member functions on the class in C++98, 71 could have been decoupled without loss of implementation efficiency.

Functional (C++)

In the context of the programming language C++, functional refers to a header file that is part of the C++ Standard Library and provides a set of predefined class templates for function objects, including operations for arithmetic, comparisons, and logic. Instances of these class templates are C++ classes that define a function call operator, and the instances of these classes can be called as if they were functions. It is possible to perform very sophisticated operations without writing a new function object, simply by combining predefined function objects and function object adaptors.

The class template std::function provided by C++11 is a general-purpose polymorphic function wrapper. Instances of std::function can store, copy, and invoke any callable target—functions, lambda expressions (expressions defining anonymous functions), bind expressions (instances of function adapters that transform functions to other functions of smaller arity by providing values for some of the arguments), or other function objects.

The algorithms provided by the C++ Standard Library do not require function objects of more than two arguments. Function objects that return Boolean values are an important special case. A unary function whose return type is bool is called a *predicate*, and a binary function whose return type is bool is called a *binary predicate*.

Adaptable Function Objects

In general, a function object has restrictions on the type of its argument. The type restrictions need not be simple, though: operator() may be overloaded or may be a member template. Similarly, there need be no way for a program to determine what those restrictions are. An adaptable function object, however, does specify what the argument and return types are, and provides nested typedefs so that those types can be named and used in programs. If a type F0 is a model of an adaptable generator, then it must define F0::result_type. Similarly, if F1 is a model of the adaptable unary function, it must define F1::argument_type and F1::result_type, and if F2 is a model of the adaptable binary function, it must define F2::first_argument_type, F2::second_argument_type, and F2::result_type. The C++ Standard Library provides base classes unary_function and binary_function to simplify the definition of adaptable unary functions and adaptable binary functions.

Adaptable function objects are important, because they can be used by function object adaptors: function objects that transform or manipulate other function objects. The C++ Standard Library provides many different function object adaptors, including unary_negate (that returns the logical complement of the value returned by a particular adaptable predicate), and unary_compose and binary_compose, which perform composition of function object.

Predefined Function Objects

The C++ Standard Library includes in the header file functional many different predefined function objects, including arithmetic operations (plus, minus, multiplies, divides, modulus, and negate), comparisons (equal_to, not_equal_to, greater, less, greater_equal, and less_equal), and logical operations (logical_and, logical_or, and logical_not).

Examples

Function wrappers can be used to make calls to ordinary functions or to functions objects created by lambda expressions.

```cpp
#include <iostream>
#include <functional>


/* Define a template function */
template <typename T> void printValue(T value)
{
        std::cout << value << std::endl;
}


int main(void)
{
        /* A function wrapper to a function */
        std::function<void (int)> funcA = printValue<int>;
        funcA(2015);


        /* A function wrapper to a function pointer */
        std::function<void (int)> funcB = &printValue<int>;
        funcB(2016);


        /* A function wapper to a lambda function. */
        std::function<void (int)> funcC = [](int value) { st-
d::cout << value << std::endl; };
        funcC(2017);


        /* A function wrapper generated by std::bind().
         * Pass a pre-defined parameter when binding.
         */
        std::function<void (void)> funcD = std::bind(printVal-
ue<std::string>, "PI is");
```

```
        funcD();


        /* A function wrapper generated by std::bind().

         * Pass a parameter when calling the function.

         */

        std::function<void (float)> funcE = std::bind(printVal-
ue<float>, std::placeholders::_1);

        funcE(3.14159);

}
```

Function wrappers also can be used to access member variables and member functions of classes.

```
#include <iostream>

#include <functional>


template <typename T> class CAnyData {

public:

        T m_value;

        CAnyData(T value) : m_value { value } {}

        void print(void) { std::cout << m_value << std::endl; }

        void printAfterAdd(T value) { std::cout << (m_value +
value) << std::endl; }

};


int main(void)

{

        /* A function wrapper to a member variable of a class
*/

        CAnyData<int> dataA { 2016 };

        std::function<int (CAnyData<int> &)> funcA = &CAny-
Data<int>::m_value;
```

```
        std::cout << funcA(dataA) << std::endl;
1       CAnyData<float> dataB { 2016.1 };
        std::function<void (CAnyData<float> &)> funcB = &CAny-
Data<float>::print;
        funcB(dataB);



        /* A function wrappter to member function with passing
a parameter */
        std::function<void (CAnyData<float> &, float)> funcC =
&CAnyData<float>::printAfterAdd;
        funcC(dataB, 0.1);



        /* A function wrappter to member function generated by
std::bind */
        std::function<void (float)> funcD = std::bind(&CAny-
Data<float>::printAfterAdd, &dataB, std::placeholders::_1);
        funcD(0.2);



        return 0;

}
```

Sequence Container (C++)

In computing, sequence containers refer to a group of container class templates in the standard library of the C++ programming language that implement storage of data elements. Being templates, they can be used to store arbitrary elements, such as integers or custom classes. One common property of all sequential containers is that the elements can be accessed sequentially. Like all other standard library components, they reside in namespace *std*.

The following containers are defined in the current revision of the C++ standard: array, vector, list, forward_list, deque. Each of these containers implements different algorithms for data storage, which means that they have different speed guarantees for different operations:

- array implements a compile-time non-resizeable array.

- vector implements an array with fast random access and an ability to automatically resize when appending elements.

- deque implements a double-ended queue with comparatively fast random access.

- list implements a doubly linked list.

- forward_list implements a singly linked list.

Since each of the containers needs to be able to copy its elements in order to function properly, the type of the elements must fulfill CopyConstructible and Assignable requirements. For a given container, all elements must belong to the same type. For instance, one cannot store data in the form of both char and int within the same container instance.

History

Originally, only vector, list, deque were defined. Until the standardization of the C++ language in 1998, they were part of the Standard Template Library, published by SGI.

The array container at first appeared in several books under various names. Later it was incorporated into boost C++ libraries and was proposed into the standard C++ library. The motivation for inclusion of array was that it solves two problems of the C-style array: the lack of STL-like interface and inability to be copied as any other object. It firstly appeared in C++ TR1 and later was incorporated into C++11.

The forward_list container has been added to C++11 as a space-efficient alternative to list when reverse iteration is not needed.

Properties

array, vector and deque all support fast random access to the elements. list supports bidirectional iteration, whereas forward_list supports only unidirectional iteration.

array does not support element insertion or removal. vector supports fast element insertion or removal at the end. Any insertion or removal of an element not at the end of the vector needs elements between the insertion position and the end of the vector to be copied. The iterators to the affected elements are thus invalidated. In fact, any insertion can potentially invalidate all iterators. Also, if the allocated storage in the vector is too small to insert elements, a new array is allocated, all elements are copied or moved to the new array, and the old array is freed. deque, list and forward_list all support fast insertion or removal of elements anywhere in the container. list and forward_list preserves validity of iterators on such operation, whereas deque invalidates all of them.

Vector

The elements of a vector are stored contiguously. Like all dynamic array implementations, vectors have low memory usage and good locality of reference and data cache utilization. Unlike other STL containers, such as deques and lists, vectors allow the user to denote an initial capacity for the container.

Vectors allow random access; that is, an element of a vector may be referenced in the same manner as elements of arrays (by array indices). Linked-lists and sets, on the other hand, do not support random access or pointer arithmetic.

The vector data structure is able to quickly and easily allocate the necessary memory needed for specific data storage, and it is able to do so in amortized constant time. This is particularly useful for storing data in lists whose length may not be known prior to setting up the list but where removal (other than, perhaps, at the end) is rare. Erasing elements from a vector or even clearing the vector entirely does not necessarily free any of the memory associated with that element.

Capacity and Reallocation

A typical vector implementation consists, internally, of a pointer to a dynamically allocated array, and possibly data members holding the capacity and size of the vector. The size of the vector refers to the actual number of elements, while the capacity refers to the size of the internal array.

When new elements are inserted, if the new size of the vector becomes larger than its capacity, *reallocation* occurs. This typically causes the vector to allocate a new region of storage, move the previously held elements to the new region of storage, and free the old region.

Because the addresses of the elements change during this process, any references or iterators to elements in the vector become invalidated. Using an invalidated reference causes undefined behaviour.

The reserve() operation may be used to prevent unnecessary reallocations. After a call to reserve(n), the vector's capacity is guaranteed to be at least n.

The vector maintains a certain order of its elements, so that when a new element is inserted at the beginning or in the middle of the vector, subsequent elements are moved backwards in terms of their assignment operator or copy constructor. Consequently, references and iterators to elements after the insertion point become invalidated.

C++ vectors do not support in-place reallocation of memory, by design; i.e., upon reallocation of a vector, the memory it held will always be copied to a new block of memory using its elements' copy constructor, and then released. This is inefficient for cases where the vector holds plain old data and additional contiguous space beyond the held block of memory is available for allocation.

Specialization for Bool

The Standard Library defines a specialization of the vector template for bool. The description of this specialization indicates that the implementation should pack the elements so that every bool only uses one bit of memory. This is widely considered a mistake. vector<bool> does not meet the requirements for a C++ Standard Library container. For instance, a container<T>::reference must be a true lvalue of type T. This is not the case with vector<bool>::reference, which is a proxy class convertible to bool. Similarly, the vector<bool>::iterator does not yield a bool& when derefer-enced. There is a general consensus among the C++ Standard Committee and the Library Working Group that vector<bool> should be deprecated and subsequently removed from the standard library, while the functionality will be reintroduced un-der a different name.

List

The list data structure implements a doubly linked list. Data is stored non-contig-uously in memory which allows the list data structure to avoid the reallocation of memory that can be necessary with vectors when new elements are inserted into the list.

The list data structure allocates and deallocates memory as needed; therefore, it does not allocate memory that it is not currently using. Memory is freed when an element is removed from the list.

Lists are efficient when inserting new elements in the list; this is an O(1) operation. No shifting is required like with vectors.

Lists do not have random access ability like vectors (O(1) operation). Accessing a node in a list is an O(n) operation that requires a list traversal to find the node that needs to be accessed.

With small data types (such as ints) the memory overhead is much more significant than that of a vector. Each node takes up sizeof(type) + 2 * sizeof(type*). Pointers are typically one word (usually four bytes under 32-bit operating systems), which means that a list of four byte integers takes up approximately three times as much memory as a vector of integers.

Deque

deque is a container class template that implements a double-ended queue. It provides similar computational complexity to vector for most operations, with the notable exception that it provides amortized constant-time insertion and removal from both ends of the element sequence. Unlike vector, deque uses discontiguous blocks of memory, and provides no means to control the capacity of the container and the moment of reallocation of memory. Like vector, deque offers support for random access iterators, and insertion and removal of elements invalidates all iterators to the deque.

Array

array implements a compile-time non-resizeable array. The size is determined at compile-time by a template parameter. By design, the container does not support allocators. Unlike the other standard containers, array does not provide constant-time swap.

Overview of Functions

The containers are defined in headers named after the names of the containers, e.g. vector is defined in header <vector>. All containers satisfy the requirements of the Container concept, which means they have begin(), end(), size(), max_size(), empty(), and swap() methods.

	array (C++11)	vector	deque	list	forward_list (C++11)	Description
	(implicit)	(constructor)	(constructor)	(constructor)	(constructor)	Constructs the container from variety of sources
	(implicit)	(destructor)	(destructor)	(destructor)	(destructor)	Destructs the container and the contained elements
	(implicit)	operator=	operator=	operator=	operator=	Assigns values to the container
	N/A	assign	assign	assign	assign	Assigns values to the container
	N/A	get_allocator	get_allocator	get_allocator	get_allocator	Returns the allocator used to allocate memory for the elements
Element access	at	at	at	N/A	N/A	Accesses specified element with bounds checking.
	operator[]	operator[]	operator[]	N/A	N/A	Accesses specified element without bounds checking.
	front	front	front	front	front	Accesses the first element
	back	back	back	back	N/A	Accesses the last element
	data	data	N/A	N/A	N/A	Accesses the underlying array
Iterators	begin	begin	begin	begin	begin	Returns an iterator to the beginning of the container
	end	end	end	end	end	Returns an iterator to the end of the container
	rbegin	rbegin	rbegin	rbegin	N/A	Returns a reverse iterator to the reverse beginning of the container
	rend	rend	rend	rend	N/A	Returns a reverse iterator to the reverse end of the container

Capacity	empty	empty	empty	empty	empty	Checks whether the container is empty
	size	size	size	size	N/A	Returns the number of elements in the container.
	max_size	max_size	max_size	max_size	max_size	Returns the maximum possible number of elements in the container.
	N/A	reserve	N/A	N/A	N/A	Reserves storage in the container
	N/A	capacity	N/A	N/A	N/A	Returns the number of elements that can be held in currently allocated storage
	N/A	shrink_to_fit	shrink_to_fit	N/A	N/A	Reduces memory usage by freeing unused memory (C++11)
Modifiers	N/A	clear	clear	clear	clear	Clears the contents
	N/A	insert	insert	insert	N/A	Inserts elements
	N/A	emplace	emplace	emplace	N/A	Constructs elements in-place (C++11)
	N/A	erase	erase	erase	N/A	Erases elements
	N/A	N/A	push_front	push_front	push_front	Inserts elements to the beginning
	N/A	N/A	emplace_front	emplace_front	emplace_front	Constructs elements in-place at the beginning (C++11)
	N/A	N/A	pop_front	pop_front	pop_front	Removes the first element
	N/A	push_back	push_back	push_back	N/A	Inserts elements to the end
	N/A	emplace_back	emplace_back	emplace_back	N/A	Constructs elements in-place at the end (C++11)
	N/A	pop_back	pop_back	pop_back	N/A	Removes the last element
	N/A	N/A	N/A	N/A	insert_after	Inserts elements after specified position (C++11)
	N/A	N/A	N/A	N/A	emplace_after	Constructs elements in-place after specified position (C++11)
	N/A	N/A	N/A	N/A	erase_after	Erases elements in-place after specified position (C++11)
	N/A	resize	resize	resize	resize	Changes the number of stored elements
	swap	swap	swap	swap	swap	Swaps the contents with another container of the same type

There are other operations that are available as a part of the list class and there are algorithms that are part of the C++ STL (Algorithm (C++)) that can be used with the list class.

- Operations

  o list::merge - Merges two sorted lists

  o list::splice - Moves elements from another list

- o list::remove - Removes elements equal to the given value

- o list::remove_if - Removes elements satisfying specific criteria

- o list::reverse - Reverses the order of the elements

- o list::unique - Removes consecutive duplicate elements

- o list::sort - Sorts the element

- Modifiers

  - o array::fill - Fills the array with the given value

Usage Example

The following example demonstrates various techniques involving a vector and C++ Standard Library algorithms, notably shuffling, sorting, finding the largest element, and erasing from a vector using the erase-remove idiom.

```cpp
#include <iostream>

#include <vector>

#include <array>

#include <algorithm> // sort, max_element, random_shuffle, re-
move_if, lower_bound

#include <functional> // greater

#include <iterator> //begin, end, cbegin, cend, distance


// used here for convenience, use judiciously in real programs.
using namespace std;

using namespace std::placeholders;


auto main(int, char**)
  -> int
{
  std::array<int,4> arr{ 1, 2, 3, 4 };
```

```cpp
// initialize a vector from an array
vector<int> numbers( cbegin(arr), cend(arr) );


// insert more numbers into the vector
numbers.push_back(5);

numbers.push_back(6);

numbers.push_back(7);

numbers.push_back(8);
// the vector currently holds { 1, 2, 3, 4, 5, 6, 7, 8 }


// randomly shuffle the elements
random_shuffle( begin(numbers), end(numbers) );


// locate the largest element, O(n)
auto largest = max_element( cbegin(numbers), cend(numbers) );


cout << "The largest number is " << *largest << "\n";
cout << "It is located at index " << distance(largest, cbegin(numbers)) << "\n";


// sort the elements
sort( begin(numbers), end(numbers) );


// find the position of the number 5 in the vector
auto five = lower_bound( cbegin(numbers), cend(numbers), 5 );
```

```
  cout << "The number 5 is located at index " << distance(five,
cbegin(numbers)) << "\n";


  // erase all the elements greater than 4

  numbers.erase( remove_if(begin(numbers), end(numbers),

    bind(greater<>{}, _1, 4) ), end(numbers) );


  // print all the remaining numbers

  for(const auto& element : numbers)

    cout << element << " ";


  return 0;

}
```

The Output will be the Following:

The largest number is 8
It is located at index 6 (implementation-dependent)
The number 5 is located at index 4
1 2 3 4

Components of C++ Standard Library

Algorithm (C++)

In the C++ Standard Library, algorithms are components that perform algorithmic operations on containers and other sequences.

The C++ standard provides some standard algorithms collected in the <algorithm> standard header. A handful of algorithms are also in the <numeric> header. All algorithms are in the std namespace.

Categories of Algorithms

The algorithms in the C++ Standard Library can be organized into the following categories.

- Non-modifying sequence operations (e.g. find_if, count, search)

- Modifying sequence operations (e.g. replace, remove, reverse)

- Sorting (e.g. sort, stable_sort, partial_sort)

- Binary search (e.g. lower_bound, upper_bound)

- Heap (e.g. make_heap, push_heap)

- Min/max (e.g. min, max)

Examples

- OutputIterator copy(InputIterator source_begin, InputIterator source_end, OutputIterator destination_begin)

- void fill(ForwardIterator destination_begin, ForwardIterator destination_end, T value)

- InputIterator find(InputIterator begin, InputIterator end, T search_obje (returns an iterator the found object or end, if the object isn't found)

- const T& max(const T& a, const T& b) returns the greater of the two arguments

- ForwardIterator max_element(ForwardIterator begin, ForwardIterator end) finds the maximum element of a range

- const T& min(const T& a, const T& b) returns the smaller of the two arguments

- ForwardIterator min_element(ForwardIterator begin, ForwardIterator end) finds the minimum element of a range

Allocator (C++)

In C++ computer programming, allocators are an important component of the C++ Standard Library. The standard library provides several data structures, such as list and set, commonly referred to as containers. A common trait among these containers is their ability to change size during the execution of the program. To achieve this, some form of dynamic memory allocation is usually required. Allocators handle all the requests for allocation and deallocation of memory for a given container. The C++ Standard Library provides general-purpose allocators that are used by default, however, custom allocators may also be supplied by the programmer.

Allocators were invented by Alexander Stepanov as part of the Standard Template Library (STL). They were originally intended as a means to make the library more flexible and independent of the underlying memory model, allowing programmers to utilize custom pointer and reference types with the library. However, in the process of adopting STL into the C++ standard, the C++ standardization committee realized that a complete abstraction of the memory model would incur unacceptable performance penalties. To remedy this, the requirements of allocators were made more restrictive. As a result, the level of customization provided by allocators is more limited than was originally envisioned by Stepanov.

Nevertheless, there are many scenarios where customized allocators are desirable. Some of the most common reasons for writing custom allocators include improving performance of allocations by using memory pools, and encapsulating access to different types of memory, like shared memory or garbage-collected memory. In particular, programs with many frequent allocations of small amounts of memory may benefit greatly from specialized allocators, both in terms of running time and memory footprint.

Background

Alexander Stepanov and Meng Lee presented the Standard Template Library to the C++ standards committee in March 1994. The library received preliminary approval, although a few issues were raised. In particular, Stepanov was requested to make the library containers independent of the underlying memory model, which led to the creation of allocators. Consequently, all of the STL container interfaces had to be rewritten to accept allocators.

In adapting STL to be included in the C++ Standard Library, Stepanov worked closely with several members of the standards committee, including Andrew Koenig and Bjarne Stroustrup, who observed that custom allocators could potentially be used to implement persistent storage STL containers, which Stepanov at the time considered an "important and interesting insight".

> From the point of view of portability, all the machine-specific things which relate to the notion of address, pointer, and so on, are encapsulated within a tiny, well-understood mechanism.
>
> —Alex Stepanov, designer of the Standard Template Library

The original allocator proposal incorporated some language features that had not yet been accepted by the committee, namely the ability to use template arguments that are themselves templates. Since these features could not be compiled by any existing compiler, there was, according to Stepanov, "an enormous demand on Bjarne [Stroustrup]'s and Andy [Koenig]'s time trying to verify that we were using these non-implemented features correctly." Where the library had previously used pointer and reference types directly, it would now only refer to the types defined by the allocator. Stepanov later described allocators as follows: "A nice feature of STL is that the only place that mentions the machine-related types (...) is encapsulated within roughly 16 lines of code."

While Stepanov had originally intended allocators to completely encapsulate the memory model, the standards committee realized that this approach would lead to unacceptable efficiency degradations. To remedy this, additional wording was added to the allocator requirements. In particular, container implementations may assume that the allocator's type definitions for pointers and related integral types are equivalent to those provided by the default allocator, and that all instances of a given allocator type always compare equal, effectively contradicting the original design goals for allocators and limiting the usefulness of allocators that carry state.

Stepanov later commented that, while allocators "are not such a bad [idea] in theory (...) [u]nfortunately they cannot work in practice". He observed that to make allocators really useful, a change to the core language with regards to references was necessary.

The 2011 revision of the C++ Standard removed the weasel words requiring that allocators of a given type always compare equal and use normal pointers. These changes make stateful allocators much more useful and allow allocators to manage out-of-process shared memory. The current purpose of allocators is to give the programmer control over memory allocation within containers, rather than to adapt the address model of the underlying hardware. In fact, the revised standard eliminated the ability of allocators to represent extensions to the C++ address model, formally (and deliberately) eliminating their original purpose.

Requirements

Any class that fulfills the *allocator requirements* can be used as an allocator. In particular, a class A capable of allocating memory for an object of type T must provide the types A::pointer, A::const_pointer, A::reference, A::const_reference, and A::value_type for generically declaring objects and references (or pointers) to objects of type T. It should also provide type A::size_type, an unsigned type which can represent the largest size for an object in the allocation model defined by A, and similarly, a signed integral A::difference_type that can represent the difference between any two pointers in the allocation model.

Although a conforming standard library implementation is allowed to assume that the allocator's A::pointer and A::const_pointer are simply typedefs for T* and T const*, library implementors are encouraged to support more general allocators.

An allocator, A, for objects of type T must have a member function with the signature A::pointer A::allocate(size_type n, A<void>::const_pointer hint = 0). This function returns a pointer to the first element of a newly allocated array large enough to contain n objects of type T; only the memory is allocated, and the objects are not constructed. Moreover, an optional pointer argument (that points to an object already allocated by A) can be used as a hint to the implementation about where the new memory should be allocated in order to improve locality. However, the implementation is free to ignore the argument.

The corresponding void A::deallocate(A::pointer p, A::size_type n) member function accepts any pointer that was returned from a previous invocation of the A::allocate member function and the number of elements to deallocate (but not destruct).

The A::max_size() member function returns the largest number of objects of type T that could be expected to be successfully allocated by an invocation of A::allocate; the value returned is typically A::size_type(-1) / sizeof(T). Also, the A::address member function returns an A::pointer denoting the address of an object, given an A::reference.

Object construction and destruction is performed separately from allocation and deal-location. The allocator is required to have two member functions, A::construct and A::destroy, which handles object construction and destruction, respectively. The se-mantics of the functions should be equivalent to the following:

```
template <typename T>

void A::construct(A::pointer p, A::const_reference t) { new
((void*) p) T(t); }
```

```
template <typename T>

void A::destroy(A::pointer p){ ((T*)p)->~T(); }
```

The above code uses the placement new syntax, and calls the destructor directly.

Allocators should be copy-constructible. An allocator for objects of type T can be con-structed from an allocator for objects of type U. If an allocator, A, allocates a region of memory, R, then R can only be deallocated by an allocator that compares equal to A.

Allocators are required to supply a template class member template <typename U> struct A::rebind { typedef A<U> other; };, which enables the possibility of obtaining a related allocator, parameterized in terms of a different type. For example, given an allocator type IntAllocator for objects of type int, a related allocator type for objects of type long could be obtained using IntAllocator::rebind<long>::other.

Custom Allocators

One of the main reasons for writing a custom allocator is performance. Utilizing a special-ized custom allocator may substantially improve the performance or memory usage, or both, of the program. The default allocator uses operator new to allocate memory. This is often implemented as a thin layer around the C heap allocation functions, which are usually optimized for infrequent allocation of large memory blocks. This approach may work well with containers that mostly allocate large chunks of memory, like vector and deque. How-ever, for containers that require frequent allocations of small objects, such as map and list, using the default allocator is generally slow. Other common problems with a malloc-based allocator include poor locality of reference, and excessive memory fragmentation.

A popular approach to improve performance is to create a memory pool-based allo-cator. Instead of allocating memory every time an item is inserted or removed from a container, a large block of memory (the memory pool) is allocated beforehand, possibly at the startup of the program. The custom allocator will serve individual allocation requests by simply returning a pointer to memory from the pool. Actual deallocation of memory can be deferred until the lifetime of the memory pool ends. An example of memory pool-based allocators can be found in the Boost C++ Libraries.

Another viable use of custom allocators is for debugging memory-related errors. This could be achieved by writing an allocator that allocates extra memory in which it places debugging information. Such an allocator could be used to ensure that memory is allocated and deallocated by the same type of allocator, and also provide limited protection against overruns.

> In short, this paragraph (...) is the Standard's "I have a dream" speech for allocators. Until that dream becomes common reality, programmers concerned about portability will limit themselves to custom allocators with no state
>
> —Scott Meyers, *Effective STL*

The subject of custom allocators has been treated by many C++ experts and authors, including Scott Meyers in *Effective STL* and Andrei Alexandrescu in *Modern C++ Design*. Meyers emphasises that C++98 requires all instances of an allocator to be equivalent, and notes that this in effect forces portable allocators to not have state. Although the C++98 Standard did encourage library implementors to support stateful allocators, Meyers calls the relevant paragraph "a lovely sentiment" that "offers you next to nothing", characterizing the restriction as "draconian".

In The C++ Programming Language, Bjarne Stroustrup, on the other hand, argues that the "apparently [d]raconian restriction against per-object information in allocators is not particularly serious", pointing out that most allocators do not need state, and have better performance without it. He mentions three use cases for custom allocators, namely, memory pool allocators, shared memory allocators, and garbage collected memory allocators. He presents an allocator implementation that uses an internal memory pool for fast allocation and deallocation of small chunks of memory, but notes that such an optimization may already be performed by the allocator provided by the implementation.

Usage

When instantiating one of the standard containers, the allocator is specified through a template argument, which defaults to std::allocator<T>:

namespace std {

```
  template <class T, class Allocator = allocator<T> > class
vector;
```

```
// ...
```

Like all C++ class templates, instantiations of standard library containers with different allocator arguments are distinct types. A function expecting an std::vector<int> argument will therefore only accept a vector instantiated with the default allocator.

Enhancements to Allocators in C++11

The C++11 standard has enhanced the allocator interface to allow "scoped" allocators, so that containers with "nested" memory allocations, such as vector of strings or a map of lists of sets of user-defined types, can ensure that all memory is sourced from the container's allocator.

Example

```
//__gnu_cxx::new_allocator< typename > Class Template Reference

//https://gcc.gnu.org/onlinedocs/gcc-4.9.0/libstdc++/api/
a00057.html

/**

processor    : 0

vendor_id    : AuthenticAMD

cpu family   : 16

model        : 6

model name   : AMD Athlon(tm) II X2 270 Processor

stepping     : 3

microcode    : 0x10000c8

cpu MHz            : 2000.000

cache size   : 1024 KB

...

processor    : 1

vendor_id    : AuthenticAMD

cpu family   : 16

model        : 6

model name   : AMD Athlon(tm) II X2 270 Processor

stepping     : 3

microcode    : 0x10000c8
```

```
 cpu MHz             : 800.000

 cache size    : 1024 KB

 ...

 Linux debian 3.14-2-686-pae #1 SMP Debian 3.14.15-2 (2014-08-
09) i686 GNU/Linux

 ...

 gcc (Debian 4.9.1-12) 4.9.1

 Copyright (C) 2014 Free Software Foundation, Inc.

 This is free software; see the source for copying conditions.
There is NO

 warranty; not even for MERCHANTABILITY or FITNESS FOR A PAR-
TICULAR PURPOSE.

 ...

java@debian:~/java/eclipse$ ldd /usr/lib/i386-linux-gnu/libst-
dc++.so.6.0.20

        linux-gate.so.1 (0xb7733000)

        libm.so.6 => /lib/i386-linux-gnu/i686/cmov/libm.so.6
(0xb75da000)

        libc.so.6 => /lib/i386-linux-gnu/i686/cmov/libc.so.6
(0xb742f000)

        /lib/ld-linux.so.2 (0xb7734000)

        libgcc_s.so.1 => /lib/i386-linux-gnu/libgcc_s.so.1
(0xb7411000)


 */

#include <iostream>

using namespace std;

using namespace __gnu_cxx;


class RequiredAllocation

{
```

```cpp
public:

        RequiredAllocation ();

        ~RequiredAllocation ();

        std::basic_string<char> s = "hello world!\n";
};


RequiredAllocation::RequiredAllocation ()

{

        cout << "RequiredAllocation::RequiredAllocation()" <<
endl;

}
RequiredAllocation::~RequiredAllocation ()

{

        cout << "RequiredAllocation::~RequiredAllocation()" <<
endl;

}


void alloc(__gnu_cxx ::new_allocator<RequiredAllocation>* all,
unsigned int size, void* pt, RequiredAllocation* t){

        try

                {

                        all->allocate (size, pt);

                        cout << all->max_size () << endl;

                        for (auto& e : t->s)

                                {

                                        cout << e;

                                }

                }

        catch (std::bad_alloc& e)
```

```
                    {
                                cout << e.what () << endl;
                    }
}


int
main ()
{


        __gnu_cxx ::new_allocator<RequiredAllocation> *all =
                        new __gnu_cxx ::new_allocator<RequiredAl-
location> ();


        RequiredAllocation t;
        void* pt = &t;


        /**
        * What happens when new can find no store to allocate?
By default, the allocator throws a stan-
        * dard-library bad_alloc exception (for an alternative,
see §11.2.4.1)
        * @C Bjarne Stroustrup  The C++ Programming language
        */
        unsigned int size = 1073741824;
        alloc(all, size, &pt, &t);


        size = 1;
        alloc(all, size, &pt, &t);


        return 0;
}
```

Standard Template Library

The Standard Template Library (STL) is a software library for the C++ programming language that influenced many parts of the C++ Standard Library. It provides four components called *algorithms, containers, functional,* and *iterators*.

The STL provides a ready-made set of common classes for C++, such as containers and associative arrays, that can be used with any built-in type and with any user-defined type that supports some elementary operations (such as copying and assignment). STL algorithms are independent of containers, which significantly reduces the complexity of the library.

The STL achieves its results through the use of templates. This approach provides compile-time polymorphism that is often more efficient than traditional run-time polymorphism. Modern C++ compilers are tuned to minimize abstraction penalty arising from heavy use of the STL.

The STL was created as the first library of generic algorithms and data structures for C++, with four ideas in mind: generic programming, abstractness without loss of efficiency, the Von Neumann computation model, and value semantics.

Composition

Containers

The STL contains sequence containers and associative containers. The Containers are objects that store data. The standard sequence containers include vector, deque, and list. The standard associative containers are set, multiset, map, multimap, hash_set, hash_map, hash_multiset and hash_multimap. There are also *container adaptors* queue, priority_queue, and stack, that are containers with specific interface, using other containers as implementation.

Container	Description
Simple containers	
pair	The pair container is a simple associative container consisting of a 2-tuple of data elements or objects, called 'first' and 'second', in that fixed order. The STL 'pair' can be assigned, copied and compared. The array of objects allocated in a map or hash_map (described below) are of type 'pair' by default, where all the 'first' elements act as the unique keys, each associated with their 'second' value objects.
Sequences (Arrays/Linked Lists): ordered collections	
vector	a dynamic array, like C array (i.e., capable of random access) with the ability to resize itself automatically when inserting or erasing an object. Inserting an element to the back of the vector at the end takes amortized constant time. Removing the last element takes only constant time, because no resizing happens. Inserting and erasing at the beginning or in the middle is linear in time.
	A specialization for type bool exists, which optimizes for space by storing bool values as bits.

list	a doubly linked list; elements are not stored in contiguous memory. Opposite performance from a vector. Slow lookup and access (linear time), but once a position has been found, quick insertion and deletion (constant time).
slist	a singly linked list; elements are not stored in contiguous memory. Opposite performance from a vector. Slow lookup and access (linear time), but once a position has been found, quick insertion and deletion (constant time). It has slightly more efficient insertion, deletion and uses less memory than a doubly linked list, but can only be iterated forwards. It is implemented in the C++ standard library as forward_list.
deque (*double-ended queue*)	a vector with insertion/erase at the beginning or end in amortized constant time, however lacking some guarantees on iterator validity after altering the deque.
Container adaptors	
queue	Provides FIFO queue interface in terms of push/pop/front/back operations. Any sequence supporting operations front(), back(), push_back(), and pop_front() can be used to instantiate queue (e.g. list and deque).
priority queue	Provides priority queue interface in terms of push/pop/top operations (the element with the highest priority is on top). Any random-access sequence supporting operations front(), push_back(), and pop_back() can be used to instantiate priority_queue (e.g. vector and deque). It is implemented using a heap. Elements should additionally support comparison (to determine which element has a higher priority and should be popped first).
stack	Provides LIFO stack interface in terms of push/pop/top operations (the last-inserted element is on top). Any sequence supporting operations back(), push_back(), and pop_back() can be used to instantiate stack (e.g. vector, list, and deque).
Associative containers: unordered collections	
set	a mathematical set; inserting/erasing elements in a set does not invalidate iterators pointing in the set. Provides set operations union, intersection, difference, symmetric difference and test of inclusion. Type of data must implement comparison operator < or custom comparator function must be specified; such comparison operator or comparator function must guarantee strict weak ordering, otherwise behavior is undefined. Typically implemented using a self-balancing binary search tree.
multiset	same as a set, but allows duplicate elements (mathematical Multiset).
map	an associative array; allows mapping from one data item (a key) to another (a value). Type of key must implement comparison operator < or custom comparator function must be specified; such comparison operator or comparator function must guarantee strict weak ordering, otherwise behavior is undefined. Typically implemented using a self-balancing binary search tree.
multimap	same as a map, but allows duplicate keys.
hash_set **hash_multiset** **hash_map** **hash_multimap**	similar to a set, multiset, map, or multimap, respectively, but implemented using a hash table; keys are not ordered, but a hash function must exist for the key type. These types were left out of the C++ standard; similar containers were standardized in C++11, but with different names (unordered_set and unordered_map).

Other types of containers	
bitset	stores series of bits similar to a fixed-sized vector of bools. Implements bitwise operations and lacks iterators. Not a sequence. Provides random access.
valarray	Another array data type, intended for numerical use (especially to represent vectors and matrices); the C++ standard allows specific optimizations for this intended purpose. According to Josuttis, valarray was badly designed, by people "who left the [C++ standard] committee a long time before the standard was finished", and expression template libraries are to be preferred. A proposed rewrite of the valarray part of the standard in this vein was rejected, instead becoming a permission to implement it using expression template.

Iterators

The STL implements five different types of iterators. These are *input iterators* (that can only be used to read a sequence of values), *output iterators* (that can only be used to write a sequence of values), *forward iterators* (that can be read, written to, and move forward), *bidirectional iterators* (that are like forward iterators, but can also move backwards) and *random access iterators* (that can move freely any number of steps in one operation).

It is possible to have bidirectional iterators act like random access iterators, so moving forward ten steps could be done by simply moving forward a step at a time a total of ten times. However, having distinct random access iterators offers efficiency advantages. For example, a vector would have a random access iterator, but a list only a bidirectional iterator.

Iterators are the major feature that allow the generality of the STL. For example, an algorithm to reverse a sequence can be implemented using bidirectional iterators, and then the same implementation can be used on lists, vectors and deques. User-created containers only have to provide an iterator that implements one of the five standard iterator interfaces, and all the algorithms provided in the STL can be used on the container.

This generality also comes at a price at times. For example, performing a search on an associative container such as a map or set can be much slower using iterators than by calling member functions offered by the container itself. This is because an associative container's methods can take advantage of knowledge of the internal structure, which is opaque to algorithms using iterators.

Algorithms

A large number of algorithms to perform activities such as searching and sorting are provided in the STL, each implemented to require a certain level of iterator (and therefore will work on any container that provides an interface by iterators). Searching algorithms like binary_search and lower_bound use binary search and like sorting algorithms require that the type of data must implement comparison operator < or custom comparator function must be specified; such comparison operator or comparator function must guarantee strict weak ordering. Apart from these, algorithms are provided for making heap from a range of elements, generating lexicographically ordered permutations of a range of elements, merge sorted ranges and perform union, intersection, difference of sorted ranges.

Functions

The STL includes classes that overload the function call operator (operator()). Instances of such classes are called functors or function objects. Functors allow the behavior of the associated function to be parameterized (e.g. through arguments passed to the functor's constructor) and can be used to keep associated per-functor state information along with the function. Since both functors and function pointers can be invoked using the syntax of a function call, they are interchangeable as arguments to templates when the corresponding parameter only appears in function call contexts.

A particularly common type of functor is the predicate. For example, algorithms like find_if take a unary predicate that operates on the elements of a sequence. Algorithms like sort, partial_sort, nth_element and all sorted containers use a binary predicate that must provide a strict weak ordering, that is, it must behave like a membership test on a transitive, non reflexive and asymmetric binary relation. If none is supplied, these algorithms and containers use less by default, which in turn calls the less-than-operator <.

History

The architecture of STL is largely the creation of Alexander Stepanov. In 1979 he began working out his initial ideas of generic programming and exploring their potential for revolutionizing software development. Although David Musser had developed and advocated some aspects of generic programming already by year 1971, it was limited to a rather specialized area of software development (computer algebra).

Stepanov recognized the full potential for generic programming and persuaded his then-colleagues at General Electric Research and Development (including, primarily, David Musser and Deepak Kapur) that generic programming should be pursued as a comprehensive basis for software development. At the time there was no real support in any programming language for generic programming.

The first major language to provide such support was Ada (ANSI standard 1983), with its generic units feature. In 1985, the Eiffel programming language became the first object-oriented language to include intrinsic support for generic classes, combined with the object-oriented notion of inheritance. By 1987 Stepanov and Musser had developed and published an Ada library for list processing that embodied the results of much of their research on generic programming. However, Ada had not achieved much acceptance outside the defense industry and C++ seemed more likely to become widely used and provide good support for generic programming even though the language was relatively immature. Another reason for turning to C++, which Stepanov recognized early on, was the C/C++ model of computation that allows very flexible access to storage via pointers, which is crucial to achieving generality without losing efficiency.

Much research and experimentation were needed, not just to develop individual components, but to develop an overall architecture for a component library based on generic programming. First at AT&T Bell Laboratories and later at Hewlett-Packard Research Labs (HP), Stepanov experimented with many architectural and algorithm formulations, first in C and later in C++. Musser collaborated in this research and in 1992 Meng Lee joined Stepanov's project at HP and became a major contributor.

This work undoubtedly would have continued for some time being just a research project or at best would have resulted in an HP proprietary library, if Andrew Koenig of Bell Labs had not become aware of the work and asked Stepanov to present the main ideas at a November 1993 meeting of the ANSI/ISO committee for C++ standardization. The committee's response was overwhelmingly favorable and led to a request from Koenig for a formal proposal in time for the March 1994 meeting. Despite the tremendous time pressure, Alex and Meng were able to produce a draft proposal that received preliminary approval at that meeting.

The committee had several requests for changes and extensions (some of them major), and a small group of committee members met with Stepanov and Lee to help work out the details. The requirements for the most significant extension (associative containers) had to be shown to be consistent by fully implementing them, a task Stepanov delegated to Musser. Stepanov and Lee produced a proposal that received final approval at the July 1994 ANSI/ISO committee meeting. (Additional details of this history can be found in Stevens.) Subsequently, the Stepanov and Lee document 17 was incorporated into the ANSI/ISO C++ draft standard (1, parts of clauses 17 through 27). It also influenced other parts of the C++ Standard Library, such as the string facilities, and some of the previously adopted standards in those areas were revised accordingly.

In spite of STL's success with the committee, there remained the question of how STL would make its way into actual availability and use. With the STL requirements part of the publicly available draft standard, compiler vendors and independent software library vendors could of course develop their own implementations and market them as separate products or as selling points for their other wares. One of the first edition's authors, Atul Saini, was among the first to recognize the commercial potential and began exploring it as a line of business for his company, Modena Software Incorporated, even before STL had been fully accepted by the committee.

The prospects for early widespread dissemination of STL were considerably improved with Hewlett-Packard's decision to make its implementation freely available on the Internet in August 1994. This implementation, developed by Stepanov, Lee, and Musser during the standardization process, became the basis of many implementations offered by compiler and library vendors today.

Criticisms

Quality of Implementation of C++ Compilers

The Quality of Implementation (QoI) of the C++ compiler has a large impact on usability of STL (and templated code in general):

- Error messages involving templates tend to be very long and difficult to decipher. This problem has been considered so severe that a number of tools have been written that simplify and prettyprint STL-related error messages to make them more comprehensible.

- Careless use of templates can lead to code bloat. This has been countered with special techniques within STL implementations (e.g. using void* containers internally and other "diet template" techniques) and improving compilers' optimization techniques. However, this symptom is similar to naively manually copying a set of functions to work with a different type, in that both can be avoided with care and good technique.

- Template instantiation can increase compilation time and memory usage, in exchange for typically reducing runtime decision-making (e.g. via virtual functions). Until the compiler technology improves enough, this problem can be only partially eliminated by careful coding, avoiding certain idioms, and simply not using templates where they are not appropriate or where compile-time performance is prioritised.

Other Issues

- Initialisation of STL containers with constants within the source code is not as easy as data structures inherited from C (addressed in C++11 with initializer lists).

- STL containers are not intended to be used as base classes (their destructors are deliberately non-virtual); deriving from a container is a common mistake.

- The concept of iterators as implemented by STL can be difficult to understand at first: for example, if a value pointed to by the iterator is deleted, the iterator itself is then no longer valid. This is a common source of errors. Most implementations of the STL provide a debug mode that is slower, but can locate such errors if used. A similar problem exists in other languages, for example Java. Ranges have been proposed as a safer, more flexible alternative to iterators.

- Certain iteration patterns do not map to the STL iterator model. For example, callback enumeration APIs cannot be made to fit the STL model without the use of coroutines, which are platform-dependent or unavailable, and are outside the C++ standard.

- Compiler compliance does not guarantee that Allocator objects, used for memory management for containers, will work with state-dependent behavior. For example, a portable library can't define an allocator type that will pull memory from different pools using different allocator objects of that type. (Meyers, p. 50) (addressed in C++11).

- The set of algorithms is not complete: for example, the copy_if algorithm was left out, though it has been added in C++11.

Implementations

- Original STL implementation by Stepanov and Lee. 1994, Hewlett-Packard. No longer maintained.

- SGI STL, based on original implementation by Stepanov & Lee. 1997, Silicon Graphics. No longer maintained.

- libstdc++ by the GNU Project (was part of libg++)

- libc++ from LLVM

- STLPort, based on SGI STL

- Rogue Wave Standard Library (HP, SGI, SunSoft, Siemens-Nixdorf)

- Dinkum STL library by P.J. Plauger

- The Microsoft STL which ships with Visual C++ is a licensed derivative of Dinkum's STL.

- Apache C++ Standard Library (The starting point for this library was the 2005 version of the Rogue Wave standard library)

- EASTL, developed by Paul Pedriana at Electronic Arts and published as part of EA Open Source.

References

- William Ford, William Topp. Data Structures with C++ and STL, Second Edition. Prentice Hall, 2002. ISBN 0-13-085850-1.

- Stroustrup, Bjarne (2009). Programming : principles and practice using C++. Upper Saddle River, NJ: Addison-Wesley. p. 729. ISBN 9780321543721. Retrieved 22 March 2012.

- Nicolai M. Josuttis (2000). The C++ Standard Library: A Tutorial and Reference. Addison-Wesley. ISBN 0-201-37926-0.

- Scott Meyers (2001). Effective STL: 50 Specific Ways to Improve Your Use of the Standard Template Library. Addison-Wesley. ISBN 0-201-74962-9.

- David Vandevoorde and Nicolai M. Josuttis (2002). C++ Templates: The Complete Guide. Addison-Wesley Professional. ISBN 0-201-73484-2.

- Meredith, Alisdair; Boehm, Hans; Crowl, Lawrence; Dimov, Peter (2008). "Concurrency Modifications to Basic String". ISO/IEC JTC 1/SC 22/WG 21. Retrieved 19 November 2015.

- "C++11 Paper N3336". Open Standards. Programming Language C++, Library Working Group. 13 Jan 2012. Retrieved 2 Nov 2013.

- Becker, Pete. "LWG Issue 1318: N2982 removes previous allocator capabilities (closed in March, 2011)". ISO. Retrieved 21 August 2012.

- Halpern, Pablo (29 February 2008). "The Scoped Allocator Model (Rev 2)" (PDF). ISO. Retrieved 21 August 2012.

- Alexander Stepanov, Meng Lee (1 August 1994). "The Standard Template Library". HP Labs. Retrieved 2 December 2011.

Permissions

Index